VISIT US AT

www.syngress.com

SYNGRESS®

HOW TO CHEAT AT

IIS 7
Server Administration

Chris Adams
Conrad Agramont Jr.
Gene Whitley

KEY	SERIAL NUMBER
001	HJIRTCV764
002	PO9873D5FG
003	829KM8NJH2
004	BAL923457U
005	CVPLQ6WQ23
006	VBP965T5T5
007	HJJJ863WD3E
008	2987GVTWMK
009	629MP5SDJT
010	IMWQ295T6T

PUBLISHED BY
Syngress Publishing, Inc.
Elsevier, Inc.
30 Corporate Drive
Burlington, MA 01803

How to Cheat at IIS 7 Server Administration

Printed in the United States of America
1 2 3 4 5 6 7 8 9 0
ISBN-13: 978-1-59749-155-6

Publisher: Amorette Pedersen
Technical Editor: Chris Adams
Project Manager: Gary Byrne
Cover Designer: Michael Kavish

Page Layout and Art: Patricia Lupien
Copy Editors: Darlene Bordwell, Judy Eby,
Mike McGee
Indexer: Richard Carlson

For information on rights, translations, and bulk sales, contact Matt Pedersen, Commercial Sales Director and Rights, at Syngress Publishing; email m.pedersen@elsevier.com.

Technical Editor

Chris Adams is a Program Manager for Microsoft Corp. Focused heavily on "customer experience," Chris spends his time working closely with customers to ensure that their voices are heard for current and shipped products. He spends most of his time focusing on building and reviewing technical content for IIS, working with IIS most valuable professionals (MVPs), and spearheading new and exciting programs to best reach customers for the IIS team. Chris has owned such things as www.iis.net, the IIS Webcast Series, and the IIS Diagnostics Tools releases while at Microsoft. Chris was formally a Microsoft Product Support Services (PSS) engineer, technical lead, and supportability lead for the IIS product and has deep technical experience in the use and functionality of IIS 4.0, 5.0, 5.1, 6.0, and 7.0. Chris is currently Microsoft certified as an MCP, MCSA, and MCSE.

Technical Editor

Conrad H Agramont Jr. is a Partner Technology Specialist with Microsoft, where he focuses on technical readiness for Microsoft Infrastructure Partners focusing on the small to midmarket enterprises. Conrad was previously the Senior Architect for a Microsoft Gold Partner, where he was responsible for product planning, software architecture, and technical evangelism, focusing on service providers worldwide. He was also a Program Manager at Microsoft, driving hosting scenarios and architecting components for the Microsoft Provisioning System, Microsoft Solutions for Hosted Messaging and Collaboration, and Windows-Based Hosting 3.0. Conrad has more than 10 years of experience working in the Microsoft automation and hosting space, speaking at public events, and publishing articles in magazines. He is also an active blogger, focusing on many Microsoft-related topics. His blog can be found at http://agramont.net/.

Conrad would like to thank his wife, Pamela, for keeping his "nontechnical" life in balance and giving him the time to geek out, write books, and write blogs; his wonderful children, Demetrius, Trey, Jayden, and Sophia; and everyone who has taken the time to help him with his technical and career journey.

Raymond Arthur Gabriel (MCSD, MCAD, MCSD .Net) formed a consulting practice, Integrated MicroSystems Design Corp (www.imicrodev.net), in 1989 to provide technical consulting services as an application architect and solution developer. He has 20 years of experience in IT, including full life-cycle experience with multitier Windows and Web application development.

Raymond holds an associate's degree in Electronic Engineering from the Cleveland Institute of Electronics and is a member of the IEEE. He currently resides in Chester County, PA, with his wife, Sharon, whose support is an eternal source of great encouragement.

Robert McLaws is a technology writer from Mesa, AZ. He currently resides in northern Phoenix, where he works as a contract software consultant. He started a Web site called LonghornBlogs.com in October 2003. The site, now called Windows-Now (www.windows-now.com/default.aspx), has received several awards, including *PC Magazine's* Top 100 Sites of 2004 and CMP Media's Top 10 Tech Blogs of 2005.

Gene Whitley (MBA, MCSE, MCSA) is the President of SiGR Solutions (www.sigrsolutions.com), a systems integrator and value-added reseller in Charlotte, NC. He entered into the systems integration and value-added reseller industry in 1995, and in 2005, he started his own company, SiGR Solutions, which provides services and product procurement for businesses of all sizes, including Fortune 1000 companies.

Gene started his IT career in 1992 with Microsoft, earning his MCP in 1993 and MCSE in 1994. He has been the lead consultant and project manager on numerous Active Directory and Exchange migration projects for companies throughout the U.S. When not working, he spends his time with his wife and best friend, Samantha. Gene holds an MBA from Winthrop University and a BSBA in Management Information Systems from the University of North Carolina at Charlotte.

Contents

Foreword

When we set out to build IIS7 back in 2003, once IIS6 and Windows Server 2003 were released, we knew we had to think "big." Not "big" in the typical version 7 way, where the product gets bloated and overengineered—in fact, quite the opposite. We knew that it was time for IIS to undertake some dramatic changes, from modularizing the core Web server to replacing the metabase with a modern configuration system and replacing the outdated administration tool. We wanted to do all that engineering on top of all public APIs so that anyone could build new or replacement features as quickly, as powerfully, and as capably as the product team could.

The result is IIS7, a massive four-year engineering effort aimed at delivering a completely modular, extensible Web server platform, with incredible new capabilities delivered in three major areas:

- **Productive development for applications and services** IIS7 includes expanded application hosting for ASP.NET, Classic ASP, PHP Web applications and XML services with Web server extensibility throughout.

- **Easy manageability** IIS7 provides more efficient administration tools, including delegated administration and shared configuration for Web farms.

- **Lower infrastructure costs** IIS7 delivers improved scalability and enhanced security and reliability with automatic application sandboxing and rapid diagnostics.

For the IT administrator, IIS7 provides a flexible, easy-to-use administration toolset that can reduce time spent on routine operational tasks. For example, you can now easily copy or share IIS configuration across multiple Web servers, providing centralized management for a Web farm. You can also delegate a constrained set of administration tasks to Web site owners or developers and allow them to configure their sites or applications without requiring administrative privileges or impacting the health of the rest of the server. With IIS7, you can also take advantage of new troubleshooting tools that speed up failure diagnostics and recovery with capabilities like real-time request monitoring and automatic request tracing. IIS7 also improves security and reliability of hosted Web sites by automatically sandboxing new sites by default.

For the developer, IIS7 expands support for Web application development through fully integrated ASP.NET hosting as well as the introduction of FastCGI for reliable and high-performance hosting of PHP and other languages. The already powerful application pool process model can now host WCF XML services over any protocol, hosted by side-by-side traditional Web applications. IIS7's new modular architecture will give you more flexibility with your Web servers. Using the new public extensibility model, you can now add, remove, or even replace core IIS features.

—Bill Staples
IIS Product Unit Manager,
Microsoft Corp.

About the Author

I've had the privilege of working with Chris Adams for many years on IIS, and I can promise you that you won't find anyone else with his combination of enthusiasm, drive, and technical expertise for how to use the product. Chris is an IIS guru most popular for his vibrant personality and dynamic speaking style that he has used to great effect in his many IIS Web casts, TechEd presentations, and his blog. Chris has worked on the IIS product in one shape or form for many years, and he brings to this book an insider's perspective on how the product works and how you can make it work for you.

—Bill Staples

Preface

Internet Information Services (IIS) has been a passion, a mini-lifestyle of sorts, since I joined Microsoft. The job titles of many colleagues have changed, as have their responsibilities, but their enthusiasm, passion for doing what is right, and desire to satisfy our customers have never changed. The dream of IIS servers dominating the Web server market is a goal that I have strived for and aimed at from the beginning.

I remember the days of uncertainty while working as a newly hired engineer at GTE Wireless: The trial-by-error approach to learning that I had, as well as the countless hours lost fiddling with various types of software. I never dreamed it would lead me to the largest software company in the world, nor did I believe it would lead me to a semi-leadership role in shaping a product produced by this large software company. Microsoft contains a sea of knowledgeable individuals with passion beyond your wildest dreams. With 70,000 employees, Microsoft is amazing because the good of customers is still prevalent in almost everyone with whom I have had the honor to work.

IIS 7.0 contains the most radical changes we ever undertook since I have been associated with the product. IIS 4.0 was a rather dramatic release with new features, but nothing compared with those offered in version 7. It is no secret that I love IIS 6.0 and will continue to put as much effort into helping others implement it as I will do for IIS 7.0—but the wave of the future is upon us.

I targeted this book at those of you who need quick-and-dirty coverage of IIS 7.0. It isn't a glamorous, all-encompassing book covering everything about IIS 7.0 down to the itty-bitty details, such as registry tweaks, knob switches, and so on. Instead, this book will fit your budget and satisfy your need for *just the facts.* It also might help you perform a job better or even land a job. After reading *How to Cheat at IIS 7.0 Server Administration*, you will walk away with everything you need to talk intelligently about IIS 7.0 with anyone—and I do mean anyone.

I have had the opportunity to work with some very talented people along the way, some of whom were crucial in helping me complete this book. Therefore, I wouldn't feel right if I didn't share the love for them, as they are the folks I depend on every day. Brian Delahunty, who took a bull by the horns when joining Microsoft, is a great program manager whose achievements I strive to emulate! Carlos Aguilar Mares is the ringleader of talented developers on the IIS product team. I don't refer to many individuals as superstars, but I most certainly consider this man to be a superhero. Thanks, Carlos, for all of your tremendous support on work related to this book as well as on projects not related to it. I also want to thank Eric Deily and Thomas Deml, the bookends to anything IIS since the day I started. These good guys are skilled workers who build super products.

Lastly, thanks go out to my family, the cornerstone, who puts up with all the bad habits, undying passion for *geeking out,* and the ones who make all of this worth it. Tracey, my wife, whom I can't thank enough for everything she is to me, for me, and what she makes me as a person. Jesse, my son, thanks for just being you…I love y'all!

This book is dedicated to my late father, Major Donald Gray Adams, who passed away October 29, 2006. He was devoted to many and loved by all, and more importantly, my hero. I miss you dad!

—Chris Adams
Program Manager.
Microsoft Corp.

Chapter 1

Getting Started with IIS 7.0

Solutions in this chapter:

- **Inside the Changes in IIS 7.0**
- **IIS 6.0 versus 7.0: The Delta**

☑ **Summary**

☑ **Solutions Fast Track**

☑ **Frequently Asked Questions**

Introduction

Many variables must be taken into account when you are considering a move to IIS 7.0 and Windows "Codename: Longhorn" server. Microsoft has gone to great lengths to reduce the obstacles and make this move as seamless as possible. This chapter prepares you for the foundation of IIS 7.0 and helps you structure it in a way that is familiar. Knowledge of IIS 6.0 helps in understanding not only "how" but also "why" the product was changed. In the following chapters, you will learn the fundamentals that are necessary to move to IIS 7.0.

Inside the Changes in IIS 7.0

In this chapter we introduce the fundamentals that are accomplished using IIS 7.0 versus past versions, especially IIS 6.0. These fundamentals include:

- An introduction to the installation changes of IIS 7.0 from a very high level, and how it sets the foundation for deploying secure applications.

- Why developers like IIS 7.0. A look inside IIS 7.0's new core server.

- The configuration. Why did Microsoft start over and rebuild what already worked?

- The administration stack is more powerful than ever before. In the past, administrators had two options "out of box" to configure IIS without script—IIS Manager and AdsUtil.vbs. IIS 7.0 has a command-console utility, IIS Manager, whose areas are developer extensible.

- The most efficient diagnostics stack. Why Request Tracing is just the butter on top of the potato or ketchup on fries.

All these fundamentals are collectively necessary and revolutionary. Never in the history of Internet Information Services (IIS) has there been so many feature redesigns as there are in IIS 7.0.

IIS 7.0 improves the features for administrators and provides a friendlier environment for developers. As a continuation of Microsoft's Trustworthy Computing effort, IIS 7.0 improves security while also achieving greater efficiency, granularity, and performance.

The differences between IIS 7.0 and its predecessors are immense. The installation is more detailed than that of IIS 6.0. Administrators now have more control over the features they want to install. The ability to delegate tasks to users without granting full administrative rights allows IIS 7.0 to be easily managed without compromising security. The IIS Manager user interface is more powerful and task oriented. Command-line capabilities have also improved with the implementation of Appcmd.exe. This utility can be used for viewing and configuring objects in IIS 7.0, making it easier for administrators who need to make many changes to their system. Windows Management Instrumentation (WMI) is friendlier than it was in version 6.0. In IIS 7.0, WMI allows access to manage multiple servers.

IIS 7.0 is modular and not so monolithic as the IIS 6.0 core was. Developers can add any functionality they like by creating their own modules and adding them to the core server. For instance, if developers do not like a certain function within IIS 7.0, they can replace it with their own by adding components that are easier to develop. The ability to do this is more convenient with the implementation of new application programming interfaces (APIs). Developers are no longer dependent on Internet Server Application Programming Interfaces (ISAPIs) and their complexity to extend server functionality. A major change in the architecture of IIS 7.0 from previous versions is that .config files now hold configuration information for the IIS instead of the metabase. The .config files also live side by side with ASP.NET settings and can be deployed with application content such as pages and images.

IIS 7.0 also has new diagnostic features. The most impressive is a feature called Failed Request Tracing (FREB), which can be enabled and used in diagnosing server request failures or delays. With FREB, you can define a failed request-tracing rule that will capture trace events for that request and log them as they occur without having to reproduce the error. Administrators no longer have to dig through large report files searching for the information they need to troubleshoot a specific failed request. FREB makes resolving request failures a lot easier.

All these changes in IIS 7.0 bring about a better platform for developers, easier management for administrators, improved server performance, and better overall security.

Installing IIS 6.0

Although more stable and secure than its predecessors, IIS 6.0 was unable to shrink its memory footprint. With previous versions of IIS, when certain features were disabled, their code remained loaded and resident in memory. For example, when an administrator installed IIS 6.0 and only chose to enable IIS Manager and Web services, code for all other features were also loaded as common files and then stored in memory. This meant that administrators would also have to be concerned about patches for all of IIS, even if a patch applied to a feature they weren't using. For administrators to remove certain features from previous versions, they had to completely uninstall IIS from the system. It was an all-or-nothing installation. While developing IIS 7.0, Microsoft felt that it had an opportunity to improve security by reducing the footprint in memory while making the platform more modular and more efficient.

After you install IIS Manager and Web services, the inetsrv directory for IIS 6.0 appears (see Figure 1.1), and the directory for IIS 7.0 appears, as shown in Figure 1.2. In examining the differences, you see that none of the subdirectories under inetsrv carry over to IIS 7.0. The only top-level subdirectories you have in IIS 7.0 are the .config files and whatever language(s) you are supporting on your server. For our purposes, we are supporting U.S. English; therefore, we have an en-US directory. All configuration changes take place in the .config subdirectory, so you have only one directory to find and manage.

Figure 1.1 Simple inetsrv Directory Structure

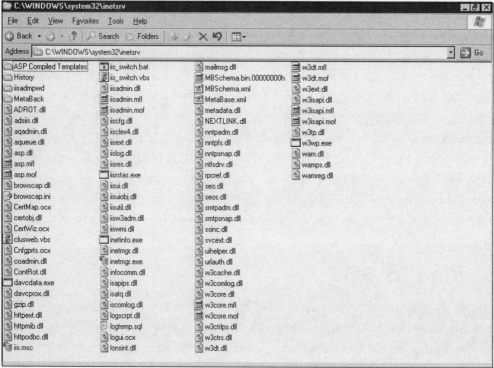

Figure 1.2 inetsrv Directory with IIS 7.0

Two options can be used to install IIS 6.0, neither of which was done by default on Windows Server 2003:

- **User Interface** Administrators could install IIS 6.0 manually via the user interface, by choosing the features they wanted.

- **Unattended Installation** Administrators had the option of conducting unattended and automated installations of IIS 6.0.

Installing IIS 6.0 via the User Interface

Although IIS 6. 0 is easy to install, learning where to install it from and getting there were difficult tasks. In the user interface of Windows Server 2003, you had to go to **Control Panel | Add or Remove Programs | Add/Remove Windows Components | Application Server**; administrators could then choose IIS and begin to enable the features they wanted. It was not very convenient or easy to find. Figure 1.3 shows the screen where IIS 6.0 selects the user interface.

Figure 1.3 IIS 6.0 Selected In User Interface

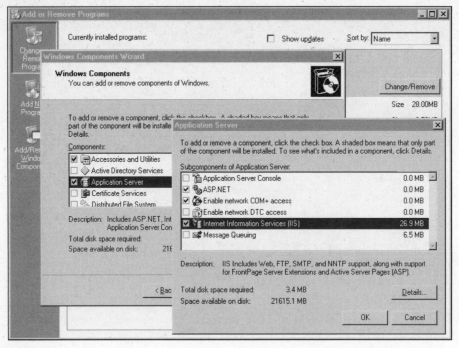

Installing IIS 6.0 Using Unattended Installation

IIS 6.0 administrators also had the option of using the unattended installation method. Information technology (IT) professionals accustomed to conducting roll-outs, are familiar with the unattended installation method of previous versions of Windows. Just like Windows, IIS 6.0 unattended installations required the creation of answer files, which contain answers to questions that can be automated during the installation process. The extent and complexity of the answer file depended on when you installed IIS 6.0. Unattended installations could be accomplished at two distinct moments:

1. **Install IIS 6.0 simultaneously with the operating system** Unattended installations could be conducted at the same time that the operating system was installed. The answer file created with standard text in this scenario can be long and complex, even for savvy veterans. Not only were administrators creating the sections for IIS, which included a Components and an optional Internet server section, they also created the sections for installing the operating system. Using the unattended installation method required using the

Winnt32.exe command. Following is the syntax required for the *Winn32.exe* command.

Winnt32 /unattend:AnswerFile /s:InstallSource

AnswerFile is the name of the file that contains the answers to questions that need to be automated, and *InstallSource* is the location of the installation files.

2. **Installing IIS 6.0 after the operating system is installed** Using the *Sysocmgr.exe* tool, administrators could install IIS 6.0 and the components they wanted from a command line, with the aid of an answer text file. Similar to the answer file for unattended installation with the operating system, the answer file here also has a Components section and optional InternetServer section, but does not include all of the options for the installation of the operating system. Following is the syntax used with the *Sysocmgr.exe* tool. Figure 1.4 shows what administrators might have in their answer files.

Sysocmgr /i:%windir%\inf\sysoc.inf /u:c:\AnswerFile.txt

The */i* switch points to the path where the *sysoc.inf* file resides, which must be read by the *sysocmgr* command. The */u* switch indicates the path to the answer file.

Figure 1.4 Example Answer File

```
[Components]
Aspnet=on
iis_common=on
iis_ftp=on
iis_asp=on
iis_www=on



[InternetServer]
SvcManualStart=www,ftp
```

In this example, the Components section of the answer file would enable ASP.NET, the IIS Common files, the File Transfer Protocol (FTP), the Active Server Pages, and Web services. The InternetServer section would set both the Web and FTP service to manual instead of automatic.

BEST PRACTICES ACCORDING TO MICROSOFT

When you are creating an answer file for operating system deployment, Microsoft suggests using the Setup Manager found on the Windows Server 2003 CD. The tool is included in the *Deploy.cab* file under the \Support\Tools folder.

SOME INDEPENDENT ADVICE

Although using the Setup Manager is the preferred way of creating answer files, the chance of error is still there. Keep your answer files short; the longer they are the greater the chance of problems. If you are just creating an answer file to install IIS 6.0, then creating it via notepad is more efficient and examples can be found throughout the Internet.

IIS 6.0 Core Server

IIS 6.0 contains several core components that perform important functions. The following are the core components with a brief description of each:

- *HTTP.sys* Implemented as a kernel mode driver. Used to receive requests and forwards them to the request queue, while also sending responses to the client.

- **Worker Processes (*w3wp.exe*)** Runs as user-mode code. Uses *HTTP.sys* to receive requests and send responses. Also runs ASP.NET applications and Extensible Markup Language (XML) Web services.

- **Web Service Administration and Monitoring** A set of features found in the Web service. Also runs in user-mode. Responsible for Hypertext Transfer Protocol (HTTP) administration and worker process management.

- *Inetinfo.exe* Runs as a user-mode component. Hosts the IIS metabase and other services such as Simple Mail Transfer Protocol (SMTP), FTP, and Network News Transfer Protocol (NNTP).

- **IIS Metabase** The data store containing all of the IIS configuration information. Saved as plain text and formatted in XML. (For more information about the metabase, see the section "Where the Metabase Took Us…and Fell Short."

HTTP.sys

A kernel mode driver and part of the Transmission Control Protocol/Internet Protocol (TCP/IP) networking subsystem, *HTTP.sys*, listens for requests that want to connect to Internet Protocol (IP) addresses and port numbers used by Web sites running on IIS. It is used by IIS for handling HTTP requests, but also fulfills several other functions including caching HTTP responses in kernel mode, managing Transmission Control Protocol (TCP) connections, implementing connection limits, time-outs, queue length limits, managing bandwidth throttling, and handling text-based logging for Web services.

Worker Processes

One of the most important changes in the core of IIS 6.0 was the use of *worker processes (w3wp.exe)*. These processes acted liked processing hosts for user-developed code. They could each host ISAPI extensions and filters, as well as Active Server Pages (ASP) applications and static content. Figure 1.5 shows the inside of a worker process (*w3wp.exe*).

With ISAPI, developers could create filters to access the core server. ISAPI filters are used to preprocess and post-process HTTP requests. ISAPI filters are driven by Web server events, not client requests. An ISAPI filter could be notified when a Read or Write event occurs and then modify the data that is to be returned to the client. ISAPI extensions are sometimes referred to as ISAPI applications, and can be called from any Web page to perform dynamic and interactive functions such as validating a form or accessing a database. ISAPI extensions and filters are written in C or C++ and are quite cumbersome to create and deploy. The deployment of ISAPI extensions and filters required server administrator rights.

By examining Figure 1.5, you see that requests can be handled by mapping them to the static file handler (default), the Common Gateway Interface (CGI) handler, or through an ISAPI extension. In Figure 1.6, requests using managed code (as shown with the solid lines) must first go through the IIS pipeline and then through an ISAPI filter before it even reaches the ASP.NET pipeline. The response (depicted as the dotted lines) then goes through the same pipeline but in reverse.

Figure 1.5 Inside a Worker Process (W3WP.EXE)

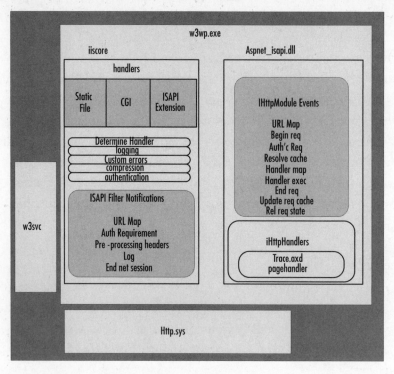

Figure 1.6 Request Going to ASP.NET Pipeline

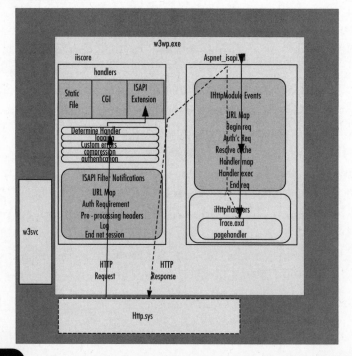

Also at issue was ISAPI deployment. In IIS 6.0 this was also cumbersome. Unfortunately, ISAPI deployment wasn't as easy as using FTP to copy the binary file to the server and have it work. To deploy ISAPI filters or extensions to the appropriate configuration for your site or application, as mentioned earlier, you had to have administrative rights on that local server and then restart the worker process that it resided in. Microsoft has resolved these issues in IIS 7.0 by making managed code a priority and allowing easier deployments of both native modules and managed code.

Web Service Administration and Monitoring

The user mode component Web Service Administration and Monitoring serves two roles in IIS:

- **HTTP Administration** By interacting with the metabase, the Web service gathers configuration data that *HTTP.sys* needs and is used to manage worker processes for application pools.

- **Managing Worker Processes** Managing worker processes includes starting, maintaining information, recycling, and the time to restart them.

Inetinfo.exe

A user mode component, *Inetinfo.exe* hosts the IIS metabase, FTP, SMTP, and NNTP services. It depends on the IIS Admin service to host the metabase.

Where the Metabase Took Us...and Fell Short

The metabase in IIS is a hierarchical structure used for storing configuration information. It was introduced in IIS 4.0 as a replacement for storing configuration information in the registry. The metabase was improved in IIS 6.0, first by formatting it into a text file using XML, and then by allowing it to be edited while running.

One of the metabase's shortcomings is that it is difficult to read and difficult to locate exactly what you're looking for. The old metabase supported outdated interfaces such as Admin Base Objects (ABOs). It also incorporated its own access control lists (ACLs); therefore, it does not use the existing ACLs from the file system. This made it very difficult to maintain. Putting in or extending the metabase schema was incredibly difficult. Figures 1.7 and 1.8 show both *metabase.xml* and *mbschema.xml*. Notice how difficult it would be to find something specific in either file.

Figure 1.7 IIS 6.0 Metabase

```xml
<?xml version="1.0" ?>
- <configuration xmlns="urn:microsoft-catalog:XML_Metabase_V64_0">
  - <MBProperty>
      <IIS_Global Location="." BINSchemaTimeStamp="527056dabc54c701" ChangeNumber="54416"
        HistoryMajorVersionNumber="16380"
        SessionKey="49634b62980000004c00000040000000102000001680000000a40000d2b61b969468!
        XMLSchemaTimeStamp="145c62dabc54c701" />
      <IIS_ROOT Location="/"
        AdminACL="49634462f0000000a400000040000000300e2e06c788e679a85ab041cf366edf87a4459
      <IIsComputer Location="/LM" EnableEditWhileRunning="0" EnableHistory="1"
        MaxBandwidth="4294967295" MaxHistoryFiles="10" />
    - <IIsConfigObject Location="/LM/DS2MB">
        <Custom Name="KeyType" ID="1002" Value="Ds2mbRoot" Type="STRING"
          UserType="IIS_MD_UT_SERVER" Attributes="NO_ATTRIBUTES" />
        <Custom Name="UnknownName_61488" ID="61488" Value="" Type="STRING"
          UserType="IIS_MD_UT_SERVER" Attributes="NO_ATTRIBUTES" />
        <Custom Name="UnknownName_61489" ID="61489" Value="" Type="STRING"
          UserType="IIS_MD_UT_SERVER" Attributes="NO_ATTRIBUTES" />
        <Custom Name="UnknownName_61491" ID="61491" Value="1" Type="DWORD"
          UserType="IIS_MD_UT_SERVER" Attributes="NO_ATTRIBUTES" />
        <Custom Name="UnknownName_61492" ID="61492" Value="sigrsolutions.com"
          Type="STRING" UserType="IIS_MD_UT_SERVER" Attributes="NO_ATTRIBUTES" />
```

Figure 1.8 IIS 6.0 Schema

```xml
<?xml version="1.0" ?>
<!-- WARNING, DO NOT EDIT THIS FILE. -->
- <MetaData xmlns="x-urn:microsoft-catalog:MetaData_V7">
  - <DatabaseMeta InternalName="METABASE">
      <ServerWiring Interceptor="Core_XMLInterceptor" />
    - <Collection InternalName="MetabaseBaseClass" MetaFlagsEx="NOTABLESCHEMAHEAPENTRY"
        MetaFlags="HIDDEN">
        <Property InternalName="Location" Type="WSTR" MetaFlags="PRIMARYKEY" />
      </Collection>
    - <Collection InternalName="IIsConfigObject" MetaFlagsEx="NOTABLESCHEMAHEAPENTRY"
        MetaFlags="HASUNKNOWNSIZES | HIDDEN">
        <Property InternalName="KeyType" ID="1002" Type="STRING"
          UserType="IIS_MD_UT_SERVER" Attributes="NO_ATTRIBUTES" MetaFlags="PRIMARYKEY"
          MetaFlagsEx="CACHE_PROPERTY_MODIFIED" DefaultValue="" />
        <Property InternalName="AdminACL" ID="6027" Type="NTACL"
          UserType="IIS_MD_UT_SERVER" Attributes="INHERIT | SECURE | REFERENCE"
          MetaFlagsEx="CACHE_PROPERTY_MODIFIED" />
        <Property InternalName="AdminACLBin" ID="6286" Type="BINARY"
          UserType="IIS_MD_UT_SERVER" Attributes="INHERIT | SECURE | REFERENCE"
          MetaFlagsEx="CACHE_PROPERTY_MODIFIED" />
        <Property InternalName="AdminEmail" ID="45060" Type="STRING"
          UserType="IIS_MD_UT_SERVER" Attributes="INHERIT"
```

Metabase backup provided a way to ensure that restoration could take place in case of corruption or if a server crashed. Although effective, the tools used in backing up the metabase in IIS 6.0 were quite old. It was not uncommon to back up the metabase and store it remotely by creating a common batch file. Using both *xcopy.exe* and *iisback.vbs*, one could automate the backup process. To run a script to conduct the backup, a user or IIS administrator had to be a member of the local Administrators group of the computer where they were backing up the metabase. Figure 1.9 is an example of what might be in a batch file that would use both *xcopy.exe* and *iisback.vbs* to back up the metabase.

Figure 1.9 Example of Backup Batch File

```
set server=servername
set name=%date%-%server%
iisback /backup /b %name% /e %password%
xcopy %windir%\system32\inetsrv\metaback\%name%.*… \\backupserver\share$\%server%
xcopy /o /x /e /h /y /c c:\web \\backupserver\share$\%server%
```

Another method of backing up the metabase in IIS 6.0 was through the IIS Manager, which would let an administrator save a copy of the metabase by right-clicking **Web Sites** and selecting **All Tasks | Save Configuration to a File.** You would then provide a filename and path for the backup. IIS 6.0 then created a machine key to encrypt some metabase parts in this file. This method then limited the backup to only being restored on the machine where it was originated. To be able to use a backup conducted in this manner on a separate machine, required the administrator to select the **Encrypt configuration using password** check box, which then substituted a password that the administrator created for the place of the machine key that was typically created. This was very easy to overlook.

Administration: A Review

IIS 6.0 administration was primarily done in the user interface with IIS Manager. Very limited in remote capabilities, administrators were required to loosen the network security settings for Distributed Component Object Model (DCOM) so that true remote administration could take place. If remote administration was required and the traffic had to go through a firewall, administrators had to open TCP 135, thereby creating another security risk.

Finally, IIS Manager dealt with administration at a high-level via category-based tabs, not task-oriented, which is more detailed, less error prone, and easier to configure. For instance, Web site security is exposed via the "Directory Security" tab as shown in Figure 1.10. This shows the lack of task-oriented security and the overall lack of organization available in IIS Manager.

Figure 1.10 Web Sites Security in IIS Manager

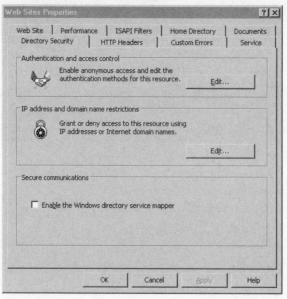

Another tool for administering IIS 6.0 was the use of *adsutil.vbs*. This utility used VBScript along with Active Directory Services Interfaces (ADSI), to modify an IIS configuration. One of the pitfalls with using *adsutil.vbs* was that first there was no ability to delegate to users, and thus you really couldn't do so without increasing security risks. *Adsutil.vbs* used old technology (ADSI); Microsoft is encouraging administrators to use WMI instead since the release of Windows Server 2003. Microsoft included eight different scripts that used WMI to help administrators manage IIS. The problem was that learning what eight different scripts did and how they made things more "simple" was counterproductive. IIS 7.0 remedies this with the implementation of *Appcmd.exe*. The following are the eight scripts that administrators needed to know:

- **iisapp.vbs**   Lists Web applications running on an IIS machine

- **iisback.vbs**   Backs up, restores, lists, and deletes IIS configurations

- **iisCnfg.vbs**   Exports and imports IIS configurations as XML file, able to copy configurations and save them to disk

- **iisext.vbs**   Enables and lists applications; adds and removes application dependencies; enables, disables, and lists Web service extensions; adds, removes, enables, disables, and lists Web service extension files

- *iisFtp.vbs* Creates, deletes, starts, stops, and lists FTP sites, and configures Active Directory user isolation for FTP sites

- *iisFtpdr.vbs* Creates and deletes virtual directories within FTP sites, and displays the virtual directories within a given root

- *iisvdir.vbs* Creates and deletes virtual directories within Web sites, and displays the virtual directories within a given root

- *iisweb.vbs* Creates, deletes, starts, stops, and lists Websites

Troubleshooting Failed Requests with IIS 6.0

Regardless of the product and the manufacturer, troubleshooting is a fact of life and a skill that improves with experience and time. IIS 6.0 improved its diagnostics capabilities from earlier versions. Still, most of the utilities used for troubleshooting were add-on tools that were not part of IIS 6.0 itself, but provided by the operating system itself or were available for download. The following is a list of tools or built-in features used for troubleshooting problems with IIS 6.0:

- *WFetch.exe* Used for troubleshooting HTTP connections. Can display the headers in HTTP Requests and HTTP Response packets sent between a client and a server.

- **File Monitor (*FileMon.exe*)** Used for viewing and capturing file system activity in real time.

- **Registry Monitor (*RegMon.exe*)** Similar to File Monitor except that it is used for viewing and capturing registry activity in real time.

- **IIS Request Monitor** Captures information about HTTP requests in IIS worker processes; good for isolating and understanding problems when worker processes become slow or unresponsive.

- **Secure Sockets Layer Diagnostic Tool (*SSLDiag*)** Useful in identifying configuration problems in the metabase, certificates, or certificate stores when running Web sites that use SSL.

- **Authentication and Access Control Diagnostics (*authdiag.exe*)** Provides the ability to review, test, and correct problems or issues with authentication and authorization

- **IIS Enterprise Tracing for Windows** New in Windows Server 2003, this tool allows you to trace HTTP requests as they move through various components in the server architecture.

- **Network Monitor** A network tracing tool that allows you to view activity on the network.

- **System Monitor** Formerly known as Performance Monitor in Windows 2000, this tool helps you to view and collect system performance data.

- **HRPlus** Provides error lookup functionality.

- **Microsoft Debugging Tools for Windows** Used in debugging and diagnosing application problems.

As can be seen, IIS 6.0 has numerous add-on tools that were quite effective in troubleshooting problems. One feature that was expanded in service pack 1 (SP1) of Windows Server 2003 was Enterprise Tracing for Windows (ETW). ETW works by implementing tracing providers used for debugging and capacity planning. It implements these providers to track HTTP requests as they move through IIS components. For instance, if an ISAPI filter causes a delay or the hanging of an HTTP request, ETW can help determine which ISAPI filter is at fault.

Conducting an ETW tracing session can be quite cumbersome. It involves everything from obtaining each provider's Globally Unique Identifier (GUID), specifying flags and levels in a text file, starting the tracing session that held numerous switches, and finally generating the tracing report. The following is an example of a command that starts up the tracing process; notice all the parameters and switches. Once the tracing report was created it was usually difficult for administrators and developers to pinpoint the cause of the failure

logman start iis_trace —pf iis_providers.guid -ets

Basically, tracing in IIS 6.0 through ETW was difficult because it didn't provide a user interface, it was very difficult to restrict to certain extensions or paths, and it was not extensible so developers could not write custom events.

IIS 6.0 versus IIS 7.0: The Delta

IIS 6.0 was a monumental step forward for the Web platform for Windows. At the highest priority stood security, followed by reliability and scalability. With IIS 7.0, Microsoft stood true to all of these important areas and delivered a rock-solid product; however, as with any release, there is still room for improvement. The following sections help us to understand the differences between IIS 6.0 and IIS 7.0, why changes were made, and what the benefits are for customers.

The major differences between IIS 6.0 and IIS 7.0 are:

- A modular core server consisting of simplified setup and a unified pipeline for request execution

- An all new delegatable, distributable configuration system allowing non-administrators as well as non-Windows credentials access to Web server configuration

- A completely rewritten IIS Manager that is task-oriented and extensible

- An extensible WMI provider that offers native access to the new configuration as well as access via Windows PowerShell

- A single, all-inclusive, command-line utility called *AppCmd.exe* that simplifies access to configuration and state information (done in individual VBS files with IIS 6.0)

- An IIS and *ASP.NET* diagnostics engine that is extensible and allows granular access to runtime-specific information about requests

- A brand-new Failed Request Tracing feature to identify causes of request failures

Modular Core Server

The biggest change in architecture between IIS 6.0 and IIS 7.0 is the modular core server. Remember that the core server in IIS 6.0 was monolithic and its installation was all or none. In IIS 7.0 all of that changes. Figure 1.11 is a diagram of the modular core server in IIS 7.0. As mentioned earlier, the new modular core allows administrators to load only what they need. Figure 1.12 shows that modules can be completely uninstalled from the server at any time.

Figure 1.11 IIS 7.0 Modular Server Core

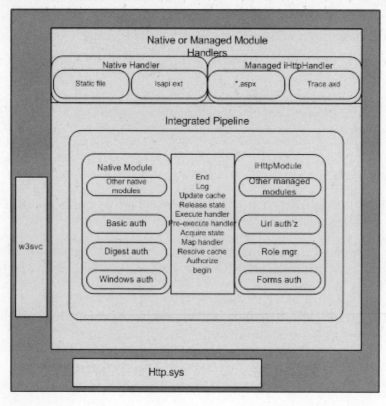

Figure 1.12 IIS 7.0 Module Selection

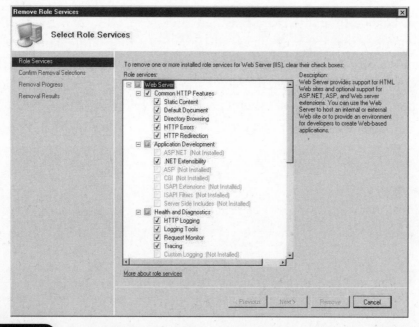

Because of the changes made to the core server in IIS 7.0, the memory footprint is smaller and the risk of loading unused code and it being available for exploitation is removed, along with achieving better performance. The ability to customize server workload will reduce its attack surface. Patching requirements are also minimized. When a patch was released in the IIS 6.0 monolithic model, the entire core was re-done and sent out. Now only those modules that require patching will receive them.

The new extensible APIs are a big improvement over the previous ISAPI model. Practically every aspect of IIS provides extensibility, thus allowing developers to tailor the server to meet their own needs, regardless of whether they use managed or native code. The new modular architecture has allowed Microsoft to eliminate duplication, and as such, IIS 7.0 has a single pipeline for all code regardless if whether it's managed or native code.

NOTE

IIS 7.0's new native API still requires users to know C\C++. Microsoft offers an additional capability by allowing a developer to use managed code to interact with the server.

Delegation: Less Is Often Better

In IIS 6.0, for a user to do any tasks on the server required administrative rights, which were a security nightmare for server administrators. Now with IIS 7.0, administrators are able to delegate tasks to users without leaving the door wide open. In IIS 7.0, administrators can delegate features in IIS Manager to Web site and Web application administrators, allowing them to manage their sites and applications remotely without having administrative access to the server.

BEST PRACTICES ACCORDING TO MICROSOFT

Microsoft recommends a strategy of starting with the minimum rights and working up. It does not recommend opening rights up completely and later locking them down. Doing so could cause applications to become unstable.

SOME INDEPENDENT ADVICE

Delegation creates a new culture in IT. When Active Directory came out, the ability to delegate administrative tasks to users was possible. For users who had administrator rights before delegation, it was considered a slap in the face. They felt as though they were no longer trusted. Although delegation is a great security tool, be prepared for the human factor, especially from those who used to have full administrative rights.

Server administrators still have complete control over what management features are delegated to application owners.

- **Feature Delegation** The ability to configure which features of a Web site or application to delegate to Web site and application administrators. Provides the ability to delegate control of specific features to site or application administrators without having to provide them with full administrative control of the server.

- **Administrators** This feature allows server administrators the ability to create site and application administrators. Server administrators include both the local server's administrators group and the members of the Domain Administrators group.

- **Management Service** A management service for IIS 7.0 that enables server, site, and application administrators the ability to connect to IIS 7.0 remotely using IIS Manager. It also allows site and application administrators the ability to connect to IIS 7.0 on the server locally, when they are a member of a Windows group.

Figure 1.13 shows the Feature Delegation screen from within the new IIS Manager.

Figure 1.13 Feature Delegation in IIS Manager

Improved User Interface for Users, Partners, and Microsoft

The interface in IIS has changed in version 7.0. It has become more task-oriented, helping administrators do exactly what they want, and not forcing them to search for the correct tab or control button. IIS Manager is extensible as is the rest of IIS 7.0. It allows you to administer most of the features in IIS 7.0 and monitor the server's operation. Administrators can manage both IIS and *ASP.NET* configuration settings, membership and user data, and runtime diagnostic information.

As seen in the previous section, the new interface can also be used to enable delegation. The new IIS Manager can remotely manage servers via Hypertext Transfer Protocol Secure sockets (HTTPS), therefore making remote management more secure friendly and not forcing IT administrators to open additional ports on firewalls. The ports for HTTPS (443), which are required for remote IIS Manager use, are typically already opened on the firewall. IIS Manager is completely extensible, allowing the creation of custom modules that add new functionality. For example, a developer could create a diagnostics module used to view event viewer data relevant to IIS. Figure 1.14 shows the new IIS Manager interface.

Figure 1.14 IIS Manager in IIS 7.0

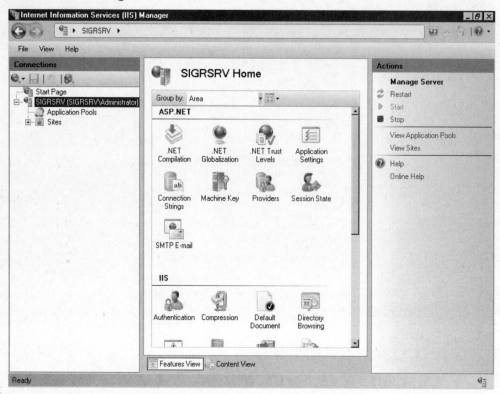

WMI with Logical Layout, Strong Support for PowerShell

IIS 7.0 includes a new WMI provider that provides access to configuration and server state information to people using VBScript, Jscript, and Windows PowerShell. Because IIS 7.0 is modularized, to take advantage of the capabilities of WMI in IIS you must enable the feature allowing you to use WMI with IIS 7.0. Figure 1.15 shows the IIS Management Scripts and Tools feature being enabled in Longhorn Server.

Figure 1.15 Enabling WMI for IIS 7.0

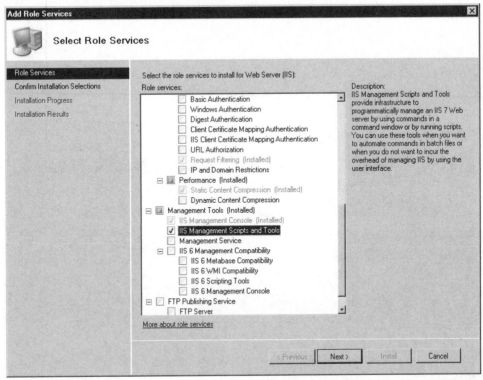

WMI is used to build scripts for Web administration, such as accessing, reading, and modifying key configuration files such as ApplicationHost.config and Web.config, the files that replaced the old metabase. Script writers have the ability to add, remove, or edit any part of the IIS 7.0 configuration. For example, WMI scripts have the ability to add modules at either the global or section level, configure custom HTTP errors, Multipurpose Internet Mail Extensions (MIME) Maps, Secure Sockets Layer (SSL) bindings, and ASP settings. WMI scripting in IIS 7.0 continues to be important for automating frequently repeated tasks, such as creating Web sites.

One can view the logical layout of WMI namespaces of IIS 7.0 by using WMI CIM studio, which can be downloaded for free at www.microsoft.com/downloads/details.aspx?FamilyID=6430f853-1120-48db-8cc5-f2abdc3ed314&DisplayLang=en.

Another way of accessing WMI is through PowerShell. PowerShell is a new command-line scripting technology created by Microsoft to provide administrators with control and automation of system administration tasks. The PowerShell script, which we will call *PowerWMI.ps1*, will retrieve information from the *Win32_Process* class and echo back the Name and WorkingSetSize for each item. The results are shown in Figure 1.16. The following is the PowerShell script.

```
$strComputer = "."
$colItems = get-wmiobject -class "Win32_Service" -namespace "root\cimv2" -
computername $strComputer

foreach ($objItem in $colItems) {
        write-host $objItem.Name, $objItem.State
}
```

Figure 1.16 Using PowerShell with WMI

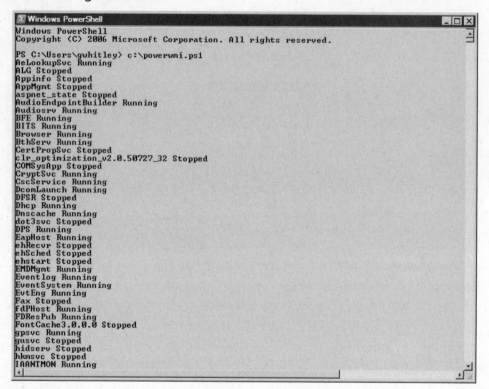

IIS 7.0 now includes a new WMI provider used to access both configuration and server state information. Developers and administrators alike can use VBScript, Jscript, and Windows PowerShell to take advantage of this. By using WMI CIM Studio, we can view the logical layout of objects and classes in a WMI namespace.

AppCmd: Swiss Army Knife for IIS Administrators and Developers

A major improvement in the administration of IIS 7.0 comes in the form of the command line utility *Appcmd.exe*. Think of the eight scripts mentioned earlier that IIS 6.0 administrators needed to know. Now think of having all of that capability tied into one command. *Appcmd.exe* provides a comprehensive set of management functionality and better support for bulk operations than the user interface. *Appcmd.exe* makes it easy to read and write configurations, access site and application pool state information, create virtual directories, and perform any other administrative task directly from the command line. Other abilities include starting and stopping sites, recycling application pools, listing the running worker processes, and examining currently executing requests. It supports linked operations like those found in Windows PowerShell, which allows multiple operations on a related set of objects to be performed together from a single command line. It's no wonder that *Appcmd.exe* is called the Swiss Army knife for IIS Administrators and Developers. Figure 1.17 shows *Appcmd.exe* performing numerous commands.

Figure 1.17 Appcmd.exe

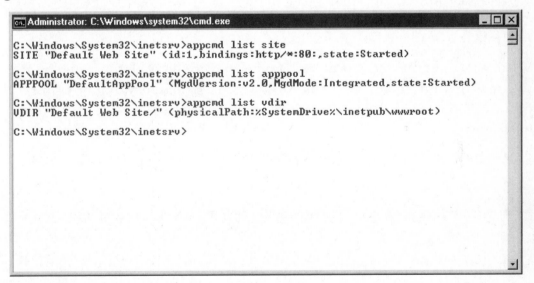

Diagnostics 101

IIS 7.0 provides new tools to help debug applications and monitor the server. The following are two new features available to both administrators and developers:

- Runtime State and Control API (RSCA)

- FREB

Runtime State and Control API (RSCA)

RSCA allows developers to see running requests on a server in real-time. This feature exposes the active state of sites and application pools and running worker processes. RSCA allows administrators to start and stop sites and recycle application pools. This capability comes in handy when investigating server issues or tuning server performance, because being able to quickly see what is going on in the system itself and controlling it while troubleshooting is powerful. To break it down, RSCA does the following:

- Provides in-process state information (current processes running, application pools process ID, currently executing requests, and AppDomains loaded)

- Real-time starting and stopping of sites

FREB

When a user informs you that there is a problem with the Web server, the first thing you do is try to reproduce the problem; however, a lot of times you can't. That's where FREB comes into play. Possibly the most anticipated feature in IIS 7.0, it does the following:

- Traces all requests through the pipeline

- Identifies requests that are stuck or failing

- Identifies time taken in each module, helping to analyze long running requests

- Provides that there be no need in reproducing the error for tracing failed requests

- Administrators can configure custom failure definitions per Universal Resource Locator (URL) based on time-taken or HTTP status and sub-status codes)

To use FREB you must create at least one failed request tracing rule where you can set the trace attributes per site or per application. This then allows you to capture an XML-formatted log of a specific problem when it occurs. As stated earlier, administrators and developers will no longer have to reproduce the problem.

FREB can also be left enabled on a server, allowing administrators and developers the ability to continuously capture trace logs for requests that have encountered a configurable failure condition, while avoiding any performance of saving trace logs. This allows you to capture information when errors occur, even if it's an intermittent problem. This eliminates the difficult task of having to conduct deep debugging of issues.

Because the tracing infrastructure is exposed to IIS modules and the server's extensible model, all components, whether they came with IIS or were developed by a third party, can emit detailed tracing information during request processing. You can even write your own modules that provide data to IIS 7.0's trace files information.

Figure 1.18 shows an example of setting up the location of where the XML-formatted log will reside after you set up FREB.

Figure 1.18 FREB Log Location

Once again, FREB is probably the most anticipated feature offered by IIS 7.0, which both developers and administrators will rely on.

Summary

Possibly the most anticipated release of IIS ever, version 7.0 rebuilt from the ground up does not disappoint. A new modular design allows administrators to load what they want without the risk of having unwanted and unused code residing in memory and creating a security concern. The new modular design also allows developers to add any functionality they wish. A new set of publicly available API's removes the reliance on ISAPI and having to know C and C++ when wanting to extend IIS. Managed code no longer has second class citizenship; it has the same access to the pipeline that native code does. WMI now provides native access to managing servers. The old metabase and its complexities have been replaced by more manageable *.config* files.

Security is improved. Server administrators can now delegate tasks to Web administrators and developers without having to provide total server administrative rights. Administrative tools are easier to use and more powerful. The new and improved IIS Manager is now task-oriented and wizard-based, thereby walking administrators through the necessary steps to achieve what they need to. IIS 7.0 now has a complete administrative command line utility in *Appcmd.exe* that can be used to view and configure objects.

Diagnostic features are now easier to use and more powerful. FREB is a feature that is able to trace all requests through the pipeline, identify stuck or failing requests, and is useful in analyzing long running scripts. FREB allows administrators to enable it, create a rule, and then never worry about having to recreate an error.

Microsoft has brought about a lot of changes to an already solid platform, and improves upon it with IIS 7.0. Both developers and administrators will benefit from its features.

Solutions Fast Track

Inside the Changes in IIS 7.0

☑ The IIS 6.0 core was monolithic and did not easily support extensions. With two pipelines present it had the possibility of producing duplication.

☑ The IIS 6.0 metabase was large and difficult to read and locate.

☑ Most diagnostic tools in IIS 6.0 were add-ons and not built into the product. These tools were difficult to use, such as ETW.

☑ FREB enables administrators and developers to trace all requests throughout the pipeline. By enabling FREB on the server, administrators and developers never have to reproduce the error.

IIS 6.0 versus 7.0: The Delta

☑ IIS 7.0 has a modular core; developers are able to add any functionality they want. Only modules that are enabled are loaded in memory, which is more efficient and more secure.

☑ Administrative delegation is available. Server administrators can now provide the access needed by Web administrators and developers without having to provide full administrative rights.

☑ IIS Manager is now more complete and robust, basically allowing any part of IIS to be managed by the user interface.

☑ Appcmd.exe provides a more comprehensive management functionality and better support for bulk operations than IIS Manager

Frequently Asked Questions

The following Frequently Asked Questions, answered by the authors of this book, are designed to both measure your understanding of the concepts presented in this chapter and to assist you with real-life implementation of these concepts. To have your questions about this chapter answered by the author, browse to **www. syngress.com/solutions** and click on the **"Ask the Author"** form.

Q: In IIS 7.0, do ISAPI filters give you any advantage over modules and managed code?

A: No. Because of the new modular core, both managed code and native code subscribe to the same events.

Q: Does IIS 7.0 run on Windows Server 2003?

A: No. IIS 7.0 will only run on certain versions of Vista and the upcoming Longhorn Server.

Q: Can I manage IIS 7.0 via the command line?

A: Yes. By using the new Appcmd.exe utility, you can manage IIS and ASP.NET

Q: I have existing ADSI and WMI scripts that work in IIS 6.0. Will they work in IIS 7.0?

A: Yes, but you must enable the IIS 6.0 Management Compatibility feature.

Q: In IIS 7.0, how do I troubleshoot hard-to-reproduce failed request issues?

A: Use FREB.

Chapter 2

Installation of IIS 7.0

Solutions in this chapter:

- Install Types Available in IIS 7.0
- Installation Features
- IIS 7.0 Modules

☑ Summary

☑ Solutions Fast Track

☑ Frequently Asked Questions

Introduction

Installation procedures were completely rewritten for Windows Vista and Longhorn Server. The previous installer, SysOcMgr.exe, has been replaced by a more modular setup process. To complicate matters, IIS 7.0 is broken down into many different feature sets, each of which has independent modules associated with it. Unlike previous versions of IIS, IIS 7.0 setup will install to your system only the selected modules and nothing more. This means that modules will not be physically present on the system. For this reason, it is imperative that you understand each feature set, and the subsequent modules, to be successful at installing only the features desired and nothing more and furthermore ensure that you do not install more than is needed.

Install Types Available in IIS 7.0

Users need to understand that installation technology has been merged together for Windows Vista and Longhorn server. For IIS 7.0, it is important to evaluate the installation method that fits your environment. The following installation types are available:

- Using Vista's Add Windows Features
- Using Vista's Command-Line Package Manager (pkgmgr.exe)
- Using Windows Server's Unattended Installation (code-named "Longhorn")

IIS 7.0 is now modular, giving administrators and developers alike complete control of the features they require while minimizing the memory footprint of the Web server. Now not only are unneeded and unwanted components disabled, they aren't even installed. Previously, even if an administrator chose not to enable certain features of IIS, the modules making up those features still ran in memory, even though they didn't execute.

Setup in IIS 7.0 includes more than 40 installable features, providing administrators the ability to deploy whatever they need. Setup for both Vista and the upcoming Longhorn Server uses what is referred to as a *declarative model,* whereby each feature of the operating system defines its own set of components and dependencies. Vista and Longhorn Server benefit from a single binary base sharing a code base between them. For this reason, the dependencies are known for all features, and depending on those features chosen by the administrator, smaller service packs and patches are possible, thus reducing the time it takes to perform updates.

Since Vista and Longhorn Server use a single component setup that unifies the OS installation, services the OS, and provides installation of optional features, administrators no longer need to use sysocmgr.exe. There are various ways of installing IIS 7.0, including the following:

- Vista's Programs and Features

- Longhorn Server's Server Manager

- Command-Line Package Manager (pkgmgr.exe)

- Unattended installation

Vista's Programs and Features

In Windows Vista, operating system features such as IIS 7.0 are installed via Programs and Features in Control Panel, which replaces Add/Remove Programs in previous versions of Windows such as Windows XP. We will walk through the installation of IIS 7.0 on Windows Vista using the Programs and Features method. You must have administrator rights or the ability to use the *runas* command and provide the administrator credentials when prompted. This installation works on Vista Home Premium, Business, and Ultimate editions. In this example we will install just the default Web server for IIS 7.0:

1. In Windows Vista, click **Start | Control Panel**, as shown in Figure 2.1.

Figure 2.1 Selecting Control Panel

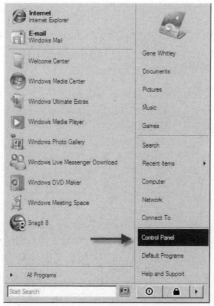

2. In Classic View of Control Panel, select **Program and Features**, as shown in Figure 2.2.

Figure 2.2 Selecting Programs and Features

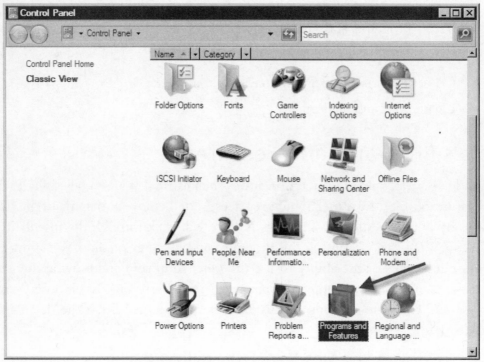

3. On the left, select **Turn Windows features on or off** (see Figure 2.3).

4. Now you should see the Windows Features box. Scroll down until you see Internet Information Services. Now choose **Internet Information Services**, as shown in Figure 2.4, and click **OK**.

Figure 2.3 Selecting Turn Windows Features On or Off

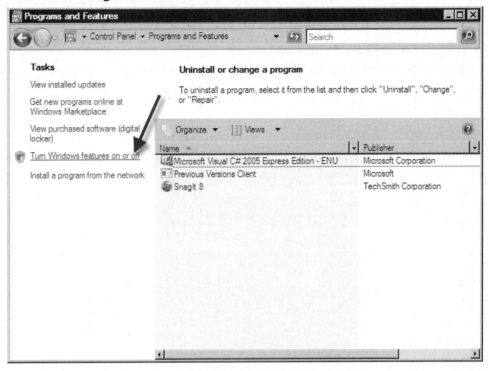

Figure 2.4 Selecting IIS

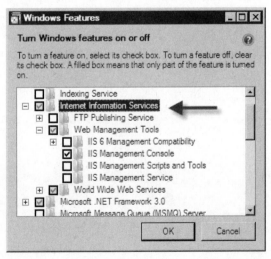

5. Close **Programs and Features**.

6. Now go to **Control Panel | Administrative Tools** and you should see the IIS Manager in the list of available tools, as shown in Figure 2.5.

Figure 2.5 Administrative Tools

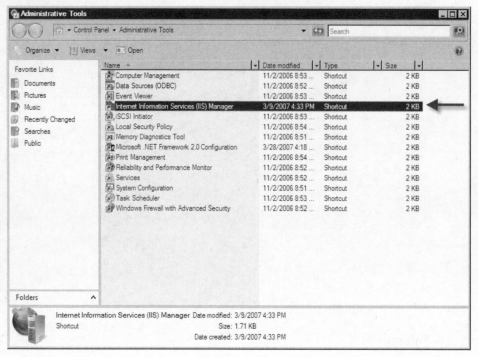

7. To test our installation, open **Internet Explorer** and go to **http://localhost**. You should see the screen shown in Figure 2.6.

Figure 2.6 Testing Localhost

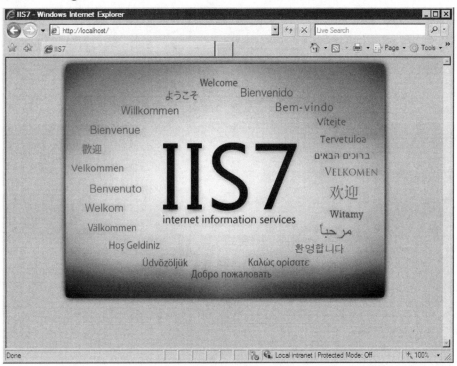

Longhorn's Server Manager

Installation using Longhorn's Server Manager provides a single interface that allows administrators to install and uninstall server roles and features. It also provides quick status on the state of installed roles and provides entry points to role management tools. To install IIS 7.0 on Longhorn Server, just as in Vista, you must have administrator rights to the system. In this example we will install the same features as the last procedure for Vista but using Longhorn Server's Server Manager:

1. Click the **Start** button and go to **Administrative Tools | Server Manager**, as shown in Figure 2.7.

2. While in Server Manager, select **Roles** in the left window pane. Afterward the Roles view is displayed, similar to Figure 2.8. As you see, we have no roles installed on our server.

Figure 2.7 Selecting Server Manager

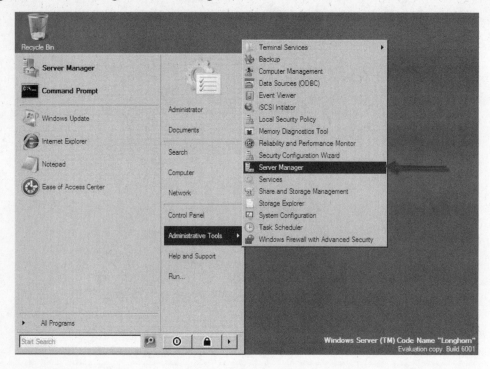

Figure 2.8 Roles View in Server Manager

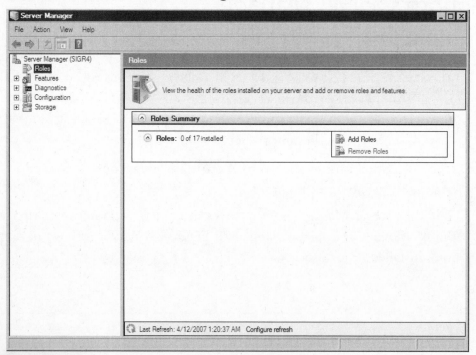

3. Now let's add the Web Server role for Longhorn Server. As shown in Figure 2.9, select **Add Roles**.

Figure 2.9 Selecting Add Roles in Server Manager

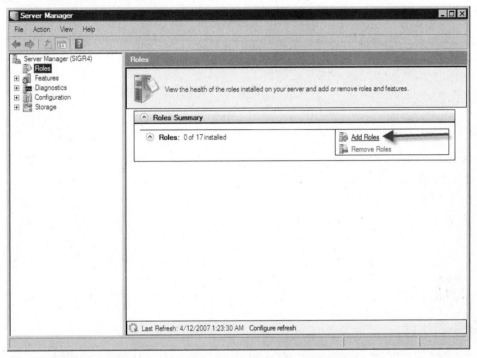

4. Now you should see the **Add Roles Wizard** in Figure 2.10. Click **Next**.

5. The **Select Server Roles** screen appears as shown in Figure 2.11. Choose **Web Server (IIS)**.

Figure 2.10 Add Roles Wizard in Longhorn Server

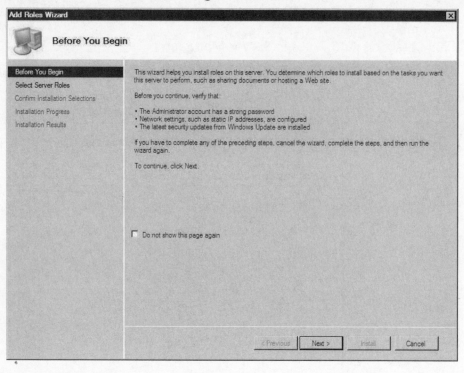

Figure 2.11 Selecting the Web Server Role

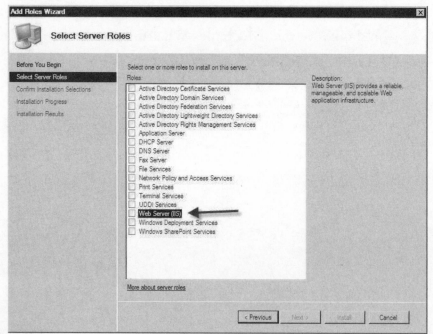

6. After you select Web Server (IIS), a popup screen like the one shown in Figure 2.12 will inform you that this role cannot be installed unless the Windows Process Activation Service is also installed. If you need to know why these features are required, simply click the **Why are these features required** link at the bottom of the dialog box. Now click **Add Required Features**. Once that's done, click **Next** back on the Select Server Roles screen.

Figure 2.12 The Features Required for Web Server (IIS) Screen

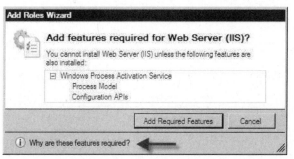

7. Now you will see the **Web Server (IIS)** screen shown in Figure 2.13, providing an introduction to the Web Server. Click **Next**.

Figure 2.13 Introduction to Web Server Wizard Screen

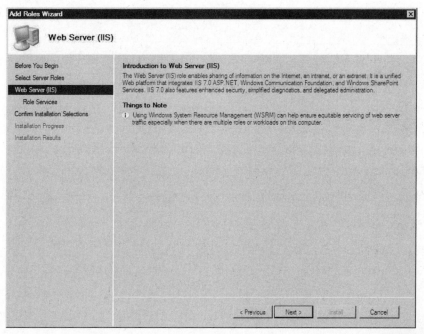

8. You will be allowed to select the features you want enabled in IIS 7.0, as shown in Figure 2.14. Since we are just taking the defaults, we won't be adding or deleting any features, so we can now click **Next**. Remember that with IIS 7.0, only the modules from the features you choose load, so the more you add, the larger the footprint becomes.

Figure 2.14 Selecting IIS 7.0 Features

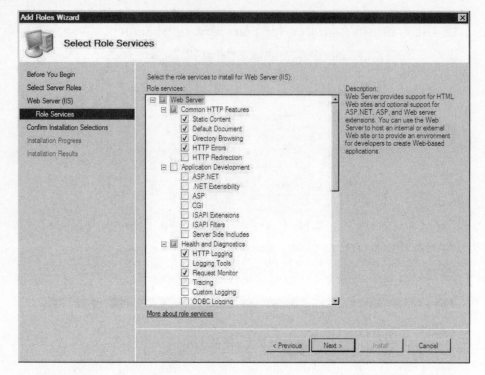

9. After selecting the features you require, the installation wizard provides you a breakdown of the roles, services, and features you are about to install, as shown in Figure 2.15. If you are sure of what you want to install, click **Install**. If not, click **Previous** and select the features you want.

10. You will now see the **Installation Progress** screen, similar to the one shown in Figure 2.16.

Figure 2.15 List of Features to Be Installed

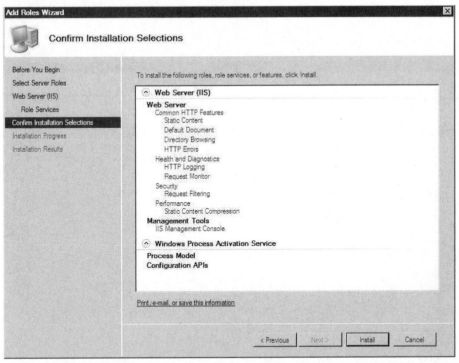

Figure 2.16 Installation Progress

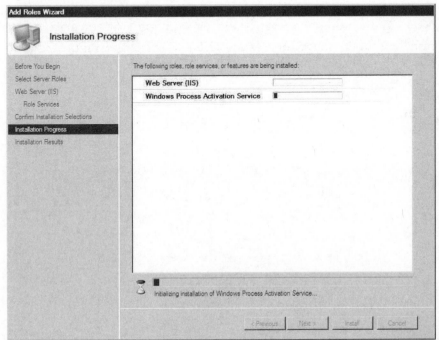

11. When the installation is complete, you will see the **Installation Results** shown in Figure 2.17. After viewing the installation results, click **Close**.

Figure 2.17 Installation Results

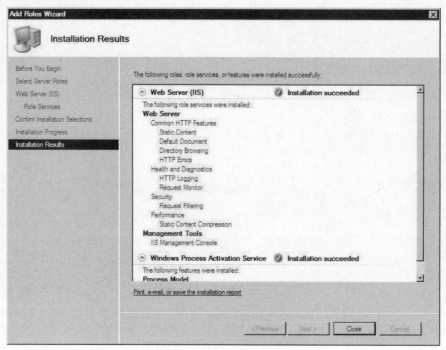

12. Now you should see Server Manager, showing that you have one role installed, that being **Web Server (IIS)**, as shown in Figure 2.18.

13. To verify that the installation was a success, just as in Vista, you can test using http://localhost. You should see the same screen as previously shown in Figure 2.6.

Figure 2.18 Web Server (IIS) Installed

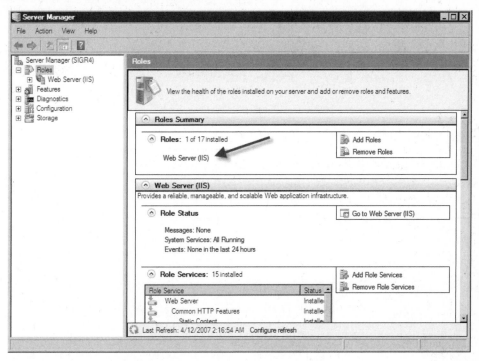

Just as in previous versions of IIS, we can install the server via the user interface, whether through Vista's Programs and Features or Longhorn Server's Server Manager. These methods are probably the easiest forms of installation. Now we will examine installing IIS 7.0 via the command line using PKGMGR.EXE.

Installing with PKGMGR.EXE

Since Windows 2000, administrators have been able to install optional features via sysocmgr.exe. Now, with both Windows Vista and Longhorn Server, command-line installation is done using pkgmgr.exe. This tool can install features directly from the command prompt or even from an XML file, which we will cover in unattended installations.

PKGMGR.EXE works with Windows Vista Home Premium, Business, Ultimate, and Longhorn Server editions. Here is the syntax for pkgmgr.exe:

```
Start /w pkgmgr.exe /iu:update1, update2…
```

And these are the commands for pkgmgr.exe:

- */iu:{update name};* Specifies updates to install.

- */uu:{update name};* Specifies updates to uninstall.

- */n:{unattended XML};* Specifies the filename of the unattended XML file.

! WARNING

Running pkgmgr.exe without the *start /w* prefix will cause pkgmgr to return without the administrator knowing when the optional feature(s) installation has completed.

Now we will install IIS 7.0 with the default features using pkgmgr.exe. Just as before, you must have administrator rights or access to the local administrator's password while using the *runas* command:

1. In Windows, open a command window as shown in Figure 2.19.

Figure 2.19 A Command Window in Vista

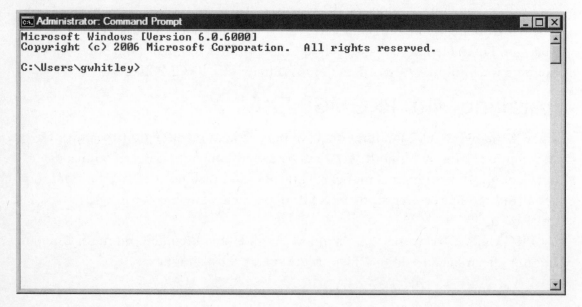

2. Now type the following command in the command window:

```
start /w pkgmgr /iu:IIS-WebServerRole;WAS-WindowsActivationService;WAS-
ProcessModel;WAS-NetFxEnvironment;WAS-ConfigurationAPI
```

Note that the command must be typed as one line and it will scroll in the command window as needed, as shown in Figure 2.20.

Figure 2.20 Pkgmgr Command

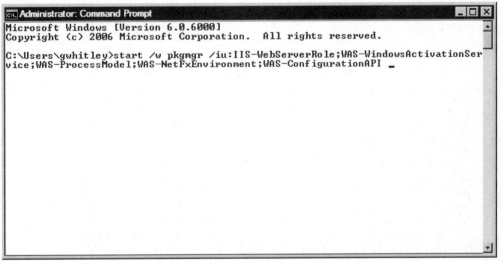

3. Press **Enter** to install IIS 7.0 with the default features. The installation can take between 1 and 5 minutes. Once it's complete, you will see a blinking cursor, as shown in Figure 2.21.

Figure 2.21 Pkgmgr.exe Installation Complete

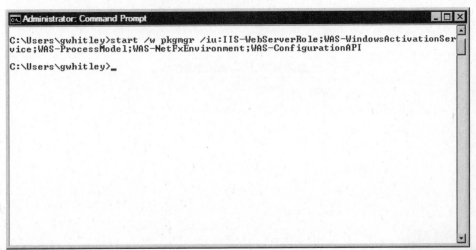

4. After you've completed the installation, you can test it by going to http://localhost, where you should see the IIS welcome screen that we saw in Figure 2.6.

Now that we know how to use the pkgmgr.exe command, let's put it in practice with an unattended XML file using Longhorn Server.

Unattended Installation

As we mentioned earlier, you can do an unattended installation for IIS 7.0 using an XML file. To do this, you will use the pkgmgr.exe command along with your XML file for the unattended installation. We won't go over how to create the XML file, but before creating it, you must obtain the build number of the operating system you are installing to:

1. Locate the **regedit.exe** file in the C:\Windows directory (assuming that you installed Windows in C:\Windows).

2. Right-click **regedit.exe** and click **Properties**.

3. Once the regedit properties come up, go to the **Details** tab and you will see the **Product version**, as shown in Figure 2.22. In our case the product version is 6.0.6001.16497. This number is used in the *<assemblyIdentity>* section of our unattend.xml file.

Figure 2.22 Obtaining the Build Number

In this example, we will install all the features available for IIS 7.0 in Longhorn Server using the unattended installation method. In a situation where as the administrator you have to deploy numerous servers with multiple if not all features for IIS 7.0, using the unattended method will likely be your best bet:

1. Create a file named unattend.xml using a text editor like Notepad or a tool such as Visual Studio, as we have in Figure 2.23.

Figure 2.23 Unattend.xml file

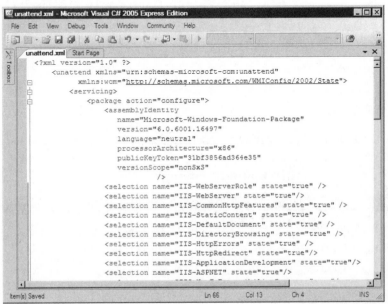

2. Now we will open a command window and install IIS 7.0 using pkgmgr as we did previously, but this time we'll call the unattend.xml file we created. So in the command window, type **start /w pkgmgr /n:C:\unattend.xml** as shown in Figure 2.24.

3. Once IIS 7.0 is installed, you will come to a blinking cursor (see Figure 2.25).

Figure 2.24 Starting Unattended Installation of IIS 7.0

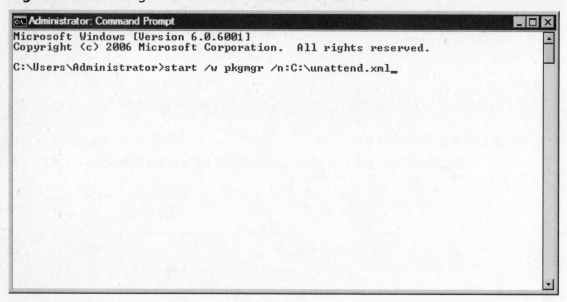

Figure 2.25 Unattended Installation Complete

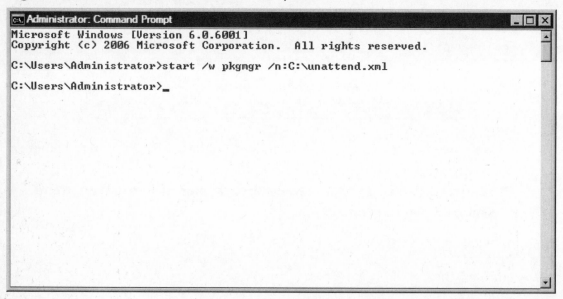

4. After installation is complete, go to http://localhost to test whether IIS is installed. If it's installed, you will see the IIS welcome screen shown in Figure 2.6, just as you've seen in the other examples. You can also verify the installation of the features by opening **Server Manager | Roles**, then

scrolling down to **Role Services** and verifying that the appropriate services and features have been installed. Figure 2.26 shows Server Manager and the role services installed.

Figure 2.26 Server Manager and Role Services Installed

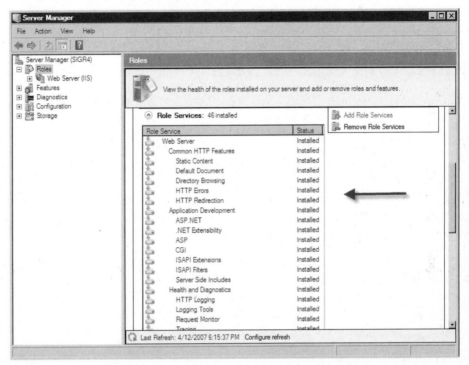

Now that we've gone over each of the installation methods, let's look at some major feature sets and what they offer users.

SOME INDEPENDENT ADVICE

Always test your unattended installation in a lab or some sort of controlled environment. Now that administrators have the responsibility of understanding setup modules in greater detail, the chances of mistakes increase. In addition, since the unattended files are XML based, the syntax becomes tighter and less forgiving.

Installation Feature Sets

Unlike any other version of IIS, IIS 7.0 is broken down into the smallest possible installable components. In IIS 7.0, these components are called *modules* and are standalone in functionality or are grouped into a larger "feature set" to help install like modules. This section discusses the major feature sets and what they offer users:

- FTP Publishing Service
- Web Management Tools
  - IIS 6.0 Management Capability
- World Wide Web Services
  - Application Development Features
  - Common HTTP Features
  - Health and Diagnostics
  - Performance Features
  - Security

It is important to understand what each feature set installs and further realize what potential risks (such as open ports) come with each feature set.

As we stated earlier in this chapter, IIS 7.0 has a modular setup allowing administrators control of what modules are installed without concern of having non-installed modules residing in memory. Modules in IIS 7.0 can be standalone or grouped into larger feature sets, helping install similar modules. For administrators who will be installing IIS via a command line or script, it is especially important that they understand the details of each feature set. In this section we cover the following feature sets:

- FTP Publishing Service
- Web Management Tools

- World Wide Web Services

The FTP Publishing Service

The FTP Publishing Service provides FTP connectivity through IIS 7.0. It is available to Windows Vista Business, Enterprise, Ultimate, and Longhorn Server. It has not changed since IIS 6.0 in that it relies on the metabase, and therefore inetinfo.exe will reside in memory if installed. The FTP Publishing Service is not installed by default and is made up of two components, FTP Server and FTP Management Console. Their modules are listed in Table 2.1 along with their descriptions.

Table 2.1 FTP Publishing Modules

Module	Description
FTPServer	Installs the FTP Service
FTPManagement	Installs the FTP Management Console for administrators

FTP Server provides support for uploading and downloading files from systems using the File Transfer Protocol. The FTP Server in IIS 7.0 is simply the same one that shipped with IIS 6.0.

The FTP Management Console is used by administrators to manage FTP servers locally and remotely. It is located in the IIS 6.0 Manager, as shown in Figure 2.27.

Figure 2.27 The FTP Management Console

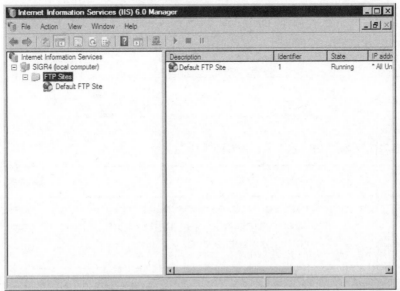

Web Management Tools

The Web Management Tools not only install IIS Manager, WMI, and Remote Management Service, but they are also responsible for loading IIS 6.0 Management Compatibility, which is not installed by default. This is important because if you or your developers have older applications that cannot be modified to take advantage of the new architecture, such as those that use Admin Base Objects (ABO) or Active Directory Service Interface (ADSI), you must install IIS 6.0 Management Compatibility so that these applications can be provided with the forward compatibility that they require to run on IIS 7.0. Figure 2.28 shows us installing Web Management Tools along with IIS 6 Management Compatibility with the IIS 6 Management Console and IIS Metabase and IIS 6 configuration compatibility in Windows Vista. Table 2.2 is a listing of the modules that make up the Web Management Tools feature set, along with their descriptions and dependencies.

Figure 2.28 Web Management Tools

Table 2.2 Web Management Tools Modules

Module	Description	Depends On
ManagementConsole	Web server management console supporting management of local and remote Web servers	ConfigurationAPI

Continued

Table 2.2 continued Web Management Tools Modules

Module	Description	Depends On
ManagementScripting	Provides the ability to manage a Web server with IIS configuration scripts	ConfigurationAPI
ManagementService	Allows the Web server to be managed remotely via the Web server management console	ManagementConsole NetFxEnvironment ConfigurationAPI
Metabase	Installs the IIS metabase and compatibility layer	—
WMICompatibility	Installs IIS 6.0 SMI scripting interface	—
LegacyScripts	Installs IIS 6.0 configuration scripts	Metabase WMICompatibility
LegacySnap-in	Installs IIS 6.0 management console	—

World Wide Web Services

The World Wide Web Services in Windows Vista and the Web Server role in Longhorn Server provide support for Web sites using HTML and optional support for ASP.NET, ASP, and other Web server extensions. This service gives servers running IIS 7.0 the ability to host Web sites and support Web-based applications. Unlike previous versions of IIS, administrators need to make informed decisions about what functionality is required for their servers.

Installation of World Wide Web Services is relatively easy using either the Programs and Features method for Windows Vista or Server Manager for Longhorn Server in that you don't have to know what dependencies are required. That is not the case for those using the command-line installation methods. When using those methods, you must know the features you want to install and their dependencies or your installations will fail.

World Wide Web Services depend on the existence of the Windows Process Activation Service (WAS). Earlier we walked through setting up IIS via Server Manager in Longhorn Server. When we went through the installation we were prompted that the features we were installing required WAS, as shown in Figure 2.12. WAS provides all necessary infrastructure for a base level of process activation and management as well as an HTTP processing infrastructure.

The World Wide Web Services feature is made up of five sections with various modules underneath each one:

- Application Development Features
- Common HTTP Features
- Health and Diagnostics
- Performance Features
- Security

The next section covers these features and their modules in more detail.

BEST PRACTICES ACCORDING TO MICROSOFT

Microsoft highly recommends learning each and every feature set, its modules, and any dependencies. This reduces the risk of mistakes that can cause instability and poor performance on Web servers.

SOME INDEPENDENT ADVICE

Examine the feature sets and modules we've listed in this chapter. Also check out Microsoft's article "IIS Setup Overview" at www.iis.net/default.aspx?tabid=2&subtabid=25&i=955 on Microsoft's IIS Web site; it provides a great deal of information on IIS 7.0 setup in general.

IIS 7.0 Modules

It is no secret that IIS 6.0 installs with a large set of components, or *dynamic linked libraries* (DLLs.) The fashion of security offered in IIS 6.0 is to not enable features that the administrator doesn't desire on a per-DLL basis. However, IIS 6.0 doesn't offer the opportunity to fully remove the unused DLL but instead just the ability to ensure it doesn't execute. This is important for administrators because they are the ones responsible for ensuring that Windows workstations and servers are patched appropriately. There is nothing more frustrating than installing patches for features not even used, yet the DLL still was installed. When you're installing IIS 7.0, selecting no feature installs the appropriate DLLs for that feature, creating an environment where administrators need not patch features not installed.

IIS 7.0 is based on more than 40 modules that cover the wide range of features offered by the Web server out of the box. In this section, we outline each module's name, purpose, and dependencies to ensure that only the correct pieces are installed.

IIS 6.0 was solid, secure, and powerful, but it wasn't modular in design. Components that were not enabled still had their DLLs loaded in memory. This increased the size of the footprint and created headaches for administrators having to patch features they weren't even using. Microsoft improved on this by loading only those modules in memory that were selected by the administrator, making them responsible for patching those specific modules only. Modules perform specific functions; they can stand alone or be part of a feature set. The onus is now on the administrator to understand the 40-plus modules offered in IIS 7.0 and correctly choosing the ones he or she needs. Although running setup through the user interface doesn't require the knowledge of the modules and their dependencies, installing IIS via scripts and the command line does. Here we cover the most important ones and their dependencies.

The Runtime Core "Bits"

Administrators installing IIS 7.0 via the command line and through scripts must understand in detail what feature sets include what modules and their dependencies. Simply forgetting a dependent module for a feature set you require can mean the difference between a smooth installation and a nightmare implementation, especially if it is on a grand scale. On the other hand, if administrators install more than they need, they have needlessly increased their security footprint, causing additional maintenance through unneeded patching and decreasing performance. In IIS 7.0, you get what you install—it's as simple as that. As the administrator, you have the control and, more important, the responsibility to install and maintain what is needed.

Figure 2.29 lists all the setup features and their associated modules in IIS 7.0. We will discuss in detail the five sections of the World Wide Web Services. We will describe each module and list any and all its dependencies.

NOTE

All IIS features have an implicit dependency with their parent. For instance, FTP Server depends on the FTP Publishing Service being enabled. Some IIS features, though, do depend on other IIS features for their functionality, and those are referred to as intra-dependencies.

Figure 2.29 IIS 7 Setup Features and Modules

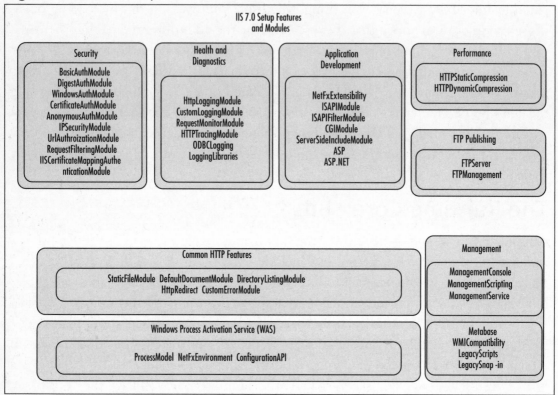

Application Development Features

The Application Development Features support the deployment of Web-based applications and dynamic content such as ASP.NET, ASP, ISAPI extensions, and filters. They also provide support for .NET extensibility, CGI executables, and files such as .stm, .shtm, and .shtml. The Application Development Features are made up of seven modules. Table 2.3 lists the modules available in the Application Development Features, with descriptions of each along with any dependencies required.

Table 2.3 Application Development Features Modules

Module	Description	Depends On
NetFxExtensibility	Enables Web servers to host .NET Framework managed module extensions	NetFxEnvironment RequestFiltering-Module
ISAPIModule	Allows ISAPI extensions to handle client requests	—
ISAPIFilterModule	Allows ISAPI filters to modify Web server behavior	—
CGIModule	Enables support for CGI executables	—
ServerSideIncludeModule	Provides support for .stm, .shtm, and .shtml include files	—
ASP	Enables Web servers to host classic ASP applications	ISAPIModule RequestFiltering-Module
ASP.NET	Enables Web servers to host ASP.NET applications	DefaultDocument-Module NetFxExtensibility NetFxEnvironment ISAPIModule ISAPIFilterModule RequestFiltering-Module

Common HTTP Features

Common HTTP Features install support for static Web server content such as HTML and image files, custom errors, and redirection. Default Document and Static Content are two of the more important modules supported here. Table 2.4 lists the modules available for the Common HTTP Features under IIS 7.0.

Table 2.4 Common HTTP Features Modules

Module	Description
StaticFileModule	Serves .htm, .html, and image files from a Web site
DefaultDocumentModule	Provides the ability to specify a default file to be loaded when users do not specify a file in a request URL
DirectoryListingModule	Allows clients to see the contents of a directory on a Web server
CustomErrorModule	Installs HTTP error files; allows you to customize the error messages returned to clients
HttpRedirect	Provides support to redirect client requests to a specific destination

Health and Diagnostics

Highly invaluable in aiding debugging and resolving issues with IIS 7.0, the Health and Diagnostics feature allows administrators and developers to monitor and manage server, site, and applications. Many administrators might not want to load this module on production systems due to performance considerations. Instead, these features may be installed on test servers, therefore not affecting user access and performance. Table 2.5 lists the modules for Health and Diagnostics and a description of each.

Table 2.5 Health and Diagnostics Modules

Module	Description
HttpLoggingModule	Enables logging of Web site activity for a particular server
CustomLoggingModule	Enables support for custom logging for Web servers, sites, and applications
RequestMointorModule	Monitors server, site, and application health
HTTPTracingModule	Enables tracing for ASP.NET applications and failed requests
ODBCLogging	Enables support for logging to an ODBC-compliant database
LoggingLibraries	Installs IIS 7.0 logging tools and scripts

Performance Features

Performance features provide for output caching by integrating dynamic output-caching capabilities of ASP.NET with the static output-caching capabilities that were present in IIS 6.0. Administrators can more effectively and efficiently use networking bandwidth by using compression mechanisms such as Gzip and Deflate. Table 2.6 lists the Performance modules and their descriptions.

Table 2.6 Performance Modules

Module	Description
HTTPStaticCompression	Compresses static content before returning it to a client
HTTPDynamicCompression	Compresses dynamic content before returning it to a client

Security

Probably the most important of all feature sets, the Security feature requires administrators to install the right modules to be assured that security in their Web servers is effective and not compromised. The Security feature set secures the Web server from both users and requests. Here is where the authentication mechanisms such as Windows Authentication, Basic Authentication, and others for IIS 7.0 are supported. The ability to filter any incoming requests and reject them without ever processing them is supported. Table 2.7 lists the modules available under the Security feature set and their descriptions.

Table 2.7 Security Modules

Module	Description
BasicAuthModule	Requires a valid Windows username and password for connection
DigestAuthModule	Authenticates clients by sending a password hash to a Windows domain controller
WindowsAuthModule	Authenticates users by using NTLM or Kerberos
CertificateAuthModule	Authenticates client certificates with Active Directory accounts

Continued

Table 2.7 continued Security Modules

Module	Description
AnonymousAuthModule	Performs Anonymous authentication when no other method succeeds
IPSecurityModule	Allows or denies content access based on IP address or domain name
UrlAuthorizationModule	Authorizes client access to the URLs that comprise a Web application
RequestFilteringModule	Configures rules to block selected client requests
IISCertificateMapping AuthenticationModule	Performs Certificate Mapping authentication using IIS certificate configuration

Summary

IIS 7.0 is modular in design, allowing administrators to take more control over the features they require. This allows them to decrease the memory footprint that IIS 7.0 uses, improving security and performance while also minimizing the amount of patching required. Administrators can install IIS 7.0 using various methods. In Windows Vista they can use the user interface via Programs and Features. Longhorn Server's Server Manager serves the same purpose through Role Services. Both Windows Vista and Longhorn Server support the use of pkgmgr.exe, a command-line tool used for installing IIS 7.0 and its various features. Administrators looking to conduct mass IIS rollouts and deployments will want to take advantage of unattended installations. This method also uses pkgmgr.exe but streamlines the installation by using an unattended XML file.

It is important that administrators understand in detail the feature sets available in IIS 7.0, their modules, and any dependencies they require. Not doing so puts their installations at risk and can cause instability and a lack of functionality at the server. IIS 7.0 empowers administrators to make it what they want, but it also gives them a great deal of responsibility as well.

Solutions Fast Track

Installation Types Available in IIS 7.0

- ☑ In Windows Vista, IIS 7.0 can be installed using Programs and Features in Control Panel.

- ☑ Server Manager in Longhorn Server allows IIS 7.0 to be installed via its user interface.

- ☑ Pkgmgr.exe is a command-line tool that can be used for installing IIS 7.0 and can save time over using the user interface when kicked off from a script.

- ☑ Administrators deploying numerous servers should use unattended installations that employ an unattended XML file and pkgmgr.exe.

Installation Features

☑ FTP Publishing Service is the same as it was in IIS 6.0 in that it looks for the existence of the metabase.

☑ Web Management Tools installs the new IIS Manager, WMI support, remote management, and IIS 6.0 Management Compatibility.

☑ World Wide Web Services provides support for Web sites using HTML, ASP.NET, ASP, and other extensions. It is made up of five sections.

IIS 7.0 Modules

☑ Modules perform specific functions; they can stand alone or be part of a feature set.

☑ Modules allow the footprint of IIS 7.0 to be small while providing the required functionality.

☑ Administrators must understand each module in IIS 7.0's setup, along with its dependencies, before using pkgmgr.exe and unattended installations.

Frequently Asked Questions

The following Frequently Asked Questions, answered by the authors of this book, are designed to both measure your understanding of the concepts presented in this chapter and to assist you with real-life implementation of these concepts. To have your questions about this chapter answered by the author, browse to **www.syngress.com/solutions** and click on the **"Ask the Author"** form.

Q: What is the best method of installation for IIS 7.0?

A: Depending on your situation, any one of the methods mentioned in this chapter could be the best. For large installations it is recommended that you use the unattended installation method. If you are installing one of two Web servers, it might be better to go through the user interface, such as Server Manager for Longhorn Server or Programs and Features for Windows Vista.

Q: Why should I learn each and every feature set, their modules, and their dependencies?

A: Administrators using pkgmgr.exe with or without an unattended XML file should know these components in great detail. Not knowing them puts at risk the stability of their servers and their performance.

Q: Why don't I simply install all the features? That way I won't miss anything.

A: You can do that, but you are putting at risk your IIS 7.0 installation by increasing the footprint in memory, possibly making it more vulnerable to attack. You are also degrading performance by loading unneeded modules and increasing the amount and frequency of patching.

Q: I thought the metabase was gone. Why does the FTP Publishing Service look for it?

A: The metabase is no longer the central repository for configuration in IIS. FTP Publishing is the same as it was in IIS 6.0, and in IIS 7.0 it believes that the metabase exists. IIS 7.0 actually translates the calls to the "old" metabase to the ApplicationHost.config file; therefore, the metabase doesn't actually exist—legacy applications and features only think it does.

Q: After I enabled IIS 6 Management Compatibility, I got the IIS 6 Management Console. Now I have two—one for IIS 7.0 and one for IIS 6.0. Why is that?

A: IIS 6.0 servers and their features must still be managed by the old IIS 6 Management Console, whereas IIS 7.0 servers can only be managed by the IIS 7 Management Console.

Chapter 3

The Extensible Core Server

Solutions in this chapter:

- **Understanding Development Advantages in IIS 7.0**

- **Extending IIS 7.0 with Native Modules**

- **Enabling Managed Code in IIS 7.0**

☑ **Summary**

☑ **Solutions Fast Track**

☑ **Frequently Asked Questions**

Introduction

There has never been so much excitement for a Microsoft Web server as there is for IIS 7.0. It is easy to understand why, when developers across all languages have the same freedoms. The parity stopped when a developer using ASP.NET attempted to garner full control of requests incoming to the Web server. This freedom wasn't allowed unless a developer knew C++ and was familiar with the complex Internet Server Application Programming Interfaces (ISAPIs) that were shipped with IIS 1.0 and later versions. These rules are changed with IIS 7.0, as developers can choose their languages of choice, and managed code developers have the same access to the same events as their C/C++ counterparts. The IIS 7.0 core server hasn't met a developer it doesn't like.

Understanding Development Advantages in IIS 7.0

This book focuses on administration more than development, but cannot avoid the fact that the landscape for development on IIS has drastically increased with IIS 7.0. Administrators should know that IIS 6.0 and previous versions were in a semi-open system where developers were offered a complex mechanism to modify the behavior of the Web server via ISAPI filters. In IIS 7.0, that barrier has been broken down and is now open to developers who write both native (C/C++) and managed (VB.NET, C#) code.

It is important to understand how native code modules are implemented and installed in IIS 7.0. Beyond that, an administrator needs to understand the implications of introducing managed code into IIS 7.0 and furthermore, how to enable them.

Although most administrators typically do not create modules themselves, it is important that they understand from a high level what changes and improvements have been made in the architecture of IIS 7.0, in particular as it applies to developers and the improvements that they will experience.

As mentioned in Chapter 1, the core server in IIS 6.0 was monolithic with two request pipelines: one for native modules and another for managed modules. The previous platform didn't provide developers with the environment they desired. Developers who used managed code such as C# or VB.NET saw their requests treated as second-class citizens, thereby not having the same freedoms as those who wrote native code such as C/C++. All was not rosy for developers using low-level languages either; they experienced a difficult and cumbersome task in extending IIS 6.0 by creating complex ISAPI filters and extensions. All of this has changed in IIS 7.0.

Administrators and developers alike need to understand that IIS 7.0 resolves these issues with a more modular architecture and unified pipeline. Whether a developer uses native or managed code, they have full access to the same events. IIS 7.0 provides a friendlier place for developers of all types. Developers need to know what is involved in extending IIS 7.0 through building native and managed modules, and administrators need to understand the different methods that are available for deploying them.

IIS 7.0 supports two different environments brought under the concept of modes. Understanding how the two modes apply to application pools and when to use either is important for both administrators and developers. The following sections examine each of the concepts mentioned in this section and go through two demonstrations.

Inside the Unified Pipeline

In earlier versions of IIS (6.0 and earlier), the development of .NET application components was allowed through ASP.NET. This was integrated via ISAPI extensions; therefore, administrators ended up having two separate pipelines—one for native code (ISAPI filters and extensions) and a second for managed code (ASP.NET). Requests to non–ASP.NET content such as static files were not visible to ASP.NET under IIS 6.0 and earlier. When running in integrated mode, IIS 7.0 allows ASP.NET to integrate with the core server, thus providing a unified pipeline for both native and managed code and allowing ASP.NET modules to be used for requesting static files and other content. No longer do developers have to depend on an ISAPI intermediary, which is difficult to write and must be done in C or C++. Now managed code can control every request going to the application to which it is mapped. Figure 3.1 depicts the core server in IIS 7.0. Notice that both native and managed code have the same access to the same events.

BEST PRACTICES ACCORDING TO MICROSOFT

When you are examining the modules loaded in w3wp.exe, Microsoft recommends using the Windows Sysinternals process explorer. Opening up the worker process in process explorer, developers can examine their modules in action, whether they are loading or not, and determine the size of their footprint in memory.

SOME INDEPENDENT ADVICE

The tools provided at Windows Sysinternals are used by many at Microsoft and have been for years, so it made sense when Microsoft acquired the group headed by Windows guru Mark Russinovich. The tools created by this group are some of the best in the industry. What's even better is that they can be downloaded for free at www.microsoft.com/technet/sysinternals/default.mspx.

Figure 3.1 IIS 7.0 Core Server

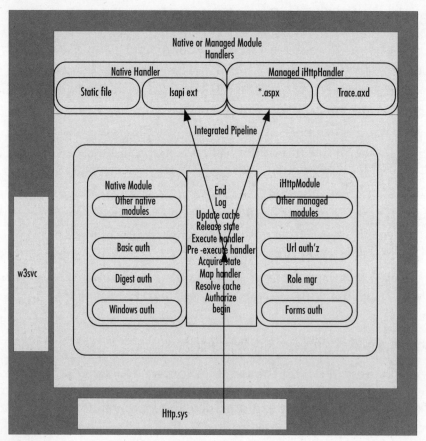

Through the use of the new native application programming interfaces (APIs) or ASP.NET, modules can be developed to extend IIS 7.0. Native code itself interacts with the IIS 7.0 request pipeline directly, without any intermediaries or shims. The advantage of this is speed and improved performance. Programmers who are used to writing ISAPI filters and extensions now have the option of using the new publicly available APIs for creating their new modules. These modules allow C and C++ programmers more freedom because they are not being bound by the tight restrictions in writing ISAPI code.

Extensibility in IIS 7.0 is also provided to manage code via webengine.dll. As we will see later, this native global module provides managed code direct access to the pipeline when running in integrated mode. Isapimodule.dll maps ISAPI calls as though modules were running in the older IIS 6.0 and earlier model in classic mode. There will be more about integrated mode versus classic mode later in this chapter.

Shortcut...

Modules and Kits

Microsoft provides sample modules and starter kits for both administrators and developers of IIS 7.0. Administrators can walk through adding and deleting modules, while developers can use the sample modules as examples for their own. These can be downloaded at www.iis.net.

Extending IIS 7.0 with Native (C\C++) Modules

Microsoft developers changed the way they developed the IIS Web server in IIS 7.0 by ensuring that they used the same APIs that were used by their customers. In IIS 7.0, the native APIs used to build features on top of the core server are the same as those used by developers. They are built and enabled the same way, and they are installed similarly.

It is important to know how a developer (or administrator) begins building a simple native module, but much more important to know how to install it correctly in IIS 7.0.

C and C++ developers do not have to deal with the difficulties of writing and debugging ISAPI filters and extensions anymore. Developers also do not need to create ISAPI code; anything they need can be accomplished by creating a module. As mentioned earlier, native code programmers can use the new server APIs that Microsoft developers used in developing IIS 7.0. Deployment is also much easier than in the past. It is important for administrators to understand how a developer goes through building native modules and what it takes to add them to IIS 7.0.

BEST PRACTICES ACCORDING TO MICROSOFT

Before modifying the applicationHost.config file, Microsoft recommends backing the file up. If after adding a native module IIS becomes unstable, it will be easier to restore to the previous file. Here is an example of performing such a backup using AppCmd.exe.
    Appcmd.exe add backup <name of backup>

SOME INDEPENDENT ADVICE

As an administrator, you may need to add modules on a regular basis. If this is the case, create a naming standard for your backups that makes sense to you. You may want to use a naming standard that mentions the module you are about to deploy. For instance, if you are about to deploy a module called MyModule, you can put it in the name of the backup. Below is an example of using the module's name, its version, and the date. This way you know that this backup was done before you added the module MyModule version 1.0.
    Appcmd.exe add backup MyModule-1.0-03-1007

Building Native Modules

Although server extensibility can now be done using managed code and the ASP.NET APIs, there still are reasons developers may want to create modules via native code. One of the biggest reasons is performance; native code runs faster than managed code. Although native and managed code strings have access to the same request pipeline, native code directly accesses it. Another reason you may want to create a native module is if you want to convert your ISAPI components into new native code modules.

A native code module contains the following:

- The RegisterModule function, which is responsible for creating a module factory and registering the module for server events.

- The implementation of the module class inheriting from the CHttpModule base class, which provides the main functionality for your created module.

- The implementation of the module factory class that implements the IHttpModuleFactory interface. It is responsible for creating instances of your newly created module.

The modules used in this example can be downloaded from Microsoft's *IIS.net* Web site at www.iis.net/downloads/default.aspx?tabid=34&g=6&i=1301. This module will be deployed as a global module in our demonstration, although any native module can be deployed at the application level just as managed modules are.

In developing a native module, the developer must implement the RegisterModule function that is started by the server when the module is loaded. In short, there are three tasks that are accomplished when implementing the RegisterModule function:

- **Saving the Global State** This is done by saving the global server instance for future use.

- **Creating the Module Factory** The module factory is responsible for creating instances of the native module for each request.

- **Registering for Server Events** This registers the module factory for the desired request processing events.

The implementing of the RegisterModule and the three tasks that are required to do so are shown in Figure 3.2 through Visual Studio 2005.

Figure 3.2 Implementing RegisterModule

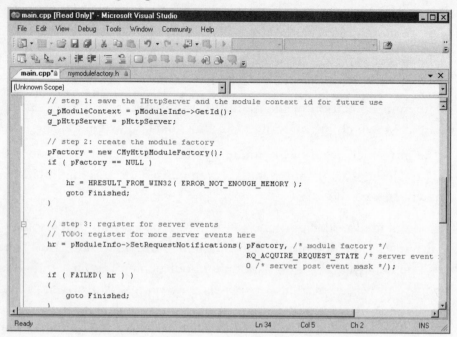

Registering a module factory is done through SetRequestNotifications. This tells the server to create the native module instance for each request using the module factory previously created, and to use the appropriate event handlers for each of the request processing stages. Once the developer has finished implementing the RegisterModule, he or she must export it to the server using a module definition file (.def). Afterward, the developer implements the module factory class. The module factory class implements the IHttpModuleFactory interface, which serves to create instances of the module on each request. Figure 3.3 shows the code for the module factory class.

Once this code is complete, the developer implements the module class, which is responsible for the main functionality of the module during any server events. The code for the main module is shown in Figure 3.4. Once complete, the developer can compile the module. Managed code, however, does not have to be compiled (we discuss managed code later in this chapter).

Figure 3.3 Module Factory Class

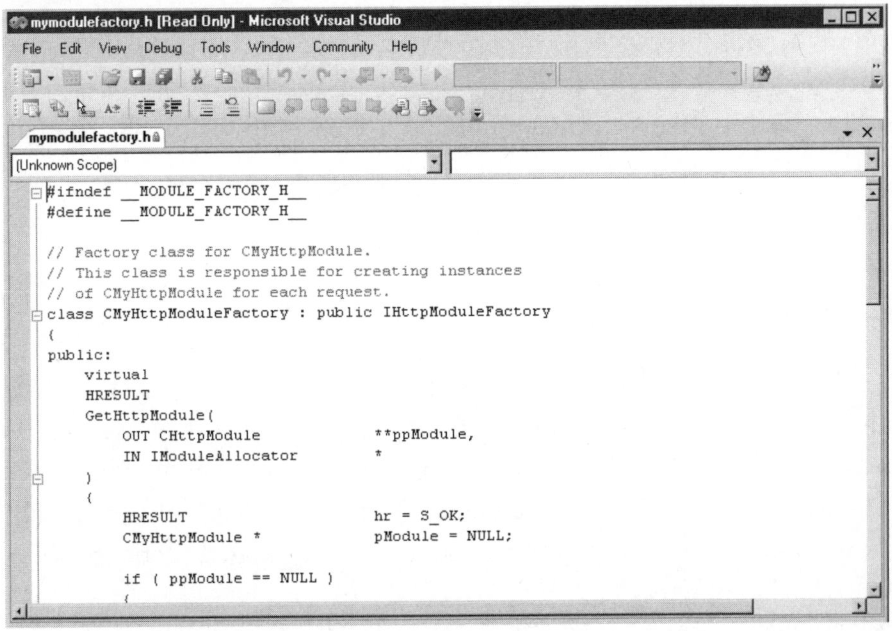

Figure 3.4 Main Native Module

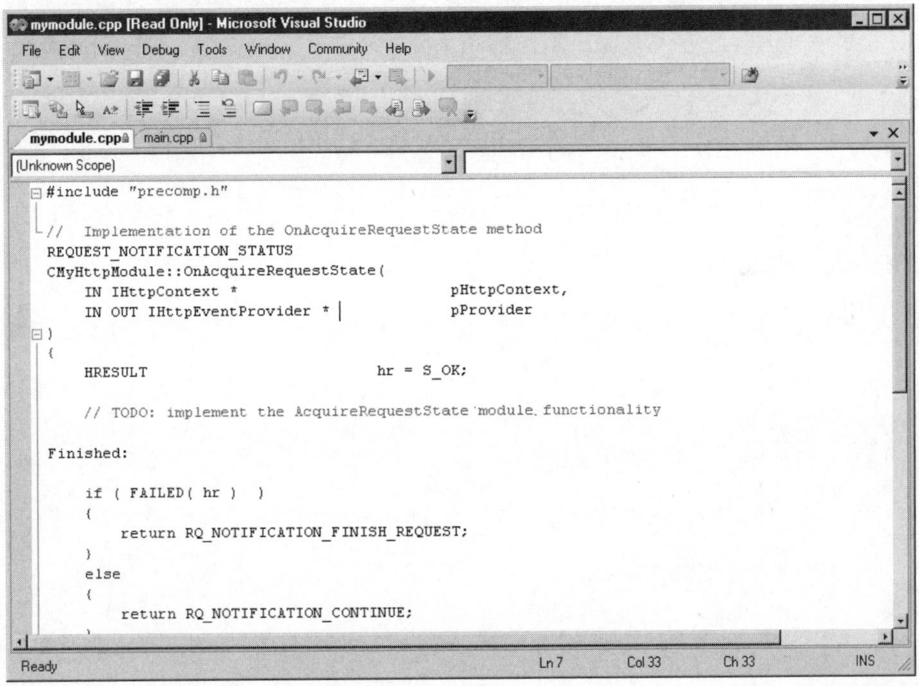

Adding Native Modules to IIS 7.0

In the previous section, we walked through what developers do to create a native module. In this section, we walk though what, as administrators, you will need to do to add these native modules to IIS 7.0. There are three ways to install a native module in IIS 7.0:

1. *APPCMD.exe*
2. IIS Manager
3. Manual Installation

Before adding the native module, you have to copy its .dll to the IIS server. There is no required location for the newly developed .dll, which in this case is called IIS7NativeModule.dll. Figure 3.5 shows that the new native module has been copied to the *C:\Native* directory, which was created on the IIS box. Now you need to deploy the module. First we will walk through using AppCmd, then IIS Manager, and finally manual deployment.

Figure 3.5 Location of the Native Module

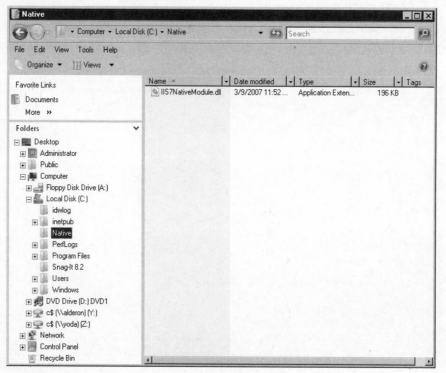

Using *APPCMD.exe* To Deploy Native Modules

As was introduced in Chapter 1, APPCMD.exe provides administrators with a new powerful command-line tool capable of managing IIS 7.0. To deploy a native module using APPCMD.exe, follow these steps:

1. Open a command prompt and go to the *%systemroot%\system32\inetsrv* directory.

2. As shown in Figure 3.6, type the command **appcmd.exe install module /name:MyModule /image:c:\Native\iis7nativemodule.dll**. Once the command has been executed, you should see a screen similar to that of Figure 3.7.

After adding the new module, you can verify that it has been added by examining the applicationHost.config file under the %systemroot%\system32\inetsrv\config folder. From the applicationHost.config file you can go to the <globalModules> section, as shown in Figure 3.8, and see that MyModule has been added.

Figure 3.6 Syntax for Using APPCMD.exe to Add a Native Module

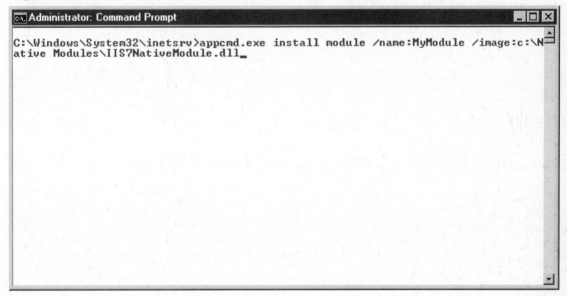

Figure 3.7 Results of Adding a Native Module with APPCMD.exe

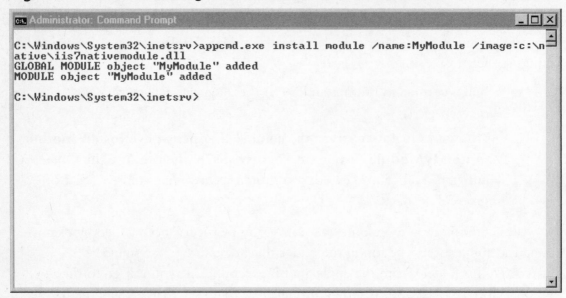

Figure 3.8 Deployed Native Module in applicationHost.config

Deploying Native Modules with IIS Manager

As shown with the APPCMD.exe command, administrators and developers can deploy native modules at the command line. Another method in IIS 7.0 is using the user interface of IIS Manager. Here are the steps to follow when you are deploying a native module in IIS 7.0 with IIS Manager.

1. Open IIS Manager. From Windows Vista this can be accomplished by clicking **Start | Run**. Type **inetmgr** and press **Enter**. The same also works for Windows "Longhorn" Server as does clicking on **Start | Administrative Tools | Internet Information Services (IIS) Manager**. Do not choose the IIS 6.0 Manager if it is installed.

2. Once in IIS Manager, go to **IIS Category | Modules**, as shown in Figure 3.9.

3. On the right side under **Actions** select **Add Native Module**, as shown in Figure 3.10.

4. Figure 3.11 shows the Add Native Module screen where you will see a list of registered modules. In this situation, the native module is not registered, so it must be registered first. On the right side of the dialog box select **Register**.

5. Under the Register Native Module dialog box (see Figure 3.12), enter the name of the module. For this instance the name is MyModule and the path is C:\Native\IIS7NativeModule.dll.

6. As shown in Figure 3.13, the native module (MyModule) is now selected from the list of registered native modules. Click **OK**.

7. Once finished you'll see the list of modules installed. You can change the view to the type of modules and then you will see that MyModule is installed as a native module, as shown in Figure 3.14.

Figure 3.9 Modules Section in IIS Manager

Figure 3.10 Add Native Module in IIS Manager

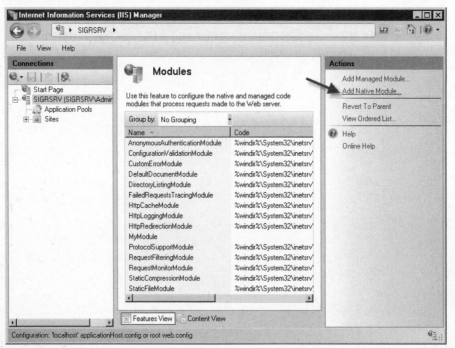

Figure 3.11 Adding an Unregistered Native Module

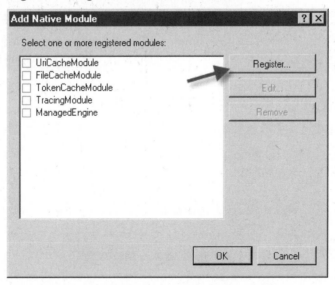

Figure 3.12 Register Native Module

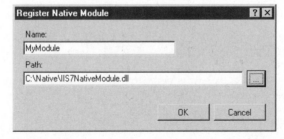

Figure 3.13 Native Module Selected

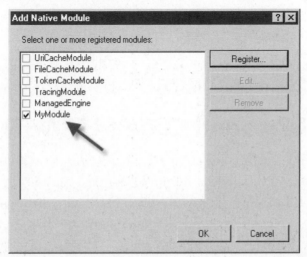

Figure 3.14 Native Module Deployed From IIS Manager

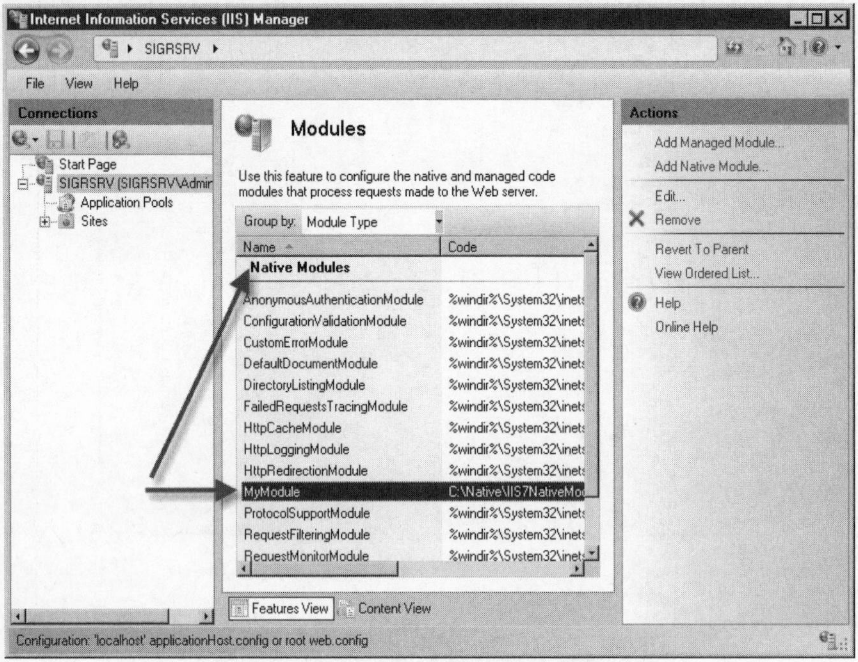

Manually Installing a Native Module

Manually deploying a native module is easier than it sounds. First, the .dll that accompanies the global module must be copied to the IIS server. After that, all it takes is editing the applicationHost.config file through any text editor such as Notepad, and entering the module information into the <globalModules> section.. The following example shows you how to install a newly created native module manually:

```
<add name="MyModule" image="c:\native\iis7nativemodule.dll"/>
```

As seen earlier, Figure 3.8 shows exactly how the aforementioned module would appear in the applicationHost.config file if it were a global module.

Enabling Managed Code (*ASP.NET*) in IIS 7.0

For the first time, managed code is a first-class citizen in IIS 7.0. In previous versions of IIS, managed code developers could not access data early in the request-processing cycle, because the IIS pipeline owned the area. Only when IIS sent the request (invoked) to ASP.NET could managed code act upon the request using a Hypertext

Transfer Protocol (HTTP) module. In IIS 7.0, a managed module has the same level of access to the request processing events as a native module has, and gives developers greater access to events.

It is important to understand how to enable managed code (i.e., *webengine.dll*), how to access request processing events and the implications of doing so.

Previously, ASP.NET features could not be applied to IIS content types (e.g., forms authentication for static files).

In versions before 7.0, managed code could not access the pipeline directly. It depended on IIS sending the request to ASP.NET, and then the managed code could act upon the request. When combined with ASP.NET, the IIS 6.0 model produced a lot of duplication, such as Universal Resource Locator (URL) mapping, authentication, and handler mapping. This meant having to configure services in two different places.

In the previous sections, we talked about and demonstrated how to install native modules in IIS 7.0. The following sections talk about and demonstrate the same with managed code. If you enable managed code in IIS 7.0, you must understand the iHttpModule interface and how its behavior depends on what mode the application pool is running in. We briefly go over both Integrated Mode and Classic Mode and when to use them.

iHttpModule Interface Support

For those unfamiliar with ASP.NET, here is a brief overview. ASP.NET is a programming model from Microsoft used for developing dynamic Web sites and Web applications. It was first released in 2002 with Visual Studio.NET. As part of the .NET Framework, which succeeded the older Active Server Pages (ASP) technology, ASP.NET is built on the Common Language Runtime (CLR) and supports numerous programming languages such as, but not limited to, C#, VB.NET, and JScript.

ASP.NET provides an interface for developers in IIS called iHttpModule. In IIS 6.0, iHttpModule housed such events as URL mapping, authentication, and handler mapping, hence a separate pipeline that could be used only for files with .aspx and .asmx extensions, not for other content such as static files.

The good news for developers of managed code is that a second pipeline is not needed. IIS 7.0 supports the iHttpModule interface, but now features powered by managed modules can be applied to *all* requests to the server, and it is handled by a single request pipeline. Unlike native modules, managed modules can be deployed with content. In IIS 7.0, managed modules are loaded in two ways:

- via webengine.dll, which is supported in integrated mode
- via isapimodule.dll, which is supported in classic mode

We cover more about the supported modes of IIS 7.0 in the next two sections. Extensibility in IIS 7.0 is now available to developers writing managed code. Before deploying a managed module, ASP.NET must be installed on the IIS server. Figures 3.15 and 3.16 show where to enable ASP.NET on Microsoft "Longhorn" Server and Windows Vista, respectively. The sample code used for demonstration purposes is from the "IIS Managed Module Starter Kit," which is provided for free by the Microsoft IIS Team and can be downloaded from www.iis.net/downloads/default.aspx?tabid=34&i=1302&g=6

Figure 3.15 Adding ASP.NET to "Longhorn" Server

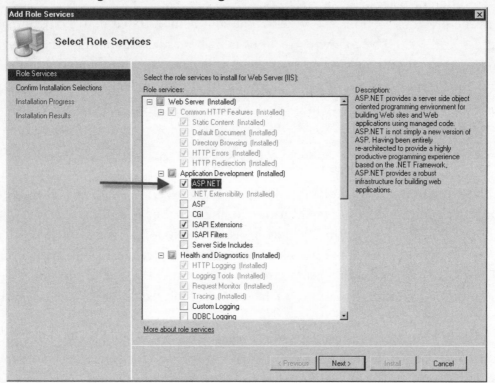

Figure 3.16 Adding ASP.NET to Windows Vista

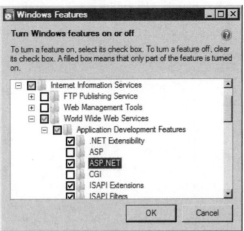

In Figure 3.17, you see some of the code for the managed module, which is written in C#. Notice IHttpModule in the code. Even if you weren't aware of the programming language used, this line shows that we are looking at a managed module and not a native one.

Although we will not go into the details of the code, it should be pointed out that the class MyModule's primary function is to register for event(s) that happen in the unified pipeline and then perform when IIS invokes the module's event handlers for its events. The Init statement sends up the module's event handler to the appropriate pipeline events. The Dispose line is used to clean up any resources after the module's instance is discarded.

After the developer compiles his or her code, the module is stored in a .dll file. In this case, it is named MyIIS7Modules.dll. Figure 3.18 shows the web.config file for this application.

Figure 3.17 Managed Code in C#

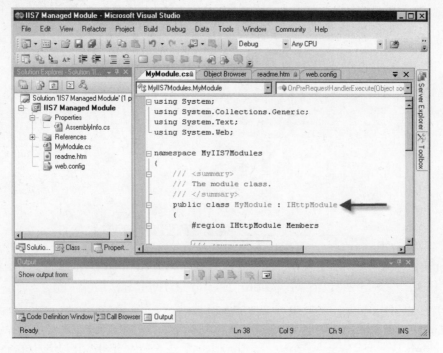

Figure 3.18 web.config

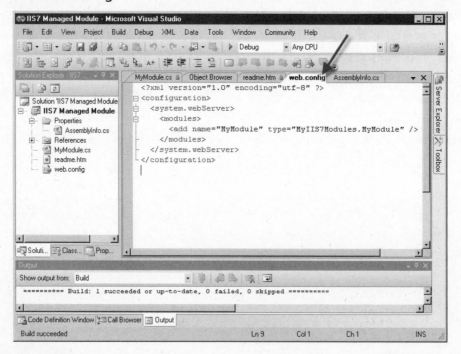

Once the code is compiled, you must deploy the module. Just as we did with the native module earlier in this chapter, copy the newly compiled .dll file somewhere on the IIS Server. In this example, we've copied it to the C:\Managed directory. Now copy the web.config file onto the server in the %systemroot%\inetpub\www-root directory. Open up IIS Manager (you can also deploy this with AppCmd.exe) and go to Modules. Under Actions, choose **Add Managed Module**, and then enter the information as shown in Figure 3.19.

NOTE

This application doesn't do anything, so for display purposes only, we chose **System.Web.Profile.ProfileModule**. After the module is added, it will appear in the list as a Managed Module under IIS Manager, as shown in Figure 3.20. You can also verify that it has been deployed by checking the <modules> section in the applicationHost.config file as shown in Figure 3.21. Please note that no managed modules will ever be added to the <globalModules> section, and that managed modules will always be loaded in the <modules> section.

Shortcut...

Managed Code Modules

Managed code modules don't have to be compiled by the developer. Simply take the application's logic in its file format (ex: .cs for C#) and drop it somewhere in the *app_code* directory on the server, and then ASP.NET will pick it up at runtime and compile it for you.

Figure 3.19 Entering Managed Module Information

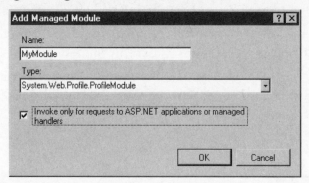

Figure 3.20 List of Managed Modules From IIS Manager

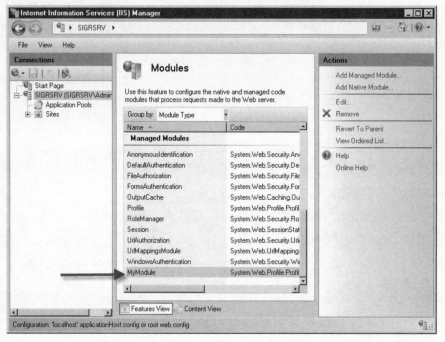

As we mentioned earlier, managed modules are loaded in IIS 7.0 in two ways and in two modes: integrated mode, which loads managed modules via webengine.dll, and classic mode, which loads via isapimodule.dll. Let's examine each.

Figure 3.21 applicationHost.config File <modules> section

Integrated Mode

Integrated mode in IIS 7.0 refers to the ability of managed code to have access to the unified pipeline. As mentioned earlier in this chapter, ASP.NET modules now have access to all content, not just from *.aspx* or *.asmx* files. So what actually creates the parity between managed code and native code in IIS 7.0? The answer is webengine.dll .

Webengine.dll is a native code module that resides under the <globalModules> section of the applicationHost.config file. It acts as a shim that allows managed code direct access to the fully integrated and unified pipeline. Developers using managed code still use the iHttpModule, but they are actually working with the shim. Webengine.dll allows managed code to be treated as a first-class citizen in IIS 7.0. To use it you must run in Integrated Mode.

Which mode you run in is determined at the application pool level. You can have some application pools running in integrated mode and others in classic. In Figure 3.22 we are creating a new application pool called MyTestApp. Notice that we can select which mode we want. In this example we've chosen **Integrated**.

Figure 3.22 MyTestApp

Classic Mode

Classic mode provides the same environment that we had in IIS 6.0. IIS 7.0 in classic mode installs both the ISAPI module and the ASPNET_ISAPI.dll ISAPI extension. In IIS 7.0 classic mode, managed modules are loaded using the isapimodule.dll file.

So, if we have this unified pipeline and the managed code is at the same parity as native code, why would we want to run in classic mode? The simple answer is if you have any custom modules defined they may not run in integrated mode. This environment is safe and robust for existing applications, and developers may see no need in converting existing applications.

- IIS 7.0 offers a new landscape for developers that was never available in IIS.

- In constructing IIS 7.0, Microsoft ensured that core processing of requests was removed from features that were implemented in individual modules.

- Access to early pipeline events, such as authenticating requests, were never possible for managed code developers until IIS 7.0.

Summary

IIS 7.0 now offers developers a better environment. It's easier than ever to extend IIS using either native or managed code. Access to a unified request pipeline now puts managed code in parity with its native brethren. IIS now ships with over 40 modules built-in for developers to take advantage of.

Extending IIS 7.0 with native modules is remarkably less stressful. No longer are native code developers dealing with the complexities of creating ISAPI filters and extensions. They now are able to make use of the same APIs that Microsoft used in creating IIS 7.0. Deployment of native modules is also easier. They can be placed anywhere on the server that they are running on. Developers and administrators also have the choice of how they want to deploy these modules. Deployments can be done from the AppCmd.exe command line utility, the IIS Manager, or by editing the applicationsHost.config file.

There are more options for developers using managed code. Managed modules can run in two different modes under IIS 7.0. Integrated mode provides the new features such as the unified request pipeline that both native and manage code share. Managed code has full access to all content not just that of ASP.NET. This available for managed modules through webengine.dll, a native global module that acts as a shim so that managed code can have direct access to the pipeline.

Developers who have applications that rely on the old IIS 6.0 architecture can do so by setting their application pools to run in classic mode. This provides the same pipeline behaviors and the limitations that come with IIS 6.0. It also provides a stable and secure environment to work in.

In IIS 7.0, Microsoft has created a much friendlier environment for developers and administrators alike.

Solutions Fast Track

Understanding Development Advantages in IIS 7.0

☑ IIS 7.0 offers a new landscape for developers never before available in IIS.

☑ In constructing IIS 7.0, Microsoft ensured that core processing of requests was removed from features that were implemented in individual modules.

☑ Access to early pipeline events, such as authenticating requests, were never possible for managed code developers until IIS 7.0.

☑ IIS 7.0 is easier to extend than ever before for developers.

☑ Because of the unified pipeline, managed code is no longer treated as a second-class citizen.

Extending IIS 7.0 with Native Modules

☑ Extending IIS with C or C++ no longer requires the creation of ISAPI extensions.

☑ Native code developers now have access to the same set of APIs that Microsoft used in developing IIS 7.0

☑ Deployment of native modules is easier because of tools such as AppCmd.exe and IIS Manager, or they can be done manually by editing the applicationHost.config file.

Enabling Managed Code in IIS 7.0

☑ ASP.NET has access to all content types.

☑ Application pools can run in one of two modes: Integrated or Classic.

☑ Integrated mode takes advantage of the new features and capabilities of IIS 7.0.

☑ Managed code running under integrated mode makes use of a native module called webengine.dll, which provides direct access to the unified pipeline.

☑ Classic mode provides the same environment of IIS 6.0 with all the stability and security that developers used for their legacy applications.

Frequently Asked Questions

The following Frequently Asked Questions, answered by the authors of this book, are designed to both measure your understanding of the concepts presented in this chapter and to assist you with real-life implementation of these concepts. To have your questions about this chapter answered by the author, browse to **www.syngress.com/solutions** and click on the **"Ask the Author"** form.

Q: If managed code now has the same direct access to the request pipeline as native code, then why would you create native modules?

A: Performance for one. Native code will always run faster with less overhead than managed code. Second, managed modules are application-specific, where as if you need to create a global module, then you must do so in native code.

Q: Which method is best when deploying native modules (AppCmd.exe, IIS Manager, or manually)?

A: It depends. If you are deploying multiple native modules at one time, then creating a script that makes use of AppCmd.exe might be your best bet. IIS Manager is an excellent choice for those who prefer a more task-oriented way of doing things. A person might deploy a native module manually if they are comfortable editing configuration files and feel using either method mentioned earlier would slow them down.

Q: If I run my managed code module in classic mode, would I need to deploy webengine.dll in the applicationHost.config file?

A: No. Only if you choose to run your code in Integrated Mode would you need webengine.dll. It allows managed modules direct access to the request pipeline.

Q: I have some applications that must run in classic mode, but I want to create newer applications that take advantage of the changes in IIS 7.0. Can I have some application pools running in classic mode and others in integrated mode on the same box?

A: Yes. When you add your application pool, choose which mode you want. In IIS Manager you will see the coexistence of integrated and classic mode pools.

Q: Why can't I have a managed module in the <globalModules> section of the applicationHost.config file?

A: Only native modules can reside in the <globalModules> section. Managed modules can only be set at the application level, not the global level.

Chapter 4

Get Started with IIS 7.0's Configuration

Solutions in this chapter:

- Introducing ApplicationHost.config
- Enabling Delegated Administration in IIS 7.0

☑ Summary

☑ Solutions Fast Track

☑ Frequently Asked Questions

Introduction

Since IIS 4.0, administrators have grown to love the metabase, whereas developers did quite the opposite. The metabase offered a complex, ID-based system, with tight security. In fact, to have write access to the metabase required that a user account have administrative privileges on the Web server. In IIS 7.0, out with the old (metabase) and in with the new (applicationHost.config, web.config) was the order of the day. IIS 7.0 built on the successful and highly popular .config infrastructure ASP.NET used to build the next-generation Web server configuration. The major items introduced to this XML configuration were the System.WebServer and the System.ApplicationHost namespaces designed to give administrators and developers a multitude of access points to configuration. IIS 7.0 also enables system administrators (Windows administrators) to delegate sections of the configuration to nonadministrators easing the burden of management on themselves. Beyond that, Web farm synchronization has never been easier than it is with IIS 7.0's distributed configuration capabilities.

Introducing ApplicationHost.config

The metabase lived a long, strong, and good life. It wasn't until security, and developer productivity, came to the forefront that the metabase's shortcomings were exposed. The metabase was not architected in a manner that offered an easy, yet productive mechanism to delegate write capabilities to nonadministrator users. Furthermore, it offered undesirable child behavior not enabled at the parent level by copying the entire parent metadata to the child—potentially doubling the size of the metabase. With the new configuration, called ApplicationHost.config, IIS 7.0 natively supports the IIS 6.0 configuration while also supporting these new robust features such as distributed configuration, as well as delegated configuration.

It is important that we outline in this section the prevalent pieces of the new configuration, including System.WebServer and System.ApplicationHost. The latter is unable to be edited by anyone other than system administrators (Windows), whereas the former can be unlocked and edited as part of the application deployment process. We will focus on offering good clarification between <sites>, <globalModules>, and other ApplicationHost-enabled features.

For years the metabase has served the world of IIS well, but as the saying goes, "the only constant in life is change," and change is exactly what IIS 7.0 offers. The old metabase was not designed in a way that was easy to read, and it did not provided a mechanism for delegating control to nonadministrators. The ApplicationHost.config file has now replaced the metabase as the primary store for IIS configuration and settings. It has definitions for locking down most IIS sections to the global level so that by default they are not overridden by lower level web.config files. The ApplicationHost.config file is an XML file that resides in the *%windir%\system32\inetsrv\config directory*. It stores lists of sites, applications, virtual directories, logging, caching, and so on. It also can be viewed or modified in any text editor.

The ApplicationHost.config file contains many sections. The first section you come to in the ApplicationHost.config file and one of the most important is *<configSections>*. This section registers all IIS and Windows Activation System (WAS) sections. It contains a list of all other sections in the file. Figure 4.1 shows the *<configSections>* section and the section groups of *<system.applicationHost>* and *<system.webServer>* of the ApplicationHost.config file. Other sections to note from the ApplicationHost.config file are:

- **<globalModules>** This section contains the collection of global modules on the server. All global modules are written in native code, such as C\C++.

  <modules> This section contains the collection of modules that are written in a supported .NET language such as C# or VB.NET. Native modules written in C\C++ can also reside here as well.

- **<sites>** This section contains the collection of site definitions.

The ApplicationHost.config file has two main section groups:

- **system.applicationHost** This group contains all settings for activation, such as the list of application pools, logging settings, listeners, and sites. It can be defined only at the global level, and only Windows systems administrators can edit it.

- **system.webServer** This group contains sections for the Web server—for example, a list of modules and ISAPI filters, ASP, CGI, and others. Most of the sections in the ApplicationHost.config file are under this section group. Settings in this section group can also be set in individual web.config files. Two notable sections within the system.webServer section group of the ApplicationHost.config file are <globalModules> and <modules>.

Figure 4.1 applicationHost.config

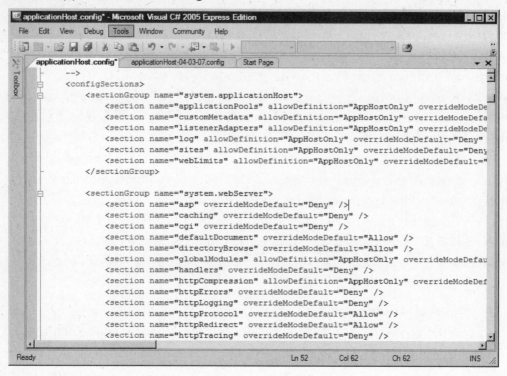

XML 101: The Basics of Configuration in IIS 7.0

There are some fundamental things that everyone needs to understand to succeed in using IIS 7.0. The IIS 7.0 configuration offers a great number of ways to edit configuration, none more useful yet unforgiving than your favorite text editor. In this section, we will spend a little time helping you become familiar with how the XML structure works in IIS 7.0. We will also discuss how to configure each of the different types of data.

For those familiar with the .NET config files and how they are laid out, some of this will be a review. The .config files used with IIS 7.0 are text files using the XML structure. Any of the .config files can be edited using any text editor such as Notepad in Windows. XML is easy to read but case sensitive, making it very strict and easy to make mistakes when you are making changes. You must keep this in mind when working with .config files. While discussing the XML structure in IIS 7.0, we'll examine the ApplicationHost.config file.

An understanding of section groups, sections, and location tags is vital to correctly edit the ApplicationHost.config file. First a *section* is a basic unit of deployment, registration, locking, searching and containment of configuration settings. Every section belongs to one section group, known as the *immediate parent*. The section group contains related sections and is used solely for the purpose of a structured hierarchy. No operations can be done on section groups. They cannot have direct configuration settings. You cannot create a section group and then begin putting configuration settings directly underneath them without the use of sections. Also, section groups can be nested, whereas sections cannot.

Because most sections are locked down by default, the recommended way to unlock them is by using tags. In IIS 7.0, you use a *location tag*. A location tag unlocks the section for the location that it specifies. In Figure 4.2 we see an example of a location tag, multiple section groups, and sections from the ApplicationHost.config file. As we just mentioned location tags can be used to unlock sections; in Figure 4.2 the location tag has unlocked all sections under the *<system.webServer>* section group; therefore, the settings under the *<security>* section group, such as the "access" section can be modified.

Figure 4.2 ApplicationHost.config Hierarchy

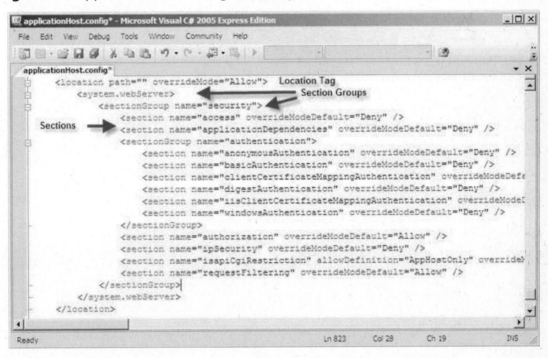

IIS 7.0 supports *distributed configuration*, which creates a unified hierarchy merged from multiple sources. Here is how it works: Values contained in the

ApplicationHost.config and web.config files are merged into an effective result for each possible URL. Those familiar with the security in NTFS can think of files inheriting rights from their parent directory and any directory above that establishing effective rights. The same principle applies to distributed configuration in IIS 7.0. Figure 4.3 is a graphical representation of the distributed configuration and hierarchy in IIS 7.0.

Figure 4.3 Distributed Configuration and Hierarchy

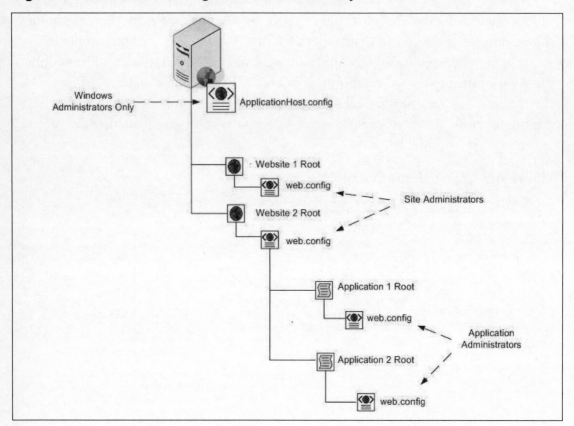

For instance, let's say that you are the site administrator (not the Windows administrator) for Web site 2. Your site has a link to a directory full of old Excel spreadsheets. People who use your site simply click this link on the Web page, and then the directory with all the Excel spreadsheets comes up. To allow this action, you must change the behavior of IIS 7.0. As the site administrator you can do this by creating your own web.config file that enables directory browsing, as shown in Figure 4.4. After you've deployed the new web.config file, users can now see the directory with all the Excel spreadsheets.

Figure 4.4 Sample web.config File

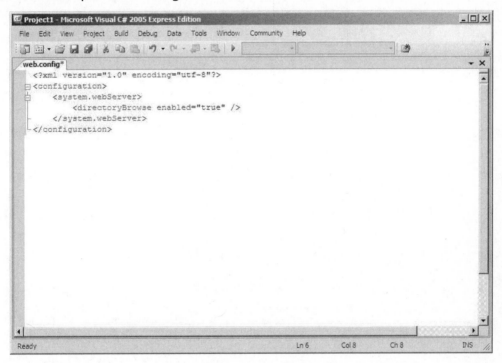

How is this possible? As the site administrator you can do this because the *overrideModeDefault* for the *directoryBrowse* setting in the ApplicationHost.config file is set to *Allow* (see Figure 4.5). This setting enables this feature to be delegated to developers or lower level administrators and allows them to change the behavior of IIS 7.0 without having to be system administrators. Reexamining Figure 4.3 shows us again how the new hierarchy in IIS 7.0 works. Notice that changes can be made at all levels, but changes can also be blocked at certain points, or for that matter, all levels in the case of denying a feature in the ApplicationHost.config file.

In our example, we stated that you were the site administrator for Web site 2. Now let's say you are the application administrator for Application 1 (refer back to Figure 4.3). Could you have accomplished the same thing? The answer is yes. As long as *directoryBrowse* was unlocked at the ApplicationHost.config file, which in our example it is, and the new site administrator for Web site 2 didn't disable it at the Web site level.

Figure 4.5 *directoryBrowse* Allowed in ApplicationHost.config

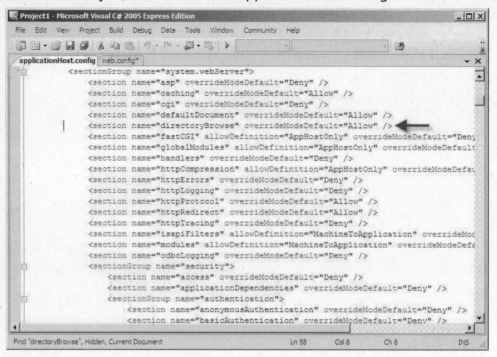

If the site administrator decided that he or she did not want the ability to browse directories available for any applications on his or her site, the administrator would simply set *<directoryBrowse enabled="false" />* in his or her web.config file (see Figure 4.6). Now no one below the site administrator for Web site 2 can use directory browsing in his or her applications. Remember that the ApplicationHost.config file unlocked the *directoryBrowse* feature, and that allowed it to be delegated to administrators and developers below the system administrator. If an administrator above you disables a feature that has been unlocked from the ApplicationHost.config file, then even if you set the feature to true in your web.config file, he or she will override you if he or she has set that same feature set to *false*.

Figure 4.6 Disabling a Feature in web.config

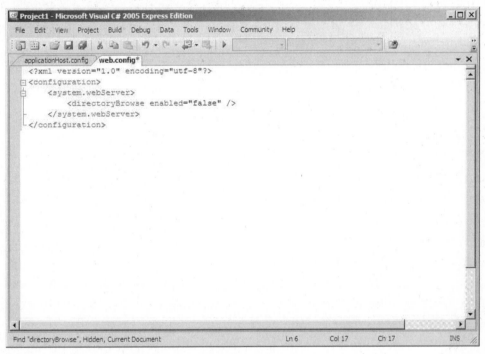

BEST PRACTICES ACCORDING TO MICROSOFT

Even though XML files can be edited via any text editor such as Notepad, Microsoft doesn't actually recommend that you use it. The reason is the strict nature of XML. XML is case sensitive and has a tight structure. Editing these files in Notepad would make it very easy to make syntax errors and difficult to find them. Microsoft recommends using a tool such as Visual Studio 2005. It makes reading XML easier. It color codes specific areas of a line and allows you to find the number of a line that might be causing a problem. Visual Studio also guides you through creating XML files such as web.config in avoiding syntax errors, making it easier on you when you are working with these files.

SOME INDEPENDENT ADVICE

Administrators who are not developers may have a tough time talking IT managers and CIOs into purchasing copies of Visual Studio for them so that they can easily edit .config files. Microsoft makes this easy for you. You can download express editions of Visual Studio for free at www.msdn.microsoft. com/vstudio/express. These are not full-blown editions of Visual Studio, but they will suffice in helping administrators who are not developers to work with these files—and at a cost any IT Manager or CIO can handle…free!

The System.ApplicationHost Section Group Purpose

We've learned what section groups and sections are in the ApplicationHost.config file. Now it's time to discuss one of the most important section groups there is: the system.ApplicationHost section group. Microsoft meticulously went through each part of the old metabase, broke it down into small pieces, and analyzed each piece from there. After the analysis, these pieces, based on functionality and purpose, were put into one of two locations: system.ApplicationHost or system.webServer section groups.

The system.ApplicationHost section group includes sections that define key parameters for a Web server. It holds sections that are used by the WAS service and are therefore defined globally. These sections include sites, application pools, applications, and virtual directories. They also contain some default settings for logging and application pools. Because it is a globally defined section group, it is protected from being delegated to nonadministrators. Figure 4.7 shows the actual system.ApplicationHost section group from the ApplicationHost.config file for IIS 7.0. Table 4.1 lists the sections and a brief explanation of each.

Table 4.1 Sections in system.ApplicationHost

Section Name	Description
applicationPools	Contains a collection of application pools.
customeMetadata	Used by the metabase compatibility component and should not be modified.
listenerAdapters	A collection of protocol adapters. Default protocol to serve is HTTP.
log	Contains global logging settings used by the WAS service.
sites	Contains the collection of site definitions.
webLimits	Contains some time-outs and limits used by the WAS service. By default this section is empty, and the defaults are taken from the schema.

Figure 4.7 System.ApplicationHost

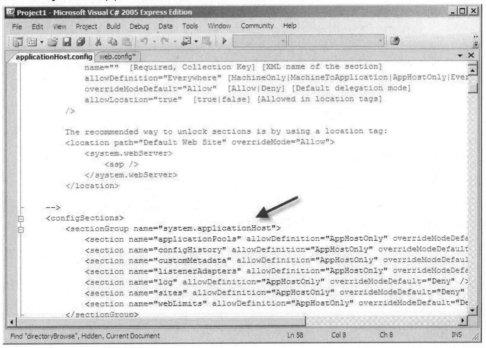

Understanding system.webserver

Considered the most powerful section group in the ApplicationHost.config file, the system.webServer section group is where the power and magic of IIS 7.0 really take place. Gone is the monolithic Web server of the past; in comes a configuration that fully supports IIS 7.0. This section group contains all the default settings for most of the more familiar metabase properties. It's also where you will see new features, such as IIS 7.0's failed request tracing. Figure 4.8 shows some of the system.webServer section group. Table 4.2 lists each of the sections in the system.webServer, and Table 4.3 lists the nested section groups and their individual sections. As we mentioned earlier, section groups can be nested within section groups; the system.webServer is a prime example of this. By default it nests three section groups with their own sections.

Figure 4.8 system.webServer

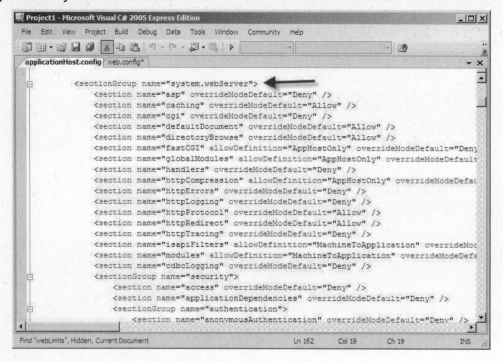

Table 4.2 system.webServer Sections

Section Name	Description
asp	Contains global defaults for ASP. By default its content is empty, and the defaults are taken from the schema.
caching	Contains cache-related configuration.
cgi	Contains the configuration for CGI.
defaultDocument	Contains the configuration for the default document functionality and the collection of files that can be served by default.
directoryBrowse	Contains the configuration for the directory listing functionality.
globalModules	Contains the collection of global native modules on the server.
handlers	Contains the collection of handlers: both native-code ISAPI extensions and managed-code HTTP handlers.
httpCompression	Contains configuration settings for both static and dynamic compression.

Continued

Table 4.2 continued system.webServer Sections

Section Name	Description
httpErrors	Contains the collection custom errors.
httpLoggins	Contains global defaults for the per-URL logging configuration.
httpProtocol	Contains the collection of HTTP custom and redirect headers.
httpRedirect	Contains the configuration settings for the client redirect functionality.
httpTracing	Contains trace-related configuration settings. By default its content is empty, and the values are taken from the schema.
isapiFilters	Contains the collection of ISAPI filters, both global filters and site filters.
modules	Contains the collection of modules, some native code and all managed code modules reside here. Can be customized per application.
odbcLogging	Contains configuration for the ODBC logging functionality. By default its content is empty, and the values are taken from the schema.
serverRuntime	Contains performance-related configuration settings that affect the runtime behavior. By default its content is empty, and values are taken from the schema.
serverSideInclude	Contains settings for the server side including functionality. By default its content is empty, and values are taken from the schema.
staticContent	Contains configuration that controls static content serving, including the collection of MIME maps.
urlCompression	Used to enable or disable per-URL and dynamic compression. By default its content is empty, and values are taken from the schema.
validation	Used to configure the validation module. It is responsible for detecting the existence of .NET Framework configuration that will be ignored by the Web server while in integrated mode.

Now we will examine the security section group which is nested within the system.webServer section group in Table 4.3. The security section group contains sections related to web server security.

Table 4.3 Security Section Group

Section	Description
access	Contains global defaults for access flags.
applicationDependencies	Contains dependencies between applications or ISAPI filters for the purpose of security lockdown. By default its content is empty and is modified as applications are installed.
authorization	Contains configuration for authorizing users and roles optionally depending on whether HTTP is being used in the request.
ipSecurity	Contains the collection of IP addresses to block from accessing the server.
isapiCgiRestriction	Contains the extension restriction list configuration to control which functionality is enabled or disabled on the server.
requestFiltering	Contains configuration for restricting requests. It contains a collection of physical directories to hide from the Web space.

We've already shown that the security section group is nested in the system.webServer. Within the security section group is another section group called authentication. This section group contains several sections for authentication. Each section corresponds to a specific authentication schema. Table 4.4 displays its sections with some description and the default setting.

Table 4.4 Authentication Section Group

Section	Description
anonymousAuthentication	Contains configuration for anonymous authentication.
basicAuthentication	Contains configuration for basic authentication.
clientCertificate-MappingAuthentication	Contains configuration for client certificate mapping authentication.
digestAuthentication	Contains configuration for digest authentication.
iisClientCertificate-MappingAuthentication	Contains configuration for IIS client certificate mapping authentication.

Continued

Table 4.4 continued Authentication Section Group

Section	Description
windowsAuthentication	Contains the configuration for Windows authentication.

Another section group is nested directly underneath the system.webServer section group: the tracing section group. The tracing section group contains sections for failed requests tracing. Table 4.5 lists its sections a description.

Table 4.5 Tracing Section Group

Section	Description
traceFailedRequests	Contains configuration for failed requests tracing. By default its content is empty.
traceProviderDefinitions	Contains the definitions for trace providers.

The IIS Schema: Your Cheat Sheet for Success

New users to IIS 7.0 are often caught off guard by errors, painful research, and unanswered questions. It isn't as though IIS 7.0 provides a cheat sheet or anything. Little do many users know that IIS 7.0's configuration is an open-book test with the answers living right inside the IIS schema. Many members of Microsoft's IIS team learned IIS 7.0 step by step using this schema as their guiding light. You should do the same thing if you want to understand the underlying configuration and how you work with it.

In this section, we will familiarize you with what the IIS schema looks like and show you how to understand what it is you are looking at.

What Is a Schema?

Before we can read the schema or extend it, we must first define is the term. A *schema* is an abstract representation of an object's characteristics and its relationship to other objects. An XML schema, such as the one in IIS 7.0, represents the interrelationship between the attributes and elements of an XML object. In IIS 7.0 the schema is declarative. In IIS 7.0, the schema is extensible in that all that needs to be done is add declarations to the system. Just like the ApplicationHost.config file, the schema is hierarchical and easy to read. The IIS 7.0 schema is located in the

%windir%\system32\inetsrv\config\schema. Those looking to extend the schema simply need to create their own schema files and drop them into the schema directory. You do not extend the schema by modifying any of the default schema files.

How to Read the Schema

Each configuration section in the schema is read as an XML element. Section groups found in the schema have no schema definition. The schema is read as follows:

```
<attribute-name>="<default-value>" [<metadata>] [<description>]
```

- **<attribute-name>** The name of the configuration attribute. Every attribute must have a name.

- **<default-value>** Value used if no other value is specified. Not all attributes have default values.

- **<metadata>** Contains several items such as the runtime type of the attribute. For example: *bool, enum, flags, int, int64, String, timeSpan.*

- **<description>** A short description of the attribute.

Section Schema

The *<sectionSchema>* is an XML element that represents the base unit of schema information. All schema information is specified underneath it. It has one direct attribute, which is *name,* and no others. The remaining parts of the schema are in subelements within the *<sectionSchema>.* Figure 4.9 shows the IIS_schema.xml file, notice the *<sectionSchema>* elements and the schema information in each.

Attribute Schema

All attributes are defined in corresponding *<attribute>* XML elements in the schema. The *<attribute>* element can be in the *<sectionSchema>,* in the element (if in a sub-element within the section), or in the *<collection>* element. The attribute schema has to specify a name and a runtime type for the attribute. It can also mark the attribute as required. For example, looking at Figure 4.9 you will find the following attribute under *<sectionSchema name="system.webServer/security/authorization">*:

```
<attribute name="accessType" type="enum" required="true">
```

Figure 4.9 IIS_schema.xml

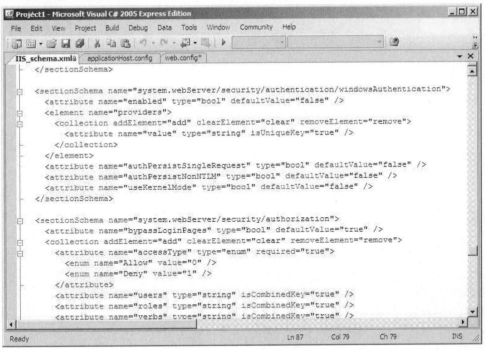

Obviously, the attribute name is *accessType*, the runtime type is *enum,* and that it is marked as required. *Enum* is a set of possible values, where only one of them can be set for the attribute. Below *accessType* you see the possible values for this attribute. We'll go over *Enum Schema* a little later. The attribute schema may also specify any of the following:

- Whether the attribute is required.

- Whether the attribute is a unique key or as part of a collection key along with other attributes.

- Whether the attribute has a default value.

- Whether the attribute is marked for automatic encryption on a disk.

- Whether the word *infinite* is allowed as a value for the attribute.

- Timespan format in seconds, minutes, or even a formatted string for timespan attributes.

- Validation rules for attributes.

Element Schema

All elements are defined in a corresponding *<element>* in the schema. The nesting of elements is supported. Simply put, an element is a container for other attributes or subelements. It is required to have a name, and it may even serve as a container of default values for collection elements. Figure 4.9 shows the *providers* element and its attributes. The syntax for the element schema is:

```
<element name="" [String, Required] [XML name of the element] isCollectionDefault=
[bool]>
```

Note, however, that *isCollectionDefault* would indicate whether the element schema has collection element default values, and not all element schemas have this.

Collection Schema

The *<collection>* XML element defines every corresponding collection in the schema. This element contains multiple elements that can be used and removed individually. Usually, its directive names are *addElement*, *removeElement*, and *clearElement*. You can see this by examining Figure 4.9 and noticing after the element *providers* is created below it, the collection schema is defined.

Enum Schema

Enum attributes must define their values to a corresponding *<enum>* XML element in the schema. Each value must have a friendly name and a numerical value. Remember our earlier example with the attribute *accessType*, the runtime type was listed as *enum*. After *accessType* was defined, we needed to define the *enum* values, which in Figure 4.9 show as:

```
<enum name="Allow" value="0" />
<enum name="Deny" value="1" />
```

Flags Schema

Every attribute of the *flags* type defines its values in corresponding *<flags>* XML element schema. They are required to have a friendly name and a numerical value. Figure 4.10 shows an example of the *flags* schema within the IIS_schema.xml file.

Figure 4.10 Example of Flags Schema

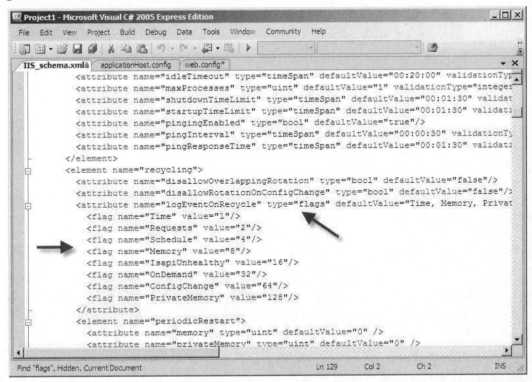

Enabling Delegated Administration in IIS 7.0

A fundamental security philosophy in the software world is to grant only what is needed, give what is necessary, and disable the rest. In IIS 7.0, the new configuration allows administrators control of features they never had before. An administrator of an IIS 7.0 server can leave the server as is and know that it is securely protected; meanwhile, another administrator has quick access to *unlock* feature by feature those that they deem necessary for nonadministrators.

It is important to understand which features are able to be delegated by default, but we should further outline how an administrator can enable delegation on a per-feature level in the configuration. It should be clearly outlined that this functionality is performed at the file level, but is also capable of being accomplished using the new IIS Manager (covered later).

Delegation Basics

You might have heard a bit about delegation prior to getting started with IIS 7.0. Delegation is a powerful feature in IIS 7.0 and one for which usage is likely in most organizations deploying IIS servers. However, you need careful planning to start to unlock feature by feature based on your environment requirements and Web application needs.

In this section, we will describe the overarching design of configuration delegation in IIS 7.0. Furthermore, we spend a great deal of time ensuring that you understand how to unlock the various pieces of configuration, such as section groups, sections, and attributes.

How It Works

As we've already discussed, IIS 7.0 supports delegation. For delegation to take place the system administrator must define the application or virtual directory from which to unlock features within the ApplicationHost.config file. Once this is done, developers or other administrators alike, then have the ability to alter the configuration of IIS for their Web sites and applications.

Figure 4.3 shows us how the hierarchy works. The system administrator creates Web sites and virtual directories, and then unlocks section groups, sections, and attributes. Site administrators can then distribute web.config files with whatever features they want to make available to developers of applications. Developers can also create their own web.config files to manipulate the configuration of IIS 7.0 to meet their needs. For IIS 7.0 to be altered by site administrators or application developers, the system administrator must unlock certain attributes and sections within the ApplicationHost.config file.

Unlocking system.webServer Section Groups

In vastly disconnected Web environments, it might be useful to completely delegate entire section groups such as security and other groups. This is useful to allow delegated management in enterprises or shared hosting environments where system administrators prefer to stay hands-off. The best way to do this is through the use of *location tags*.

Location tags specify path specific configurations and are used for locking and unlocking sections. The location tag for a path is set in a parent level in the configuration hierarchy, and considered to be at that parent level. This becomes important when it comes to locking semantics and what level can specify what sections. Unlocking can be done only at the level where the lock was defined.

If we wanted to unlock the *<security>* section group, we could place underneath a location tag similar to Figure 4.11. Just cut it from its current location in the ApplicationHost.config file and paste it to a location tag you create and a path you specify.

BEST PRACTICES ACCORDING TO MICROSOFT

Microsoft highly recommends creating a backup of the ApplicationHost.config file before you modify it. This can be done via the APPCMD command-line feature or simply by going to *%windir%\system32\inetsrv\config* and copying the file to another location.

SOME INDEPENDENT ADVICE

Encourage the system administrator to enable VSS (volume shadowing) if they haven't already done so, just in case they forget to manually backup the ApplicationHost.config file before modifying it. That way, if problems occur they can recover quickly to a working ApplicationHost.config file by choosing the last one that worked.

Figure 4.11 <security> and Location Tag

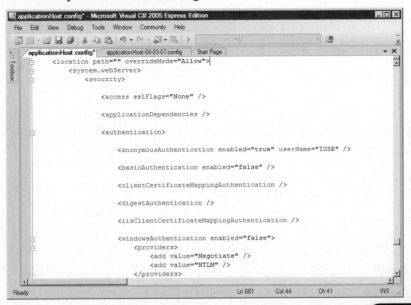

Section and Attribute locking in IIS 7.0

In more microscopic environments where system administrators desire some level of granular control, IIS' configuration offers section and attribute locking. For example, it might be necessary to allow developers to control just a simple section rather than an entire section group. Furthermore, system administrators might wish to keep control of the actual section while allowing application owners more control over particular settings for a section, in our case their attributes.

Unlocking Configuration Sections

As the system administrator you can unlock configuration sections for numerous situations. Here we will go through step by step where we need to add an application to our existing Default Web Site in IIS 7.0, and by unlocking configuration sections for delegation, we will be able to control certain settings via a web.config file. Before you start, do the following:

1. Back up the ApplicationHost.config file sitting in the *%windir%\system32\inetsrv\config* directory.

2. Create a directory to hold our web.config file that we will create later. In this example we are storing it in the C:\Test directory.

> **NOTE**
>
> For the purposes of this exercise we disabled directoryBrowse in our ApplicationHost.config file.

Now we will demonstrate how to unlock configuration sections in IIS 7.0.

1. First, you will add an application called *app* to your Default Web Site. To do this pull up IIS Manager; do not use the IIS 6.0 Manager. Open the site and highlight **Default Web Site**, as shown in Figure 4.12.

Figure 4.12 Default Web Site in IIS Manager

2. Right click **Default Web Site** and choose **Add Application**.

3. In the Add Application dialog box, enter the information as shown in Figure 4.13, then click **OK**.

Figure 4.13 Add Application Information

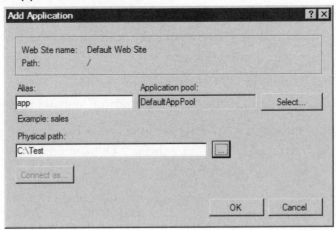

4. You should now see your application listed below Default Web Site in IIS Manager (see Figure 4.14).

Figure 4.14 Application app in IIS Manager

5. Now click on the server's name in the far left pane. In our example the server's name is **ALDERON**.

6. In the middle pane of IIS Manager, scroll down to the IIS Group and double-click **Directory Browsing**. After doing so you should see a screen similar to the one shown in Figure 4.15.

7. On the right side under **Actions**, select **Enable**. This will now allow directory browsing to be available to site administrators and application developers.

8. Open a text editor or Visual Studio and create a web.config file similar to the one in Figure 4.16. Save it in the C:\Test directory. Notice that in the web.config file has *directoryBrowse* enabled.

Figure 4.15 Authentication Section Group

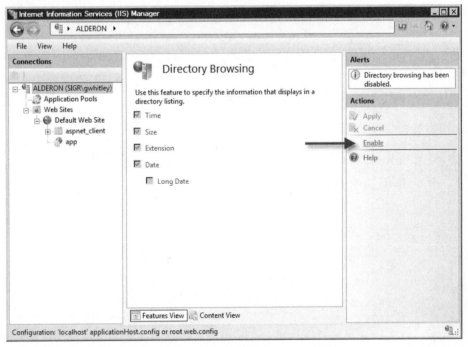

Figure 4.16 New Location Tag in ApplicationHost.config

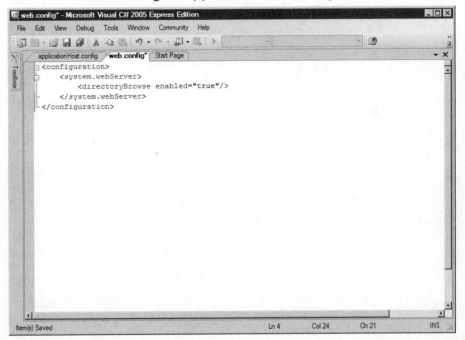

9. Now open Internet Explorer to the following URL: http://localhost/app.

10. You should now see the C:\Test directory with your web.config file in it (see Figure 4.17).

Figure 4.17 Results of Unlocking Configuration Sections

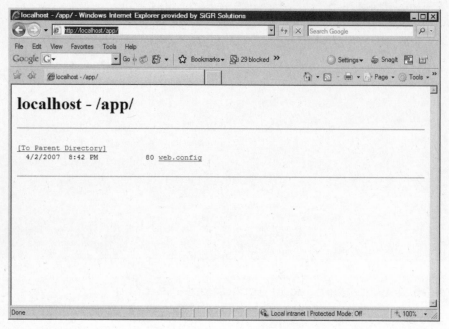

11. To disable it in your web.config change *<directoryBrowse enabled="false"/>*, as you did in Figure 4.18.

12. After disabling *<directoryBrowse>* refresh Internet Explorer, and you should see a screen similar to the one shown in Figure 4.19.

Figure 4.18 Disabling Directory Browsing in Web.config

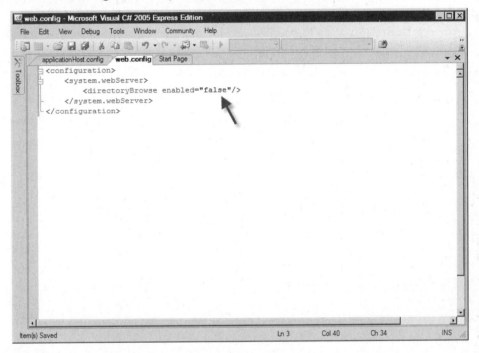

Figure 4.19 Testing Directory Browsing Disabled

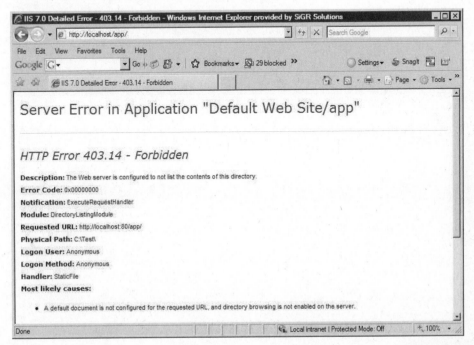

So why is delegation so important in IIS 7.0? First, IIS 7.0 configurations may now exist side by side with ASP.NET configurations. This means that Web server and application configurations can be deployed along with content. Another reason that delegation is so important is that security is not compromised. Administrators can pick and choose the features they make available for modification without having to provide system administrator rights to developers or lower level administrators; thus, everyone is more productive and efficient.

Summary

The old metabase was loved by some but hated by most because it was difficult to read and provided no mechanism for delegating to nonadministrators. It has been replaced by the XML configuration file ApplicationHost.config, which is easier to read and to configure. Within the ApplicationHost.config file are two important section groups: system.ApplicationHost and system.webServer. The system.ApplicationHost section group includes sections that define key parameters for a Web server. It holds sections that are used by the WAS service and are therefore defined globally. The system.webServer section group is where all the action is. It contains all the default settings and new features for IIS 7.0.

The schema in IIS 7.0 represents the interrelationship between the attributes and elements of each object. In IIS 7.0 the schema is hierarchical and easy to read, just as the ApplicationHost.config file is. A major improvement in IIS 7.0 over previous versions is delegation. Developers no longer need to have full administrative rights on the server to customize the behavior of IIS for their sites and applications. System administrators can simply delegate section groups or sections to developers, and then they are able to do the rest, easing the burden on administrators.

Solutions Fast Track

Introducing ApplicationHost.config

- ☑ ApplicationHost.config offers a level of configuration never before available in IIS

- ☑ Understanding who (security) can modify which configuration section, ApplicationHost versus WebServer is imperative to deploying a secure IIS 7.0

- ☑ Replaces the old hard-to-read metabase.

- ☑ It is the main configuration file in IIS 7.0.

- ☑ From within the file, administrators are able to delegate to non-administrators.

Enabling Delegated Administration in IIS 7.0

☑ Delegation is a powerful management tool and a much-needed feature in IIS 7.0.

☑ Able to unlock section groups, sections, and attributes.

☑ In xcopy scenarios, delegation is important where administrators simplify global configurations, allowing distributed and delegated configurations to exist on a per-site basis, thereby simplifying centralized management.

☑ Delegating administrative capabilities is accomplished in ApplicationHost.config, and yet some features are already enabled for delegation.

Frequently Asked Questions

The following Frequently Asked Questions, answered by the authors of this book, are designed to both measure your understanding of the concepts presented in this chapter and to assist you with real-life implementation of these concepts. To have your questions about this chapter answered by the author, browse to **www.syngress.com/solutions** and click on the **"Ask the Author"** form.

Q: What is the difference between ApplicationHost.config file and a web.config file?

A: The ApplicationHost.config file is the main configuration file for IIS 7.0. It holds global information about the server. The web.config file is used mostly by developers for applications that need to alter some specific behavior of IIS.

Q: Can anyone change the ApplicationHost.config file?

A: No. Only Windows system administrators (server administrators) can.

Q: What exactly is a section group?

A: A section group contains related sections and is used solely for the purpose of a structured hierarchy in a .config file.

Q: Can you explain what a location tag is?

A: Location tags specify path-specific configurations and are used for locking and unlocking sections. They are used at various levels of the configuration stack, such as: ApplicationHost.config, site, virtual directories, physical directories, and file level.

Chapter 5

Administration of an IIS 7.0 Web Server

Solutions in this chapter:

- **Accomplishing Tasks Using IIS Manager**

- **Accessing Information Using AppCmd.exe**

- **Writing Scripts Using the New WMI Provider**

- **Managed Code Administration: Inside Microsoft.Web.Administration**

☑ **Summary**

☑ **Solutions Fast Track**

☑ **Frequently Asked Questions**

Introduction

The IIS Manager of the past, albeit familiar by now, was clunky and difficult to familiarize yourself with. The goals of the IIS 7.0 user interface took the strong points of the old MMC-based user interface and added intuitive, useful scenario-based usage patterns. So out came the all-new IIS Manager, built to be task-based and extensible in order to ensure that Web administrators could tackle the most common tasks with little effort.

For many, IIS Manager simply doesn't scale since it isn't capable of managing large Web farms where a multitude of Web servers exist for a single site or application. The environments need more automated ways of making changes, and to do so as quickly, and with as few errors, as possible. IIS 7.0 offers users a plethora of options in this space with AppCmd.exe, WMI, and Microsoft's Web.Administration API for managed code.

Accomplishing Tasks Using IIS Manager

With a rewritten user interface, the first question that arises is how one can accomplish the same tasks using this new IIS Manager. The IIS Manager included with IIS 7.0 gets away from tabs (like IIS 6.0's IIS Manager) and uses feature-based access for its configuration. To configure the most popular features, a wizard will walk you through step-by-step instructions to fully enable the feature.

It is important to understand how to do the most important tasks, such as creating new Web sites, application pools, and applications. Beyond that, the most common task is to change the security settings and diagnostics settings using the IIS Manager.

Best Practices According to Microsoft

The all-new IIS Manager is available for Windows XP, Windows 2003, Windows Vista, and also for Windows Server "Codenamed" Longhorn. To use IIS Manager on Windows XP and Windows 2003, download the IIS Manager from www.iis.net/downloads/default.aspx&tabid=3.

IIS Manager: Getting Started

IIS Manager in IIS 7.0 gets away from the Microsoft Management Console (MMC) and instead was built using .NET's Windows Form technology. It offers most of the features available in the IIS 6.0 Manager, yet accessing these features is drastically different. Based on categories, the features are easily exposed at different levels of IIS Manager, such as the server, site, or application level.

Beyond that, IIS Manager fully supports IIS 7.0's delegation features at the various levels. A typical example of the delegation is allowing the server administrator to delegate administration to other users such as modifying authentication, default document settings, and much, much more.

Lastly, IIS Manager is built using managed code and is constructed on a nicely formed Web services architecture that allows developers to build custom modules and add them to IIS Manager to help you better manage their custom features. This is very useful for administrators since you can do tasks in IIS Manager for built-in IIS features and also for custom applications added later that are not part of IIS.

The one downside to the new IIS Manager is that it only supports administering IIS 7.0 servers. It doesn't support connecting to previous versions of IIS and making configuration changes. For customers needing this functionality, you should install the IIS 6.0 Management Tools. The end result is that you can have both IIS Manager for IIS 6.0 as well as the new IIS Manager.

The IIS Manager Overview

IIS Manager will always provide you with a view of only the objects you have permission to access. These permissions, though, do not change the primary view you will always see when using IIS Manager. The user interface is divided into three columns, with a left, center, and right column. In the left column, you will always be presented with a tree hierarchy, as shown in Figure 5.1. Based on your selection in the left column, the appropriate screen will appear in the center column (Figure 5.2), often referred to as the home page. The right column (Figure 5.3) is your task pane, offering you options based on your selection as well as helpful alerts, such as warning and informational text.

Figure 5.1 IIS Manager

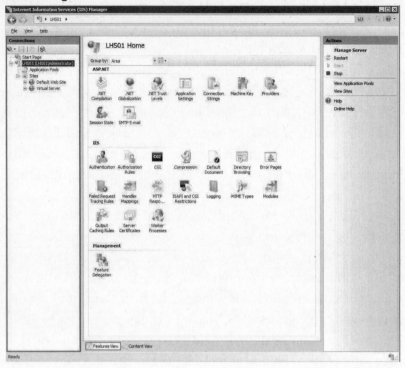

Figure 5.2 IIS Manager Center Column (e.g., Home Page)

Figure 5.3 IIS Manager's Task Pane

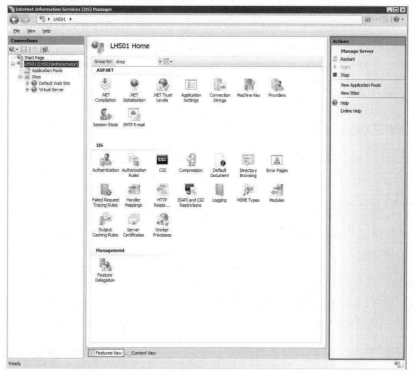

Adding Connections

In IIS 7.0, you can emulate the MMC behavior of having a single IIS Manager with multiple connections to servers. Beyond that, you can have connections directly to sites or applications all contained within the same IIS Manager. These connections, along with other preferences you select, are maintained even after shutting down the user interface.

The preferences, as well as modules and other relevant information, are stored in IIS Manager's configuration file named administration.config. This file is located in the %windir%\system32\inetsrv\config directory like other key IIS 7.0 files such as applicationhost.config.

NOTE

In Windows Vista, IIS Manager doesn't support connections to sites and applications. This is by design because IIS 7.0 in Windows Vista was tuned to developers, and the connection functionality is built for administrators and delegated administration. Instead, Windows Vista's IIS 7.0 IIS Manager supports server-level connections only.

In Windows Server "Codenamed" Longhorn, the connections user interface is available to allow users to connect to sites and applications specifically.

To add connections to a site or application in IIS Manager on Windows Server "Codenamed" Longhorn:

1. Right-click **Start Page**.

2. Click the option based on your selection (e.g., Server, Site, or Application). See Figure 5.4.

3. Enter the server, site name, and\or application in the **Add... Wizard**.

4. Click **OK**.

Figure 5.4 The IIS Manager Connection Manager in Windows Server "Codenamed" Longhorn

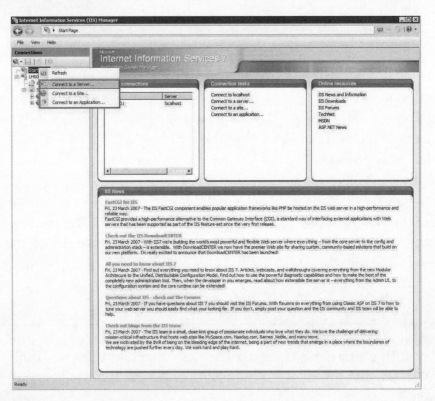

Sorting IIS Manager

IIS Manager in IIS 6.0 was heavily limited because of its hosted nature in the MMC. On the other hand, IIS Manager in IIS 7.0 offers you the ability to sort (group) the center column based on your preference. There are two sort-types and they are by area or category.

The area type will sort the features based on what that feature relates too, such as IIS or ASP.NET. Unlike any previous versions of IIS, IIS Manager is a consolidated user interface for both IIS and ASP.NET. Hence, this sorting will put IIS features under a heading called IIS, while ASP.NET is under a heading called ASP.NET, as shown in Figure 5.5.

In some cases, you are only interested in seeing them sorted, not based on technology, but rather by category. The category sorting will sort by the area per feature, such as application development, health and diagnostics, and so forth.

Lastly, you can choose to use No Sorting, which will present each feature as shown in Figure 5.4.

Figure 5.5 Selecting IIS Manager Sorting and Group By

Accomplishing the Most Common Tasks Using IIS Manager

It isn't very helpful to just look at IIS Manager. Rather, it is more important to know how to use IIS Manager. It is fairly intuitive to accomplish the high-level tasks you will often use IIS Manager for, such as creating Web sites, virtual directories, application pools, and applications. However, if you are new to IIS, then these tasks might not be as trivial as a veteran user so we will make sure you know how to easily accomplish these tasks so you can get started hosting your sites immediately.

Beyond that, you will need to manage your server's Secure Socket Layer (SSL) certificates and other settings. You will need to know how to enable these features in IIS Manager after you have created your sites or applications and we will show you how to do this.

Creating Web Sites

This is the most fundamental piece of the entire IIS 7.0 product. Without Web sites, you will not be interested in anything further about IIS 7.0. Web sites are simply containers for content such as application code, images, and style sheets. By default, IIS 7.0 provides you with a Web site called the Default Web Site. This site's default content path is located on %systemdrive%\inetpub\wwwroot.

To create a new Web site, do the following:

1. Right-click the server and select **Add Web Site**.

2. In the **Add Web Site Wizard**, enter the appropriate site name, content path, and binding information.

3. Click **OK**.

SOME INDEPENDENT ADVICE

When creating sites, you have three options of bindings. In IIS 7.0, you will need to ensure that the Ip:Port:HostHeader combination must be unique for both HTTP and HTTPS. You can select to bind a Web site to a single IP address, an IP address using a unique port, or using an IP address with a unique host header.

For SSL-enabled Web sites, you will need to ensure they are uniquely bound as well to a specific IP:Port unless you are using Wildcard SSL certificates.

Creating Virtual Directories

Virtual directories traditionally were created in IIS's Web sites to add content that lives outside the Web sites' root path. For example, if you are interested in adding content to your Default Web Site called app2 that exists in d:\MySecondApp, then you would create a virtual directory and point it to this path. Then, your Web clients can access this content using the Web sites URL plus /app2.

In IIS 7.0, virtual directories also define applications. For example, when you create a new virtual directory in IIS Manager, you will create a new application root for that directory. This behavior is slightly different than in previous versions of IIS. The important change is that virtual directories in IIS 6.0 were typically assigned to the application of their parent, where IIS 7.0 creates a new root application.

To create a new virtual directory, you do the following:

1. In the left column, select the Web site where you would like to create a virtual directory.
2. Right-click the Web site—for example, Default Web Site.
3. Click **Add Virtual Directory…**
4. In the **Add Virtual Directory Wizard**, type **alias** and enter the path.
5. Click **OK**.

Creating Applications

Many veteran IIS administrators were very familiar with the concepts sites and virtual directories, though, not nearly as familiar with applications. On the other hand, Web developers typically are the opposite and are focused on applications. IIS 7.0 brings the concept of applications to the forefront and makes applications first-class citizens. This isn't to say they haven't been important in the past, just that they typically weren't the focal point—something that is certainly different in IIS 7.0.

The key concept to grasp about applications is that applications are the fundamental building blocks of your Web sites. They are where your developers or Web business-logic is executed and where applications are assigned to a specific application pool. To isolate them fully, you would have one application per application pool, though you can certainly have many applications all participating in the same application pool.

To create a new application, do the following:

1. In the left column, select the Web site where you would like to create a virtual directory.

2. Right-click the Web site—for example, Default Web Site.

3. Click **Add Application...**

4. In the **Add Application Wizard**, type **alias**, select an application pool, and enter the path.

5. Click **OK**.

Creating Application Pools

Application pools is a concept that was added in IIS 6.0. In IIS 7.0, it changed very little and is basically the same and defines what applications run within what worker process. This is IIS's isolation functionality and is where you can recycle, change process identity security, and view health and diagnostics information. By default, IIS 7.0 provides you with a single application pool called DefaultAppPool.

SOME INDEPENDENT ADVICE

The default behavior for adding new Web sites in Windows Vista is to add it to the DefaultAppPool. This behavior is by design since Windows Vista is a client environment and isolating each Web site and its root application into its own application pool would hinder the performance of the client.

In Windows Server "Codenamed" Longhorn, though, each time you create a new Web site using IIS Manager it will create a new application pool. This behavior is expected and creates maximum isolation of your Web applications and is a good security practice.

To create an application pool, do the following:

1. In the IIS Manager **Connections** pane, expand the server node and click **Application Pools**.

2. On the **Application Pools** node, right-click and choose **Add Application Pool...**

3. In the **Add Application Pool** dialog, provide a name for the application pool in the **Name** field.

4. From the **.NET Framework version** list, select the version required by your managed applications. Otherwise, choose **No Managed Code** if the applications in this pool don't require the .NET Framework.

5. From the **Managed pipeline mode** list, select the ASP request processing mode.

6. Select the **Start application pool immediately** check box to start the pool when the WWW service is started.

7. Click **OK** to create the new Application Pool.

NOTE

The Actions pane provides the same "right click" functionality for the Application Pools.

Changing Authentication Settings

You can take several actions in the security space, such as changing the authentication type for your Web site or application. The needs of your Web applications often differ even though they are running on the same server and it is important to understand how to change authentication settings.

Authentication in IIS 7.0

IIS 7.0 offers several options like previous versions of IIS for authenticating to your Web server. The default behavior for a typical installation of IIS 7.0 is to have all authentication types disabled except anonymous authentication.

Enabling Basic Authentication

Basic authentication is a standards-based authentication for HTTP clients. It is a popular authentication when protected by SSL, but should not be used on the Internet without protecting the authentication with SSL since it will expose your user's credentials, given it is an insecure protocol.

To enable Basic authentication, click the left column of your Web site, then follow these steps:

1. On the Web site home page, double-click **Authentication**.

2. Select **Basic Authentication** by clicking it.

3. In the right-column, click **Enable** in the Actions.

Enabling Windows Authentication

In Intranet environments, it is common to disable anonymous authentication and enable Windows authentication. In IIS 6.0, Windows authentication was enabled by default but this isn't the case in IIS 7.0. There is often a lot of confusion around Windows authentication because it has a couple of authentication protocols in it, namely NT Challenge\Response (NTLM) and Kerberos. The default setting is to allow both in IIS 7.0 and let the client select the protocol to use.

To enable Windows authentication:

1. Click your **Web site** in the left column.

2. On the Web site home page, double-click **Authentication**.

3. Select **Windows Authentication** by clicking it.

4. In the right-column, click **Enable** in the Actions.

SOME INDEPENDENT ADVICE

It is possible that when viewing Authentication in IIS Manager you will not see all the supported IIS 7.0 authentications in the list. This is what happens when you have chosen not to install the authentication during setup. If you do not see the authentication type you want, use setup to add the features binaries and then restart IIS Manager.

Enabling Digest Authentication

Digest authentication is a standards-based authentication protocol defined in RFC 2617 (www.ietf.org/rfc/rfc2617.txt). In IIS 7.0, there is only one version of digest authentication, unlike in IIS 6.0. For more information on digest authentication, see the following Microsoft Webcast www.iis.net/default.aspx?tabid=2&subtabid=26&i=67.

To enable Digest authentication:

1. Click the left column of your Web site.

2. On the Web site home page, double-click **Authentication**.

3. Select **Digest Authentication** by clicking it.

4. In the right-column, click **Enable** in the Actions pane.

Enabling Forms Authentication

The integration between IIS and ASP.NET is unprecedented in IIS 7.0. This integration lets you protect all your content using ASP.NET's forms-based authentication. This cookie or cookie-less-based authentication allows Web applications to be authenticated using credentials other than Windows. For more information on forms authentication, see the following http://msdn2.microsoft.com/en-us/library/aa480476.aspx.

To enable forms authentication:

1. Click the left column of your Web site.

2. On the Web site home page, double-click **Authentication**.

3. Select **Forms Authentication** by clicking it.

4. In the right-column, click **Enable** in the Actions pane.

SOME INDEPENDENT ADVICE

When using Forms Authentication, you will need to do a bit more work than just enabling it in IIS. You are required to create a default login page using ASP.NET's login control and save that page. The default settings for Forms Authentication are available in IIS Manager by clicking Edit after selecting Forms Authentication.

Viewing Worker Process Details

IIS 7.0 gives administrators some incredible information about what is occurring in IIS's worker processes. This includes giving you the ability to see what requests are currently executing within a worker process and other details, like how long it has been executing. This is all available by viewing worker process details in IIS Manager.

To view currently executing requests within a worker process:

1. Click the left column of the server.

2. Select **Worker Processes** on the home page.

3. Click **DefaultAppPool**.

4. In the **Actions** pane, click **View Current Requests**.

Changing Diagnostic Settings

IIS 7.0 offers some powerful diagnostics capabilities, in particular the all-new Failed Request Tracing. You will learn more about failed request tracing in Chapter 6, but for our purposes here we will show you how to enable failed request tracing to assist you in troubleshooting your Web applications.

Failed request tracing is a two-step process when using IIS Manager. The first step is to enable tracing for the server, and then configure your rule for tracing to capture the data.

Do the following to enable Failed Request Tracing:

1. Click the left column of your Web site.

2. In the right column, click **Failed Request Tracing** under Configure.

3. In the **Edit Web Site Failed Request Tracing Settings**, check **Enable** and choose a path for your log files.

4. Choose the number of log files to maintain in the Maximum number of trace files.

5. Click **OK**.

Best Practices from Microsoft

For Web sites that are heavily used with hundreds of requests per second, it is recommended you set the Maximum number of trace files much higher than the default of 50. This will aid you in ensuring that when your problem occurs you will not have lost the data because of the busy nature of the site.

Selecting Rules for Failed Request Tracing

The key step to ensuring you capture the right data is to set up the right rule. You will learn later that you can set up multiple rules for your server, site, or application to assist you in troubleshooting your problem. The key step to understand is how to narrow your rule to capture only the data you need, nothing more.

In our example, we will show how to use a simple rule for capturing data when a HTTP 500 error occurs. HTTP 500 errors are defined as server failures and come in various flavors.

To create an HTTP 500 Error for All ASP.NET Pages:

1. Click the server in IIS Manager.

2. On the IIS Manager server home page, double-click **Failed Request Tracing**, as shown in Figure 5.6.

Figure 5.6 IIS Manager Failed Request Tracing

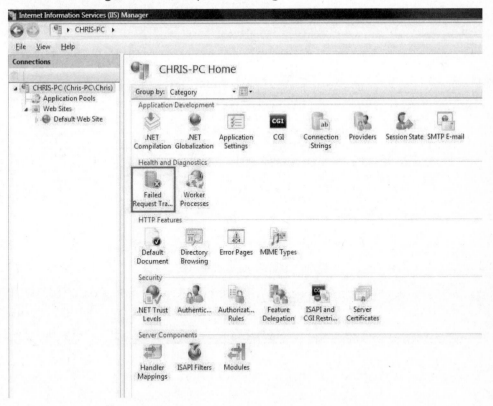

3. Click **Add** under **Actions** to start the Add Rule Wizard.

4. Select the content you would like traced—for example, ASPX pages (e.g., ASP.NET requests).

5. Choose what criteria, either HTTP status code or time-taken, to trace requests. Select **500** and click **Next**.

6. Select what providers to choose from—in your case, pick all providers, including ASP, ISAPI Extension, and WWW Server, as shown in Figure 5.7.

7. Click **Finish**.

Figure 5.7

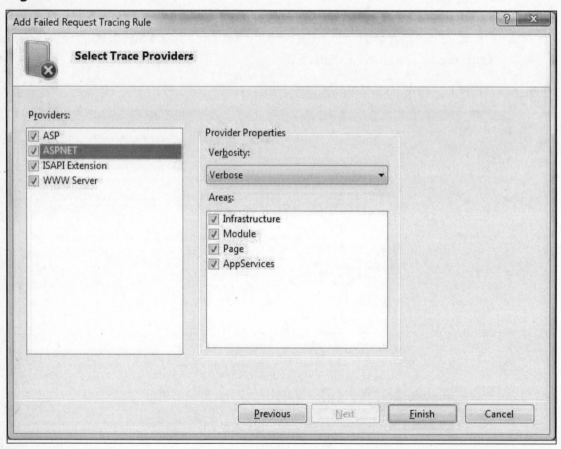

SOME INDEPENDENT ADVICE

In Windows Vista, the ASP.NET Provider is missing from IIS Manager. This provider exists in the configuration and is available. In a recent blog post, Microsoft acknowledged this problem and displays how to correct it. For more information, see http://blogs.iis.net/chrisad/archive/2007/04/10/tracing-asp-net-provider-on-windows-vista.aspx.

Accessing Information Using AppCmd.exe

AppCmd.exe is a convenient utility offered as an alternative to using IIS Manager, writing code, or building a script. Sometimes, you may be interested in making one or two changes to IIS's configuration but don't want to click this or that in IIS Manager. Or maybe the actual configuration isn't even available in IIS Manager, leaving you with no other choice. AppCmd solves this problem by using a familiar approach that employs verbs and objects. It combines much of the past power of the Visual Basic scripts (.vbs) shipped with IIS while providing a much more powerful functionality than ever offered by these scripts. Understanding how to use it will prove a strong and useful tool in managing your IIS servers.

BEST PRACTICES ACCORDING TO MICROSOFT

IIS 7.0 supports direct editing of the configuration files, including applicationHost.config and web.config files. This is a powerful ability considering that you can use your favorite text editor to build your custom server's configuration.

However, it is not recommended you directly edit the configuration using tools such as Notepad without first testing that your configuration is valid on your Web server. When using the text editor, there is no validation that your configuration is correct, something which can possibly render your Web server, sites, or applications unavailable.

This is where administration tools such as AppCmd.exe come in handy. They will not write invalid configurations but instead will return an error.

SOME INDEPENDENT ADVICE

AppCmd.exe does not work remotely. In order to successfully use AppCmd.exe, you must connect directly to your IIS 7.0 server. This is capable of being done using Terminal Services, such as using the command *mstsc /console /v:yourIIS7Server*, where *yourIIS7Server* is the name of your Web server.

An Introduction to AppCmd.exe

In IIS 6.0, you had a large list of toolsets available to you to make changes at the command line to the configuration. These were included in various Visual Basic scripts (.vbs) located in %windir%\system32 or in %systemdriver%\inetpub\admin-scripts. The downside, though, was that they were specialized and each had different verb syntaxes and object manipulation styles. In IIS 7.0, your command-line experience is combined to a single application called AppCmd.exe. In this section, you are introduced to this powerful command-line tool aimed at simplifying your experience.

Server Management Objects and Commands

AppCmd allows you to create/configure Web sites, applications, application pools, and virtual directories. You can start and stop sites, recycle application pools, list worker processes, and examine currently executing requests. You can also search, manipulate, import, and export IIS and ASP.NET configuration data.

SOME INDEPENDENT ADVICE

AppCmd.exe is not located in the system path, but instead in %windir%\system32\inetsrv. If you want quick access to the IIS 7.0 configuration runtime information, add inetsrv to the system path.

To use AppCmd in changing directories, type:
set path=%path%;%windir%\system32\inetsrv
If you're not logged on as a member of the Administrator group, run this command in an elevated cmd window from Start | All Programs | Accessories | Command Prompt. Right-click and choose **Run as administrator**.

Command syntax is based on server management objects that expose methods to perform actions and properties that reflect the current state. Most objects provide list, add, and delete methods. Site objects have start/stop methods and properties that can be read, written, or searched. All commands provide a list of object instances and property values.

You execute AppCmd commands on server management objects with parameters to control command behavior, such as the following:

```
APPCMD <COMMAND> <OBJECT> <ID> [ /parameter:value ]
```

<COMMAND> specifies a command supported by the object.

The following basic commands are supported by most objects:

LIST	Displays all objects on the machine. Optional <ID> specifies a unique object.
ADD	Creates a new object with specified property values.
DELETE	Deletes specified objects by <ID>.
SET	Sets parameters specified by <ID>.

The *Site* object supports *START* and *STOP* commands.

<OBJECT> specifies a server management object:

SITE	Administration of virtual sites
APP	Administration of applications
VDIR	Administration of virtual directories
APPPOOL	Administration of application pools
CONFIG	Administration of general configuration sections
BACKUP	Management of server configuration backups
WP	Administration of worker processes
REQUEST	Display of active HTTP requests
MODULE	Administration of server modules
TRACE	Management of server trace logs

<ID> is the identifier for the object. The format is specific to each object.

[/parameter:value] specifies optional parameter(s) that depend on the object. Usually, commands that search objects or manipulate properties allow properties specified as a parameter.

Creating Web Sites

As we showed earlier, you can use IIS Manager to create Web sites. However, in some cases you might want an easier way to do this other than using a user interface. AppCmd.exe fills this void nicely and you can quickly get a site up and running using AppCmd.exe.

Before starting, you must have the name, path, and bindings to successfully create a new Web site with a root Web application using AppCmd.

To create a new Web site using AppCmd.exe, type the following:

```
AppCmd add site /name:"My First AppCmd Website"
/bindings:http/*:80:www.myfirstsite.com
```

Creating Virtual Directories

As we said earlier, virtual directories are an important concept in IIS 7.0 because they are the definition of a root application. Thus, although we have created a new site in the preceding example, we haven't defined a new root application. We will do so in this example. If you do not define an application, or virtual directory physical path, then the site will run as part of IIS 7.0's default application pool.

```
AppCmd add site /name:"My First AppCmd Website"
/bindings:http/*:80:www.myfirstsite.com /physicalPath:"c:\inetpub\myfirstsite"
```

Creating Application Pools

The important step in creating an application pool is having applications read to define or run within your newly created application pool. Thus, after creating an application pool, you will want to assign your application to that application pool.

The syntax for creating a new application pool is the following:

```
appcmd add apppool /name:appPoolName
```

In the preceding case, *appPoolName* specifies the name of your new application pool.

By default, IIS adds application pools that run integrated managed pipeline mode and use .NET Framework version 2.0 for managed code execution. Otherwise, you can specify the .NET Framework version and managed code request-processing mode.

To add an application pool to a Web server with different settings, use the following:

```
appcmd add apppool /name:appPoolName /managedRuntimeVersion:dotNetVersion
/managedPipelineMode:pipelineMode
```

In this example, *dotNetVersion* equals the .NET Framework version the application pool runs. The possible options are v1.0, v1.1, v2.0, or blank for no managed code support.

Lastly, we set the application pool to run in either IIS 7.0's new *pipelineMode* as *Integrated* or the IIS 6.0 with ASP.NET mode called *Classic*.

Enter the following command to create an application pool that does not run managed code and uses classic mode:

```
appcmd add apppool /name:ClassicASPApp /managedRuntimeVersion:
/managedPipelineMode:Classic
```

Notice */managedRuntimeVersion:* is followed by a blank (space).

Managing Backups

IIS 7.0 configuration data stored in the administration.config, applicationHost.config, metabase.xml, and mbschema.xml files should be routinely backed up to provide quick and simple recovery to a known state or to recover from an unexpected loss. The metabase.xml and mbschema.xml files support IIS 6.0 compatibility and/or the FTP service and exist if one or both of these IIS features are selected.

While the Web application and web.config files are normally under version control, the IIS 7.0 configuration backup files could also be version controlled to aid deployment and to track changes

The AppCmd's *BACKUP* statement allows you to easily manage server configuration data by copying the current configuration files to the specified backup folder.

To view *BACKUP* command syntax, execute:

```
C:\Windows\System32\inetsrv>AppCmd Backup /?
```

The syntax when using AppCmd and using the object *Backup* is the following:

```
APPCMD (command) BACKUP <identifier> <-parameter1:value1 ...>
```

The supported verbs (or commands) include the following:

List	Lists existing configuration backups
Add	Creates a configuration backup
Delete	Deletes a configuration backup
Restore	Restores a configuration backup

Creating a Backup

To create an IIS configuration backup in a subfolder named MyFirstBackup, execute the following:

```
AppCmd Add Backup "MyFirstBackup"
```

To create a backup folder named according to the current date and time, execute:

```
AppCmd Add Backup
```

This creates the folder, C:\Windows\System32\inetsrv\backup\ 20070325T191919\ into which the configuration files are copied.

Managing Existing Backups

To List existing backups, execute:

```
AppCmd List Backup
```

To delete a backup named, MyFirstBackup, execute:

```
AppCmd Delete Backup "MyFirstBackup"
```

To restore a backup named, 20070325T191919, execute:

```
AppCmd Restore Backup "20070325T191919"
```

By default, *Restore Backup* stops IIS, overwrites the configuration files, and completes by restarting IIS services. You can prevent the restart by adding */stop:false* to the *Restore Backup* command. Otherwise, other IIS components will detect configuration changes automatically without a restart.

Making Configuration Changes with AppCmd.exe

AppCmd can quickly list your current, or default, configuration for sections or section groups. It can find unique information in the configuration or go further, such as to modify the configuration setting for a particular, granular setting. Furthermore, it can help migrating customers solve problems with their ASP.NET applications by migrating their applications over to IIS 7.0 for use in the new integrated mode. As you can see, the list is long but powerful and this section will demystify much of that by opening your world to all new horizons.

Modifying Sections Using AppCmd.exe

Sections and section groups play an important role in the IIS 7.0 configuration as we have already learned. If you need to modify these configuration settings you can easily do so using AppCmd. As with any usage of AppCmd.exe, you can view the syntax for modifying configuration using AppCmd's help for configuration. To view configuration object help, do the following:

```
Appcmd config /?
```

The configuration stack in IIS 7.0 is complex and because of this, AppCmd has an extensive list of verbs to support this complexity. AppCmd.exe is the Swiss army knife for the configuration allowing just about any action capable of being performed against the configuration stack. This is why it is important to quickly reference all of the verbs to familiarize you with them and their function. The following table will show the verbs and their description:

Verb	Description
List	Lists the current configuration sections
Set	Writes the configuration to the appropriate section
Search	Finds the configuration paths where setting(s) are defined
Lock	Locks the configuration section
Unlock	Unlocks the configuration section
Clear	Clears the configuration section
Reset	Clears the current configuration and set to default values
Migrate	Migrates a legacy configuration to IIS 7.0

In our case, we will start simply by listing configuration sections' settings and then follow up by modifying this same section to another value.

SOME INDEPENDENT ADVICE

The configuration in IIS 7.0 is tightly tied to the IIS 7.0 schema. If you are unfamiliar with the configuration section or attributes you desire to change, start with the IIS schema file. The IIS schema provides not only the element names but also their possible settings, such as strings, dwords, and so on. The IIS schema file is located in %windir%\system32\inetsrv\config\schema.

To list the current settings for the configuration section authentication, input the following:

```
Appcmd list config /section:windowsAuthentication
```

This will return you to the XML section information for the section you asked for based on its location. In our example, it will return the status for the section *windowsAuthentication*, as shown next:

```
<system.webServer>
  <security>
    <authentication>
      <windowsAuthentication enabled="false">
        <providers>
          <add value="Negotiate" />
          <add value="NTLM" />
        </providers>
      </windowsAuthentication>
    </authentication>
  </security>
</system.webServer>
```

In our case, we would like to enable Windows Authentication for the Default Web Site to support our Web application. Using AppCmd.exe, simply issue the following command:

```
Appcmd set config "Default Web Site/" /section:windowsAuthentication /enabled:true
```

This would effectively enable Windows Authentication for the Default Web Site.

SOME INDEPENDENT ADVICE

To successfully set section values, such as *windowsAuthentication* at a specific path like "Default Web Site/" requires delegation for that section to be enabled. By default, only four sections are unlocked on Windows Vista and they do not include the authentication section group. To unlock the entire group, or just the individual section (such as *windowsAuthentication*), you must change the *allowOverride* value in the configuration. You can do this using any of the administration tools.

To allow this example given, unlock this section using IIS Manager. You can do this by opening the **Feature Delegation** area at the server level and changing *windowsAuthentication* to *Read\Write* in the **Actions** pane.

After your testing is done, it is suggested you then re-lock the section unless you have a specific business need justifying it to be open. To do so, simply change the feature to read-only and it will be locked again.

Modifying Attributes Using AppCmd.exe

It becomes necessary to sometimes go lower than within a section and set a particular attribute. This is a low-level configuration setting defining a particular section, such as *authPersistSingleRequest* for the *windowsAuthentication* section. Using AppCmd.exe, you can modify this value using the following syntax:

```
Appcmd set config
```

Moving ASP.NET 2.0 Applications to IIS 7.0 Using AppCmd

As mentioned earlier, AppCmd.exe provides a convenient method for helping users move to IIS 7.0's new integrated mode. By default, ASP.NET configuration typically had configuration sections called httpModules and httpHandlers, while IIS used ScriptMaps and Isapi filters. The new integrated nature of IIS 7.0 with ASP.NET 2.0 combines these similar functioning features into a consolidated list called modules and handlers.

In some situations, a developer might deploy their custom module or handler in their web.config in IIS 6.0 using the old section name (e.g., httpModules or httpHandlers). This will cause a failure when using IIS 7.0 if the application pool is running in integrated mode. To correct this, AppCmd.exe can find use of these old section names and make the correct modifications to integrate them with IIS 7.0's modules and handlers sections.

To correct a problem with the ASP.NET configuration for use in IIS 7.0 using AppCmd, do the following:

```
Appcmd migrate config "Default Web Site/" /section:httpModules
```

In this example, we would migrate for the root application for the Default Web Site any configuration defined for *httpModules* to the IIS 7.0 configuration section modules. This would allow an application to run in Integrated mode; otherwise, the configuration itself would fail and require Classic mode.

Viewing IIS 7.0 Runtime Data Using AppCmd

Particular pieces of data aren't stored, or persisted, in a file, yet are still very important to many system administrators. This data comes as part of IIS 7.0's runtime information as well as the controls. You might, for example, be looking for the currently running sites on a particular server—no problem. On the other hand, you could be interested in shutting down a site for maintenance, yet not forcefully do so, and need to pause it. This data isn't stored in a single file somewhere; nevertheless, it is there and very much real. In this section, we will help you understand how to effectively view, set, or change this volatile data stored in the W3SVC service.

Viewing Currently Executing Requests with AppCmd

As we learned earlier, IIS 7.0 comes with some powerful diagnostics features that the administration tools can take advantage. The first nice functionality is the ability to review the currently executing requests occurring in an IIS worker process.

This is exposed using the *request* object and has the following syntax:

```
APPCMD list REQUESTS <identifier> <-parameter1:value1 ...>
```

The identifier and parameter values will help you narrow down the command to locate the specific type of requests you want to see.

To see all currently executing requests in all IIS application pools, enter the following:

```
Appcmd list requests
```

This command, though, isn't as useful on busy servers since it will return large amounts of data in which it is difficult to find what you are looking for. AppCmd.exe will make this easier by allowing you to narrow down the scope of your search by providing a site name or application pool.

To see all currently executing requests in the *DefaultAppPool*, enter the following:

```
Appcmd list requests /apppool.name:DefaultAppPool
```

To further narrow your search, you can use a parameter that allows you to ask only for show requests that match the following criteria (such as to request executing elapsed time) and AppCmd.exe will return this information to you. In the following example, we will attempt to locate requests that are currently executing in the *DefaultAppPool*, but that are still executing after 10 milliseconds.

To see all requests executing in *DefaultAppPool* that have elapsed for greater than 10 milliseconds, enter:

```
AppCmd list requests /apppool.name:DefaultAppPool /elapsed:10
```

As you have hopefully seen, AppCmd.exe provides you with some powerful command-line capabilities and insight into the Web server runtime. If you use this wisely, you will be well ahead in the troubleshooting and diagnostics in IIS 7.0.

Configuring and Using Trace Log Data with AppCmd

IIS 7.0 introduces Failed Request Tracing to help administrators and developers locate failures. As we mentioned earlier, setting up tracing requires you to enable this for the server, site, or application and then define a tracing rule. You can use AppCmd's *Trace* object to help you enable log files, set up rules, and even inspect your trace log files.

Enabling or Disabling Failed Request Tracing

Compared to IIS Manager, AppCmd is unique in allowing you to either enable or disable tracing with or without defining a tracing rule. This is nice because you can predefine rules and have them ready should they be needed. In this case, you would simply enable tracing and the existing rules will be used.

However, you might need to enable tracing for the URL but also define new rules at the same time. In IIS Manager, you had to take two separate actions, but with AppCmd.exe you can define all within a single command.

To enable tracing and define a rule, enter the following:

```
appcmd configure trace "Default Web Site/" /enable /path:*.aspx
```

To disable tracing for a URL, type:

```
appcmd configure trace "Default Web Site/" /disable /path:*.aspx
```

Viewing Trace Log Files Using AppCmd

As we mentioned earlier, you can also use AppCmd.exe to inspect previously created trace log files. This is a nice, handy feature but requires some insight into how tracing is designed and works. You will learn more about how tracing works in the next chapter, but for our purposes here let's define how you would view a trace log file. It is important to note that it is much easier to use Internet Explorer to view trace log files since it assists you in viewing the various errors, warnings, or informational data stored in the log files.

To view a trace log file using AppCmd, use the following syntax:

```
appcmd inspect trace "Default Web Site/fr000001.xml"
```

Writing Scripts Using the New WMI Provider

The first question asked by many when they hear there is a completely rewritten WMI provider in IIS 7.0 is why. You are surely asking the same if you are familiar with IIS 6.0's WMI provider. The reason is fundamental and centered on the IIS 6.0 provider more than anything else. The resources and work it would take to rewrite the IIS 6.0 provider to understand the brand-new configuration in IIS 7.0 was terribly expensive and potentially risky. Beyond that, the WMI provider in IIS 6.0 wasn't built with extensibility in mind, and building in extensibility after the fact is difficult.

The current provider in IIS 6.0 as well would be difficult to keep it compatible if you embarked on re-architecting it to support IIS 7.0.

Instead, Microsoft built a new WMI provider from the ground up that supported the new configuration as well as extensibility. Let's learn more about this new WMI provider.

Getting Started with WMI

Let's get started by familiarizing you with the objects available in the WMI provider, and then apply that learning to accomplish common tasks using that provider. WMI scripts start with a specific creation process where objects, methods, and wisdom come together.

The power of WMI is the fact that it has remoting built in to allow you to connect directly to a remote computer and manipulate its configuration. This is the downside to AppCmd.exe because it can't work remotely.

Starting Fresh with WMI in IIS 7.0

IIS 6.0 shipped with a WMI provider, and in fact, most of the command-line scripts were built using this provider. We mentioned though that the new provider in IIS 7.0 is completely new and provides a new object model to simplify the usage of WMI.

To learn WMI, you should start with simple, straightforward tasks and build upon them until you have a fully functional script to accomplish your Web deployment.

In our example, we will use similar heuristics as we did for IIS Manager and AppCmd.exe, where we do the following:

1. Create Web sites.

2. Add Virtual Directories to our Web sites.

3. Create an application pool.

4. Enable an authentication type for our Web site.

5. Set up tracing for our new Web site.

Creating Web Sites Using WMI

You might typically not work with single Web sites and need to manage or create multiple sites on your IIS 7.0 server. This administration task can be accomplished using IIS Manager, or AppCmd.exe, yet they require a little more work than one might want. Beyond that, they aren't reusable in the future. This is possible using WMI.

In this case, you can easily adapt using WMI, and with simple steps can start building your deployment automation.

To create a Web site using WMI, type this code and save it as **CreateWebsite.vbs**:

```
Set oIIS = GetObject("winmgmts:root\WebAdministration")

' Create a binding for the site

Set oBinding = oIIS.Get("BindingElement").SpawnInstance_

oBinding.BindingInformation = "*:80:www.myFirstWMISite.com"

oBinding.Protocol = "http"

' These are the parameters we will pass to the Create method

name = "My First WMI Site"

physicalPath = "C:\inetpub\wwwroot"

arrBindings = array(oBinding)
```

```
' Get the Site object definition

Set oSiteDefn = oIIS.Get("Site")

' Create site!!

oSiteDefn.Create name, arrBindings, physicalPath
```

Creating Virtual Directories Using WMI

To take the next step, you should now define your first virtual directory using WMI to allow you to further expand your arsenal of tools. In this example, you will add to your script the ability to create a virtual directory and define your first root application using WMI.

Add the following WMI script to your *CreateWebsite.vbs* to add a virtual directory:

```
Set oIIS = GetObject("winmgmts:root\WebAdministration")

' Define the Path, SiteName, and PhysicalPath for the new application.

strApplicationPath = "/NewApp"

strSiteName = "My First WMI Site"

strPhysicalPath = "D:\inetpub\NewApp"

' Create the new application

oIIS.Get("Application").Create strApplicationPath, strSiteName,_ strPhysicalPath
```

Using WMI to Create Application Pools

The goal is to step up your script to allow it to isolate your Web applications in IIS 7.0. In this next step, we will add script to allow you to create a new application pool and assign your root application for your new site to this application pool.

To create your application pool and assign an application to it, copy the following and save it as **CreateAppPool.vbs**:

```
Set oIIS = GetObject("winmgmts:root\WebAdministration")

oIIS.Get("ApplicationPool").Create("MyAppPool")
```

To assign your application, /NewApp, to your application pool, add this to CreateAppPool.vbs:

```
' Retrieve the NewApp application.

Set oApp = oWebAdmin.Get("Application.SiteName='My First WMI Site',Path='/NewApp'")


' Specify the new application pool name.

oApp.ApplicationPool = "MyAppPool"


' Save the change.

oApp.Put_


' Display the new application pool name.

WScript.Echo

WScript.Echo "New application pool: " & oApp.ApplicationPool
```

Setting Authentication Using WMI

After you have created your Web site, root application, and virtual directory, the next major step is to modify the default configuration settings for your Web site. This sample could reach very, very far and is usable for many different properties or attributes in your Web site. In your case, you will start by modifying the default settings of your new Web site's authentication to support Windows authentication.

To change "My First WMI Site" authentication using WMI, copy the following and save it as **SetWindowsAuthentication.vbs**:

```
siteName = "Default Web Site"


Set oWmiProvider = GetObject("winmgmts:root\WebAdministration")
Set oAnonAuth =
oWmiProvider.Get("AnonymousAuthenticationSection.Path='MACHINE/WEBROOT/APPHOST',Loc
ation='" + siteName + "'")
Set oWinAuth =
oWmiProvider.Get("WindowsAuthenticationSection.Path='MACHINE/WEBROOT/APPHOST',Locat
ion='" + siteName + "'")
```

```
oAnonAuth.Enabled = false
oAnonAuth.Put_
oAnonAuth.Refresh_

oWinAuth.Enabled = true
oWinAuth.Put_
oAnonAuth.Refresh_
```

Enabling Failed Request Tracing Using WMI

Last, it is important to prepare yourself for any potential diagnostics you might need to do for your new Web site and application. The last step to perform will set up Failed Request Tracing for your new Web site.

To enable Failed Request Tracing using WMI, copy the following and save it as **EnableFREB.vbs**:

```
siteName = "Default Web Site"
myFrebDirectory = "%SystemDrive%\MyFrebDir"

Set oWmiProvider = GetObject("winmgmts:root\WebAdministration")
Set oSite = oWmiProvider.Get("Site.Name='" + siteName + "'")

oSite.TraceFailedRequestsLogging.Enabled = true
oSite.TraceFailedRequestsLogging.Directory = myFrebDirectory

oSite.Put_
oSite.Refresh_
```

Managed Code Administration: Inside Microsoft.Web.Administration

Microsoft's .NET Framework and its supporting development platforms offered yet another opportunity to manage your IIS Web servers. IIS 7.0 offers a new, robust, managed-code API aimed at empowering the manage code community of developers with the ability to not only build Web applications but also configure their IIS 7.0 servers.

Using your language of choice, you can quickly add the Microsoft.Web.Administration (MWA) binary to your Visual Studio project and modify your IIS 7.0 configuration. In this section, we will help you understand how MWA interacts with IIS 7.0 and give you a starter course on using it.

The Microsoft.Web.Administration Object Model

In this section, we will familiarize users with the object model that is available using MWA. It is also important to understand how to build scripts using MWA and we will help you get started with the most common tasks highlighted thus far in this chapter. The beauty of this administration stack is its powerful capabilities supporting all the .NET Framework languages. If you prefer VB.NET over C# then just set up the project and off you go using MWA—with your favorite development language.

In our examples, we will use C# to manipulate the IIS 7.0 configuration and also access runtime information all from within a console application. This makes the code reusable since it will be compiled to an EXE that can be reused on all your IIS 7.0 Web servers.

MWA, like all of our other toolsets, can only work against an IIS 7.0 server, thus causing you to use other administration tools to administer previous versions of IIS.

Getting Started with MWA

Using Microsoft.Web.Administration isn't necessarily the most convenient methodology for many administrators. However, there are a great deal of developers who would like to set up packages for their Web applications using Visual Studio, and MWA makes this extremely simple. Imagine you are a developer for your company and you have an HR application you have built and would like to create the setup so that all administrators are required to do is click setup.exe. With your project in Visual Studio, you can easily add a reference in your setup project to MWA and add logic to execute configuration changes to IIS 7.0.

You also can build console applications that would allow you to interface with the various server objects to give you quick access to executing requests, site status, or ASP.NET application domains.

In our example, we will take you through doing some simple administration using a compiled executable that is reusable throughout your Web infrastructure.

Using C# Express to Create a Console Application

The first step is to download a flavor of Visual Studio 2005 that works for you. For many, you already have Visual Studio 2005 and can't skip this step. However, if you do not have access to Visual Studio, you can download one of the Visual Studio Express Editions, such as Visual C# Express (available for download at http://msdn.microsoft.com/vstudio/express/visualcsharp/).

To create a console application project in C# express, add a reference to the Microsoft.Web.Administration library. To do this, perform the following steps:

1. Open Visual Studio 2005 or Visual C# Express Edition.

2. Enter your project name and select your save location.

3. Click **Project** and Select **Add Reference**.

4. Click the **Browse** tab.

5. Browse to **%windir%\system32\inetsrv**.

6. Select **Microsoft.Web.Administration.dll**.

7. Click **OK**.

SOME INDEPENDENT ADVICE

Microsoft.Web.Administration shipped as part of Windows Vista. The entire API documentation is available on Microsoft's MSDN Web site at http://msdn2.microsoft.com/en-us/library/microsoft.web.administration.

Figure 5.8 Create Your MWA Project

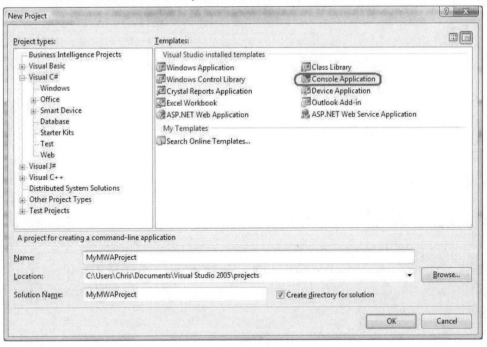

Figure 5.9 Add an MWA Reference on Windows Vista

Accessing Runtime Information with MWA

As you have learned, MWA is simple and easy to use to create Web sites, application pools, and applications. It can also be used easily access configuration attributes and properties on those Web sites such as authentication, default documents, and much more.

IIS 7.0 offers more than just configuration data—server objects and runtime data are also accessible using MWA. This includes server objects such as site status, application pool status, and ASP.NET application domains. These state objects are not represented in any configuration file and instead are stored within the worker process or Web Application Services (WAS) process.

Creating a Web Site Using MWA

It is a fundamental first step as we have seen when doing administration to create a Web site. You will need to understand how to instantiate the MWA objects and create the new site. Lastly, you will call the commit method to ensure that the new changes are committed to file.

```
using System;
using System.Collections.Generic;
using System.Text;
using Microsoft.Web.Administration;

namespace MSWebAdmin_Application
{
    private static void CreateSite()
        {
            using (ServerManager serverManager = new ServerManager())
            {
                Site site = serverManager.Sites.Add("My First MWA Site",
@"%SystemDrive%\inetpub\wwwroot", 8080);
                site.ServerAutoStart = true;

                serverManager.CommitChanges();
            }
        }
}
```

In this sample, we grabbed the *ServerManager* object and created a new instance. After that, we simply set the variable (*myFirstMWASite*) so we can use it later while also creating the new site using the *Add* method. Lastly, we set the site auto start status to True so that after creating the site it will automatically be started.

Shortcut...

Setting the Auto Start Status

This is often a confusing concept for IIS veterans. What exactly does the term site status mean? It is important to understand that it is possible to have a site created though not running. This is often the case in staging or development environments. When *ServerAutoStart* is set to false, you cannot access the Web site using the bindings (e.g., URL) until the administrator or site administrator enables it.

This step isn't required since the site will auto-start when you create it unless you explicitly set it to false. It should be noted that if you are creating a site without providing bindings that are unique, you should set *ServerAutoStart* to false until you set the bindings to be unique.

Creating Virtual Directories Using MWA

```
using System;
using System.Collections.Generic;
using System.Text;
using Microsoft.Web.Administration;


namespace MSWebAdmin_Application
{
      Class CreateVirtualDirectory("My First MWA Site","/", "/VDir", "C:\\temp");


private static void CreateVirtualDirectory(string siteName, string applicationPath,
string virtualDirectoryPath, string physicalPath)
      {
          using (ServerManager serverManager = new ServerManager())
          {
              Site site = serverManager.Sites[siteName];

              Application app = site.Applications[applicationPath];
```

```
            app.VirtualDirectories.Add(virtualDirectoryPath, physicalPath);

            serverManager.CommitChanges();
        }
    }
```

In this example, we create a virtual directory called for the site My First MWA site with the one single application. In this case, we point the root application and virtual directory content path to c:\temp.

Adding Application Pools Using MWA

In order to set My First MWA Site to run as isolated and in its own application pool, you must create the application pool and then assign the site's root application to run in this newly created application pool.

In this example, we will accomplish two goals:

1. Create a new application pool.
2. Assign the path My First MWA Site/ (root application) to your new application pool.

To create a new application pool, use the following:

```
using System;
using System.Collections.Generic;
using System.Text;
using Microsoft.Web.Administration;

namespace MSWebAdmin_Application
{
    class CreateApplicationPool()
    {
     private static void CreateApplicationPool()
     {
        using (ServerManager serverManager = new ServerManager())
        {
            ApplicationPool appPool = serverManager.ApplicationPools.Add("My
First MWA AppPool");
            appPool.ProcessModel.UserName = "<User>";
            appPool.ProcessModel.Password = "<Password>";
        }
     }
```

}

   Assign My First MWA Site to the new application pool:

```
using System;
using System.Collections.Generic;
using System.Text;
using Microsoft.Web.Administration;

namespace MSWebAdmin_Application
{
      class AssignApplicatonPoolToSite("My First MWA Site", "/", "My First MWA
AppPool");
               private static void AssignApplicationPoolToSite(string siteName,
string applicationPath, string applicationPoolName)
      {
          using (ServerManager serverManager = new ServerManager())
          {

serverManager.Sites[siteName].Applications[applicationPath].ApplicationPoolName =
applicationPoolName;

              serverManager.CommitChanges();
          }
      }

}
```

Changing the Authentication Type for a Web Site Using MWA

Multiple properties are customizable for your Web sites, yet many times you will not touch them. The principles often are the thing to grasp, and in this illustration we will touch on one of those often changed settings: authentication. The goal though is to get away from creating sites or virtual directories and modifying actual site settings. This could stretch to things like adding modules, handlers, default documents, and much, much more.

   In this example, you will enable Windows authentication for our newly created Web site.

```
using System;
using System.Collections.Generic;
```

```
using System.Text;
using Microsoft.Web.Administration;

namespace MSWebAdmin_Application
{
      class EnableWindowsAuthentication("My First MWA Site")
      private static void EnableWindowsAuthentication(string siteName)
       {
            using (ServerManager serverManager = new ServerManager())
            {
                Configuration appHostConfig =
serverManager.GetApplicationHostConfiguration();

                // Enable Windows Authentication
                ConfigurationSection windowsAuthentication =

appHostConfig.GetSection("system.webServer/security/authentication/windowsAuthentica
tion", siteName);
                windowsAuthentication.SetAttributeValue("enabled", true);

                // Disable Anonymous Authentication
                ConfigurationSection anonymousAuthentication =

appHostConfig.GetSection("system.webServer/security/authentication/anonymousAuthenti
cation", siteName);
                anonymousAuthentication.SetAttributeValue("enabled", false);

                serverManager.CommitChanges();
            }
      }
}
```

Viewing Currently Executing Requests Using MWA

To access currently executing requests in IIS 7.0 using MWA, you do much of what you did earlier except you change the object you are using so it points to IIS 7.0 runtime objects. In this example, you will need to ensure you have executing requests running to ensure that data is returned.

In this example, you will view any currently executing requests occurring in IIS 7.0:

```
using System;
using System.Collections.Generic;
using System.Text;
using Microsoft.Web.Administration;

namespace MSWebAdmin_Application
{
      class DisplayRequests ()
       private static void DisplayRequests()
        {
            using (ServerManager serverManager = new ServerManager())
             {
                 foreach (WorkerProcess workerProcess in
serverManager.WorkerProcesses)
                  {
                      Console.WriteLine(workerProcess.ProcessId);

                      foreach (Request request in workerProcess.GetRequests(0))
                      {
                          Console.WriteLine("{0} - {1} - {2}", request.Url,
request.PipelineState, request.TimeElapsed);
                      }
                  }
             }
        }
}
```

Summary

Like Baskin Robbins' 31 flavors, IIS 7.0 has a talented array of administration features. Whether you subscribe to the user interface flavor, command line, or writing scripts or code, there is a flavor for everyone. Unlike previous IIS versions, there has never been such a powerful lineup of configuration opportunities for Microsoft's Web platform. As an administrator or developer, you must pick the tool that is right for your environment. You can select IIS Manager for a user interface experience, AppCmd.exe when using the command line, or use WMI or *Microsoft.Web.Administration* for scripting changes in IIS 7.0's configuration and to access runtime data.

In this chapter, you have gained insight into the powerful stack of administration capabilities built directly into IIS 7.0. There is a method for manipulating the IIS 7.0 configuration that fits any flavor of administrator from the user interface to the managed-code administrator. This isn't to say that IIS 7.0 has everything in-between.

It was important to start with the most common toolset used for day-to-day administration: IIS Manager. IIS Manager, re-built from the ground up, provides a new look and feel while maintaining most of the necessary tools to completely manage IIS. It offers you the ability to manage both IIS and ASP.NET settings in a consolidated, grouped, approach as well as provide you with delegated administration.

IIS Manager supports both previous clients such as Windows XP and Windows 2003 Server, along with Windows Vista and Windows Server "Codenamed" Longhorn. You can download IIS Manager from the IIS.NET DownloadCENTER at www.iis.net/downloads/default.aspx?tabid=3.

For some, the experience of learning IIS Manager is tedious and not what they desire to do. They prefer to use the command line to improve their experience with IIS 7.0's configuration. IIS 7.0 offers a powerful desktop command-line interface called AppCmd.exe that offers access using simple syntax and strong object support. From creating Web sites to viewing currently executed requests or migrating legacy configuration, AppCmd.exe offers a Swiss-army-knife-like experience for those desiring command-line support.

The reality in the Web server world is in deployments, not in doing individual tasks that IIS Manager and AppCmd.exe specialize in. For those desiring automated, deployable, and maintainable scripts, IIS 7.0 offers you the ability to use WMI and MWA.

In the end, IIS 7.0 provides a complete end-to-end story in the administration space, offering the best lineup of toolsets ever shipped with IIS.

Solutions Fast Track

Accomplishing Tasks Using IIS Manager

☑ IIS Manager offers easy access to all relevant features in an excellent three-column view.

☑ Creating Web sites, virtual directories, and much more is simple and intuitive with the redesign of IIS Manager.

☑ IIS Manager in IIS 7.0 offers a consolidated interface for managing IIS and ASP.NET settings.

Accessing Information Using AppCmd.exe

☑ AppCmd.exe offers command-line access to IIS 7.0 configuration, server objects, and runtime data, such as requests executing.

☑ AppCmd.exe offers powerful object access, including creating and managing configuration backups for applicationhost.config.

☑ AppCmd.exe is available in %windir%\system32\inetsrv, but is easily addable to the system path for quick access

Writing Scripts Using the New WMI Provider

☑ WMI is rewritten in IIS 7.0 to support IIS's new configuration as well as extensibility.

☑ WMI is a nice means of automating tasks that are repetitive and usable across many machines.

☑ WMI can perform all the same tasks as IIS Manager and AppCmd.exe, all from a scripting, remotable interface.

Managed Code Administration: Inside Microsoft.Web.Administration

- ☑ Microsoft.Web.Administration (MWA) offers managed-code users the ability to manage IIS 7.0 configuration and other data.

- ☑ MWA supports all the .NET Framework languages and is easy to add as a reference in Visual Studio.

- ☑ MWA, like all other toolsets, is capable of creating Web sites, virtual directories, applications, and much, much more.

Frequently Asked Questions

The following Frequently Asked Questions, answered by the authors of this book, are designed to both measure your understanding of the concepts presented in this chapter and to assist you with real-life implementation of these concepts. To have your questions about this chapter answered by the author, browse to **www.syngress.com/solutions** and click on the **"Ask the Author"** form.

Q: There seem to be differences in several tools when comparing the version that is part of Windows Vista versus the one that is part of Windows Server Codenamed "Longhorn". How does one determine how to choose?

A: This is a common question and it's easy to address. Microsoft released Windows Vista and IIS 7.0 as a ready product for the developer audience and optimized for that scenario. The features built for administration in production environments will be part of "Longhorn" Server and Windows Vista Service Pack 1. The nice thing is that Microsoft is building the products simultaneously and will release them at identical points, thus bringing Windows Vista RTM users up to the IIS 7.0 server level.

Q: Can remote administration in IIS Manager be used in Windows Vista?

A: No. Unfortunately, it can't and is only supported in "Longhorn" Server and Windows Vista Service Pack 1.

Q: Can AppCmd.exe be used from client workstations connecting to IIS 7.0 servers?

A: No, unfortunately it does not have any remote capabilities and is only available on the server you want to manage. To provide remote support, use WMI or MWA.

Q: Why did Microsoft rebuild the WMI provider when they had one in IIS 6.0?

A: The new provider provided users the ability to manage IIS 7.0 in a familiar environment (WMI) while not interfering with current scripts aimed at managing IIS 6.0. In fact, the WMI provider that is part of IIS 6.0 is completely available to be used in IIS 7.0 alongside the new provider.

Q: If I am not familiar with managed code development is there any reason to learn MWA?

A: No. IIS 7.0 offers a plethora of options for managing its configuration, server objects, and runtime data for this very reason. The toolsets as a whole should have very close feature capabilities, minus IIS Manager, which obviously can't expose everything to users and still maintain usability.

Chapter 6

Troubleshooting 101: Diagnostics in IIS 7.0

Solutions in this chapter:

- **Using IIS 7.0's Custom Detailed Errors**
- **Inside IIS 7.0's Failed Request Tracing**
- **Breakpoints: Extending IIS 7.0's Tracing**
- **Reality: Inside What Tracing Can't Do in IIS 7.0**

☑ **Summary**

☑ **Solutions Fast Track**

☑ **Frequently Asked Questions**

Introduction

No area in IIS 6.0 is more in need of improvement than diagnostics. Many users referred to IIS as a "black box" into which requests went, yet never came out. To complicate the matter further, administrators and developers were often left without any avenue to reproduce and hence correct IIS because there were no means to access request-based information at the point of failure.

In contrast, it has never been so easy to detect and isolate an error than in IIS 7.0, which offers detailed error messages that outline step-by-step instructions on what to try if a request fails. In the event that the error messages don't help, you can use IIS 7.0's new Failed Request Tracing. This new instrumentation offers a step-by-step output as requests, one by one, enter and exit the IIS request pipeline. This detailed tracing can be enabled based on HTTP error messages or by time taken, two of the most common troubleshooting starting points. Beyond that, developers can build on IIS 7.0's tracing to include their individual code "eventing" that allows administrators to see their status alongside IIS 7.0's status. This makes debugging failures of IIS and custom code a reality without attaching a debugger.

As great as IIS 7.0's diagnostics are, there are still areas where it can't help. It is important to understand these areas and ensure that you tackle them with the right tools to succeed.

Using IIS 7.0's Custom Detailed Errors

IIS 6.0 and previous versions included custom yet not very detailed errors. Unlike previous versions, IIS 7.0 includes Custom Detailed Errors that offer administrators console access to the most detailed error messages, such as the module processor and request state, and some steps to resolve the problems.

It is important to understand the default behavior to show only custom detailed errors for console (127.0.0.1) requests. However, it is possible to enable detailed error messages for nonconsole requests; we will outline how to accomplish this goal effectively.

Configuring Custom Error Messages

Custom errors are a powerful method for creating customized, styled, yet useful error messages for your users. HTTP errors are a rather unpleasant side effect of the Web experience, but custom error messages can improve this typically unpleasant experience. There is a wide array of configurable settings for custom errors, such as using a specific file, redirection to another URL, or executing another URL. We will help simplify how each works and furthermore tell you how you can configure IIS7.0 to use custom error pages other than the default shipped by Microsoft.

First, let's start by taking a look at a custom error message. As you can see in Figure 6.1, the custom error message is pretty simple.

Figure 6.1 IIS 7.0 Standard HTTP Custom Error Message

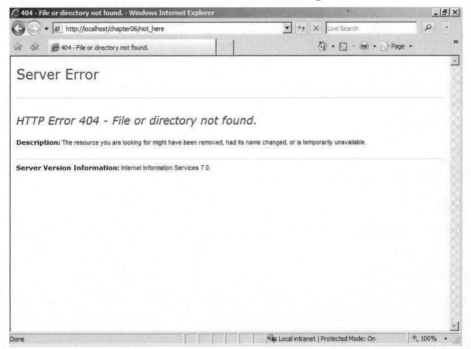

The custom error page is pretty basic and really only a placeholder until a developer can create an error page, or better yet handle the errors, that fits with the user experience and navigation that fits the rest of their application.

Now let's take a look at a detailed error message based on navigating to the same page from the IIS7 server console (see Figure 6.2).

Figure 6.2 IIS 7.0 Detailed HTTP Error Message

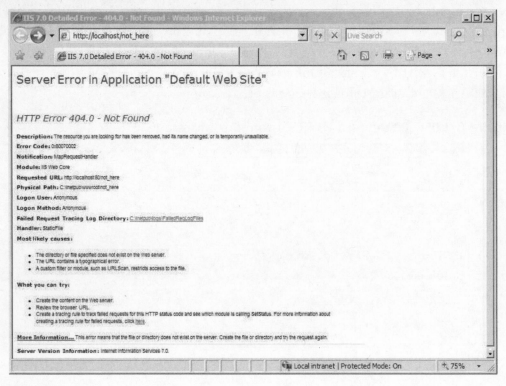

As you can see, there is quite a bit of information available that can help a developer or administrator work toward finding the root issue. As interesting as this information is for a developer or administrator, it's equally interesting for a malicious user or hacker. As a best practice, you should not expose this information to end users unless you are in a development and testing phase.

There are a number of options to suppress this generic custom error and provide our own custom error page. As an administrator or developer, you'll have the ability to override the default error handling in IIS 7.0 using a redirection to a URL, custom static error page, or custom dynamic error page. The following section will explain how to define these by server, site, and/or application.

Configuring Custom Error Messages Using IIS Manager

Let's first take a look at viewing and updating the Custom Errors pages using IIS Manager.

After opening and connecting to an IIS 7 server, click the **Error Pages** icon in the IIS section and then click **Open Feature** from the Actions pane (or simply double-click the **Error Pages** icon), as shown in Figure 6.3. These are the default Error Pages defined for the entire Web server. Any changes done at this level will impact the error pages settings for all the sites supported on that IIS 7 server, except where a site or application overrides those values.

Figure 6.3 The IIS Manager

There are a number of options available at this point from a Status Code perspective. You can add a Status Code by clicking **Add…** in the Actions pane (see Figure 6.4).

The Add Custom Error Page dialog box will allow you to provide a Status Code (e.g., 404) or a Substatus Code (e.g., 404.14). The Path Type field allows you to define the kind of action to take based on the value in the path (see Figure 6.4). Table 6.1 provides details on the available path types.

Figure 6.4 The Add Custom Error Page

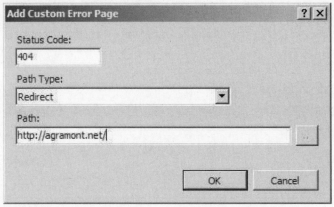

Table 6.1 Available Path Types

Path Type	Description	Path Examples
File	Points to a static file	404.htm
Execute URL	Points to a dynamic file	Error.aspx
Redirect	Redirects the client browser to a different URL	http://<URL>

Controlling the custom errors can be done at a variety of locations within IIS 7, and thus it's important to understand where these settings are actually being stored. For the entire Web server, those changes are done in the applicationHost.config file, which is which is located in the \Windows\System32\Inetsrv\Config folder. Additionally, when you're managing a given Web site, those changes can also be stored in the applicationHost.config file, or they can be managed within the web.config for the site.

HTTP error responses can be defined for the following IIS levels:

- Web server
- Web site
- Web application
- Physical directory
- Virtual directory
- File (URL)

These settings were previously available in IIS 6.0 but were not widely known and utilized. In IIS 6.0, this was done by setting a number of properties (HTTPErrorCode, HTTPErrorSubcode, URL, HandlerURL, FILE, or Filename) and using the proper combination, depending on the type of redirection you where going to use. With IIS 7.0, this is much easier to implement in the User Interface and via XML configuration.

<httpErrors> Configuration

With the rich integration between ASP.NET and IIS 7.0, a developer or administrator can define the httpError configuration at the server, Web site, or virtual directory level. This provides a greater amount of control versus what was previously available in IIS. The default *<httpErrors>* section is defined in the applicationHost.config file. (More information on the location and use of the applicationHost.config file can be found in Chapter 4.)

```
<httpErrors>
          <error statusCode="401"
prefixLanguageFilePath="%SystemDrive%\inetpub\custerr" path="401.htm" />
          <error statusCode="403"
prefixLanguageFilePath="%SystemDrive%\inetpub\custerr" path="403.htm" />
          <error statusCode="404"
prefixLanguageFilePath="%SystemDrive%\inetpub\custerr" path="404.htm" />
          <error statusCode="405"
prefixLanguageFilePath="%SystemDrive%\inetpub\custerr" path="405.htm" />
          <error statusCode="406"
prefixLanguageFilePath="%SystemDrive%\inetpub\custerr" path="406.htm" />
          <error statusCode="412"
prefixLanguageFilePath="%SystemDrive%\inetpub\custerr" path="412.htm" />
          <error statusCode="500"
prefixLanguageFilePath="%SystemDrive%\inetpub\custerr" path="500.htm" />
          <error statusCode="501"
prefixLanguageFilePath="%SystemDrive%\inetpub\custerr" path="501.htm" />
          <error statusCode="502"
prefixLanguageFilePath="%SystemDrive%\inetpub\custerr" path="502.htm" />
      </httpErrors>
```

The default location for the custom error pages is %SystemDrive%\inetpub\custerr. Within that folder will be additional folders that map to a localized code. For U.S. English, that subfolder is labeled "en-US." The localized version that will be used for the response will be defined by the actual browser setting that is set by the end user.

The *<httpErrors>* node defines the base values for all the child *<error>* nodes (see Table 6.2).

Table 6.2 Child <error> Node Attributes and Values

Attribute Name	Value
defaultPath	Default path to the HTTP error file or URL that will be used within the child *<error>* node.
detailedMoreInformationLink	At the bottom of a Detailed error page, a "More Information" link redirects the user to a Microsoft Support article. Setting the DetailedMoreInformationLink property can override the base URL for this link. This can be extremely useful if you want to capture these errors, even for internal testing, to store in a database or provide a response using an internal Knowledge Base article that directly references a particular product or module (Default= "http://go.microsoft.com/fwlink/?LinkID=62293").
defaultResponseMode	Used to define the default Response Mode that will be used within the child *<error>* node (Default= File): **File** Static file will be used. **ExecuteURL** Points to a URL within the same server. For this to work, it must be a URL that points to a dynamic page (e.g., ASPX page) that resides within the same application pool that generated the error. Needless to say, you might not want to set this at the server level if you host a number of sites with more than one application pool. By default, you will receive an error if you attempt to do this to a location outside the appPool. However, you can actually get around this and allow it to happen with an appropriate registry key. Read the "Some Independent Advice" sidebar for more details. **Redirect** Redirects to a specific URL. The URL can be on the same server or a completely different server or site.
errorMode	Defines whether a Custom Error page or Detailed Error page is used upon a given error being generated (Default=DetailedLocalOnly).

Continued

Table 6.2 continued Child <error> Node Attributes and Values

Attribute Name	Value
	DetailedLocalOnly A detailed error will only be displayed when the request comes from the local machine.
	Custom Custom pages will be used upon an error.
	Detailed A detailed error response will be provided regardless of a custom page being assigned or outside the local machine.
existingResponse	ASP.NET and IIS 7 are not integrated when it comes to error responses. Thus this value allows you to control the way you want to handle error responses (Default=Auto):
	Auto IIS 7.0 will go through a series of checks to decide which error response will be used:
	1. If the IHttpResponse::SetStatus method was called with the fTrySkipCustomErrors flag, the existing response is passed through, and no detailed or custom error is shown.
	2. If the ErrorMode property is set to Custom, the response is replaced.
	3. If ErrorMode is set to Detailed and there is an existing response, the response is passed through.
	4. If ErrorMode is set to Detailed and there is no existing response, the response is replaced with a detailed error message.
	Replace When an error message is generated (e.g., 404, File not Found), IIS will take over the error and call the appropriate custom error page or URL.
	PassThrough When an error message is generated (e.g., 404, File not Found), IIS will not call out to the custom page but will allow the error to be handled by a module. For example, when calling a page that doesn't exist *and* has an extension of .aspx, which results in a 404 File not Found error, the error response will be created by ASP.NET and *not* IIS. So in this case, the custom page or detailed page, as defined in the web.config, will not be generated.

Some Independent Advice

For a site or application to leverage an error page that's in a different application pool than its own, the following registry change will need to be made. Keep in mind that this is a serverwide change and could open the attack surface on a Web server that is "hosting" a number of different Web sites.

Note: It is recommended that you back up your registry before modifying the registry with the new data. If you use Registry Editor (Regedit.exe) incorrectly, you could cause serious problems that might require you to reinstall your operating system.

1. Open Regedit.exe (you can quickly find this using Windows Vista search by clicking the **Windows** button and typing in **RegEdit**).

2. Navigate to the following key: **HKEY_LOCAL_MACHINE\SYSTEM\CurrentControlSet\Services\W3SVC**.

3. Within the W3SVC key, create a new DWORD called **IgnoreAppPoolForCustomErrors** and with a value of **1**.

4. For this change to take effect, you'll need to restart IIS 7.0.

The child nodes for *<httpErrors>* are *<error>*, *<remove>*, and *<clear>*. The *<error>* node defines a set of properties for a given error code. As you can see, each error code is then mapped to a specific file, which then provides appropriate error response. A number of options are available by error code, including handling suberror codes.

Table 6.3 provides details on the available attributes that can be used as part of the *<error>* XML node.

Table 6.3 <error> XML Node Attributes and Values

Attribute Name	Value Type	Value
statusCode	String	Primary status code for a given error.
subStatusCode	Integer	Substatus code for a given error that is a "child" of a high-level code.
prefixLanguageFilePath	String	Location of language-specific error code folders.
Path	String	Actual filename for the given page that will be used to provide the error message to the user.

Continued

Table 6.3 continued <error> XML Node Attributes and Values

Attribute Name	Value Type	Value
responseMode	String	Defines the type of response that will be given. This will also treat the value in *Path* a bit differently. This is the same as Path Type as defined in the IIS Manager.

Within a given error code, additional suberror codes provide an even greater amount of detail.

The following XML node can be added to the *<httpErrors>* node to handle a suberror code:

```
<error statusCode="404" subStatusCode=14
prefixLanguageFilePath="%SystemDrive%\inetpub\custerr" path="404-14.htm" />
```

This XML looks much like the previous XML, except it uses a new XML attribute, subStatusCode, which takes an integer and is the suberror code. Thus, the preceding XML is capturing the 404.14 statusCode and is then being redirected to the 404-14.htm file. If an error code is raised and it's actually a suberror code, but no subStatusCode is defined in the *<httpErrors>* XML, the "parent" statusCode will be used.

The following URL points to a Microsoft Support page that provides a general list and description of Error Codes used by IIS 6.0 and 7.0: http://support.microsoft.com/kb/318380

The prefixLanguageFilePath attribute provides a pointer to a folder that holds additional folders with the language-specific error pages. For example, the default error code pages are located at ="%SystemDrive%\inetpub\custerr and contain a child folder named en-US. The en-US folder contains all of the individual error pages, such as 404-14.htm. The syntax (folder name) and acceptable languages that can be used here are defined in RFC 1766 (www.ietf.org/rfc/rfc1766.txt).

Overriding for a Site

Until now, we've focused mainly on configuring the errors page and behavior at the server level. As stated earlier, error configuration can be delegated down to the site and application/virtual directory level. This gives a Web site administrator and Web developer a greater amount of control than in the past, to define and manage how errors are handled for their site.

The following is a simple web.config file that overrides the default behavior when a file isn't found (404 error):

```
<configuration>
    <system.webServer>
            <httpErrors errorMode="Custom">
                    <remove statusCode="404" subStatusCode="-1" />
                    <error statusCode="404" prefixLanguageFilePath=""
path="http://agramont.net/" responseMode="Redirect" />
            </httpErrors>
    </system.webServer>
</configuration>
```

You'll notice that there are two XML nodes within the *<httpErrors>* node. Before you can add an error node that overrides a previously defined node, such as the default error nodes, you must first remove it using the *<remove>* node. Only then can you add the *<remove>* node that redefines that setting. When the preceding XML code is defined in the web.config, you'll see the information shown in Figure 6.5 represented in the IIS Manager.

Figure 6.5 HTTP Errors

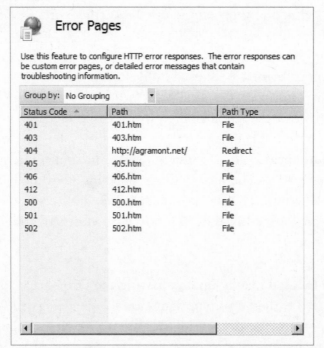

The IIS Manager provides a list of all the error pages defined for this given site. This also includes an aggregated view of the inherited and explicit (defined as "Local" in the Entry Type column) error pages and their associated values.

Understanding and Reading Custom Error Messages in IIS 7.0

In IIS 7.0, the data shared in custom errors is more robust than ever. IIS 7.0 offers detailed information about the request information itself as well as reasons that the failure might have occurred. In an unprecedented feature never available in custom errors in previous versions, step-by-step instructions provide information on how to further troubleshoot or fix the error. It is important to understand how to read the information IIS provides as well as how to further your research if the recommended steps don't resolve your problem.

The detailed error provides a wealth of information that can help a Web administrator or developer quickly narrow down the root cause of a given error. There are a number of helpful pieces of information on the Detailed Error page. Although the Error Code value provides the actual error code that was raised, it's only one piece of the puzzle. The other properties listed here provide additional context to the request that generated the error:

- **Description** A user-friendly description of the error.
- **Error Code** The actual error code.
- **Notification** Event handler within the Module (see next bullet) that generated the error.
- **Module** A pointer to the module that generated the error.
- **Requested URL** The URL that was used by the end user. This will also include any information in the query string as well.
- **Physical Path** A pointer to the actual physical path of the page that generated the error. This could be an ASP, ASPX, or even HTML page. This is useful if a user was trying to browse a given page (e.g., cart.aspx) and then was redirected to a different page that generated the actual error (e.g., newcart.aspx).
- **Logon User** The username that was used by IIS 7.0 and Windows in performing the request.

- **Logon Method** Defines the type of authentication method that was used as part of this request. For most public sites, this will be set to Anonymous.

- **Failed Request Tracing Log Directory** A pointer to the directory that will hold the trace file for this error. This doesn't tell you the actual file-name, which is a good thing from a security perspective.

- **Handler** The Handler within IIS 7.0 that raised the error.

- **Most likely causes** IIS 7.0 provides a list of pointers for each status code that can help you troubleshoot the issue or at least give you an idea of where to look next.

- **What you can try** This field provides some helpful troubleshooting tasks that the developer or administrator can perform.

- **More Information** This field provides yet another set of ideas on what the issue might be and how you could resolve it. What's interesting is that by clicking the "More Information" link, you'll be routed to a Microsoft sup-port article that will provide—yes, you guessed it—more information.

Delegating Custom Errors

This detailed error data doesn't have security in mind, hence they aren't sent to any clients other than requests started at the IIS server console. However, in some situations, it is useful to have some of the custom errors delegated to clients other than the just the console. This section outlines ways you can carefully delegate custom errors and the security risks associated with doing so.

Controlling custom errors is, by default, a server-specific setting and can only be controlled by the Web server administrator. The great thing about IIS 7 is that it pro-vides the ability to allow a Web site administrator or developer to control their own custom errors. To do this, you first must allow the ability to "override" the default settings that are defined in the applicationHost.config XML file.

Within the applicationHost.config file, you must make a change to the following XML node and change the overrideModeDefault from Deny to Allow:

```
<section name="httpErrors" overrideModeDefault="Deny" />
```

NOTE

Although shown here directly changing the XML configuration files, you can also do this in IIS Manager by clicking **Feature Delegation (Under Management Area) | Error Pages** and changing to **Read\Write**.

If you neglect to make this change before proceeding to the next set of steps, you'll get an "HTTP Error 500.19—Internal Server Error" error message from IIS that proceeds to tell you that overrideModeDefault needs to be changed.

Making a change to the Custom Errors properties using IIS Manager for a virtual directory named Chapter06 within the Default Web Site will result in the following XML being stored within the applicationHost.config file:

```
<location path="Default Web Site/Chapter06">
        <system.webServer>
            <httpErrors>
                <remove statusCode="500" subStatusCode="-1" />
                <error statusCode="500" prefixLanguageFilePath="" path="D:\
\web\Chapter06\Error.aspx" responseMode="File" />
            </httpErrors>
        </system.webServer>
    </location>
```

Let's say that we don't want to host this particular information within the applicationHost.config file, but we want the Web site developer/administrator to control it from their end. To do this, we could easily remove this XML from the applicationHost.config file and move it into the web.config file, which should be at the root folder for that application. The web.config should now look like the following XML:

```
<configuration>
    <system.webServer>
        <httpErrors>
                <remove statusCode="500" subStatusCode="-1" />
                <error statusCode="500" prefixLanguageFilePath="" path="D:\
\web\Chapter06\Error.aspx" responseMode="File" />
            </httpErrors>
    </system.webServer>
</configuration>
```

Custom Error Module

What drives the custom errors is the CustomErrorModule module, which is defined as a default module in the applicationHost.config file.

The following is a snapshot of a simple web.config file that will override the applicationHost.config file setting by removing the CustomErrorModule from the list of modules that will be used per request:

```
<configuration>
    <system.webServer>
        <modules>
            <remove name="CustomErrorModule" />
        </modules>
    </system.webServer>
</configuration>
```

If you now navigate to a file or folder that doesn't exist at http://*<site with above web.config>*/file_not_here, you'll get a blank page. This is because the web.config removed the only module that would capture the error and provide a response.

If you remove the CustomErrorModule at a Web site or application level using IIS Manager, you'll end up with the following web.config (assuming that no other changes were made to the Web application):

```
<configuration>
    <system.webServer>
        <modules>
            <clear />
            <add name="HttpCacheModule" type="" preCondition="" />
            <add name="StaticCompressionModule" type="" preCondition="" />
            <add name="DefaultDocumentModule" type="" preCondition="" />
            <add name="DirectoryListingModule" type="" preCondition="" />
            <add name="ProtocolSupportModule" type="" preCondition="" />
            <add name="StaticFileModule" type="" preCondition="" />
            <add name="AnonymousAuthenticationModule" type="" preCondition="" />
            <add name="RequestFilteringModule" type="" preCondition="" />
            <add name="CustomErrorModule" type="" preCondition="" />
            <add name="IsapiModule" type="" preCondition="" />
            <add name="BasicAuthenticationModule" type="" preCondition="" />
            <add name="HttpLoggingModule" type="" preCondition="" />
            <add name="RequestMonitorModule" type="" preCondition="" />
            <add name="IsapiFilterModule" type="" preCondition="" />
```

```
                <add name="ConfigurationValidationModule" type="" preCondition="" />
                <add name="OutputCache" type="System.Web.Caching.OutputCacheModule"
preCondition="managedHandler" />
                <add name="Session" type="System.Web.SessionState.SessionStateModule"
preCondition="managedHandler" />
                <add name="WindowsAuthentication"
type="System.Web.Security.WindowsAuthenticationModule"
preCondition="managedHandler" />
                <add name="FormsAuthentication"
type="System.Web.Security.FormsAuthenticationModule" preCondition="managedHandler" />
                <add name="DefaultAuthentication"
type="System.Web.Security.DefaultAuthenticationModule"
preCondition="managedHandler" />
                <add name="RoleManager" type="System.Web.Security.RoleManagerModule"
preCondition="managedHandler" />
                <add name="UrlAuthorization"
type="System.Web.Security.UrlAuthorizationModule" preCondition="managedHandler" />
                <add name="FileAuthorization"
type="System.Web.Security.FileAuthorizationModule" preCondition="managedHandler" />
                <add name="AnonymousIdentification"
type="System.Web.Security.AnonymousIdentificationModule"
preCondition="managedHandler" />
                <add name="Profile" type="System.Web.Profile.ProfileModule"
preCondition="managedHandler" />
                <add name="UrlMappingsModule" type="System.Web.UrlMappingsModule"
preCondition="managedHandler" />
                <add name="WindowsAuthenticationModule" type="" preCondition="" />
                <add name="IpRestrictionModule" type="" preCondition="" />
                <add name="CustomLoggingModule" type="" preCondition="" />
                <add name="FailedRequestsTracingModule" type="" preCondition="" />
        </modules>
    </system.webServer>
</configuration>
```

This web.config starts off by clearing all previously defined modules that would have be inherited by the web.config of the Default Web Site (because this application is within that particular site) and the applicationHost.config file. The IIS Manager then explicitly defines each additional module for us but does not add in the one module we wanted to remove.

Let's say we use the same web.config and now navigate to http://*<site with above web.config>*/file_not_here.aspx (see Figure 6.6).

Figure 6.6 A Server Error

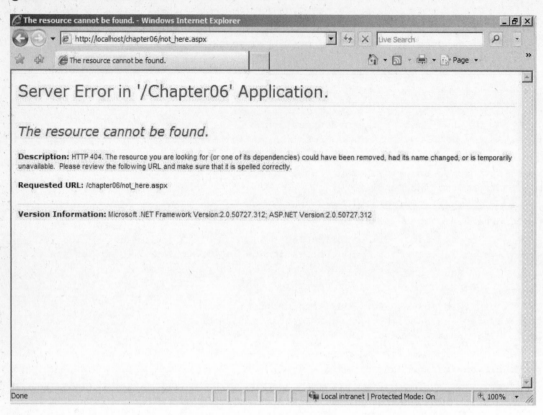

You now see that you'll get an error response from ASP.NET. Even if you set existingResponse to a value of Replace, which would normally have IIS do the error response instead of ASP.NET when an error is generated by ASP.NET, the response will still be handled by ASP.NET. This is because the previous web.config setting removed the module that would have handled the error. Thus, ASP.NET will continue to generate the error.

Inside IIS 7.0's Failed Request Tracing

Getting the current state of a request made to an IIS 7.0 server is easier than ever before when we use IIS 7.0's Failed Request Tracing. This feature allows an inside view to particular requests that are currently in process and how long they have been executing.

IIS's failed request tracing was designed in such a way that you shouldn't need to be present when a problem occurs; rather, you should simply be prepared for the problem if it arises. The success of this new feature depends solely on your ability to configure the appropriate rules for your Web applications prior to failures.

Failed Request Tracing Architecture

Although the underlying feature behind failed request tracing was introduced in Windows Server 2003 (Enterprise Tracing for Windows), its awareness and usability didn't become first class for IIS customers until IIS 7.0. The key to using this new feature is to understand how IIS 7.0's modularized core server emits events that are captured and stored for later retrieval.

At the heart of what allows Failed Request Tracing (FRT) is Enterprise Tracing for Windows (ETW), a platform component of the Windows Operation System. ETW was first leveraged by IIS with IIS 6.0 Service Pack 1. ETW is a kernel mode component that will keep track of all tracing events within nonpaged memory and will flush out the events to disk in a nonsequential order (important to note for navigating the trace files later). ETW provides a mechanism for applications to plug into the tracing infrastructure via a provider model. Each provider will have the opportunity to write relevant data per session or page requests as it relates to IIS 7.0.

With IIS 6.0/Service Pack 1, administrators had to interact directly with ETW via the command line to use ETW tracing with IIS. In addition, the ETL log file was difficult to use and often needed tools such as Log Parser (part of the IIS Diagnostics Toolkit at www.iisdiagnostics.com) to get to the relevant tracing information. Furthermore, a limited set of providers were available for tracing in IIS 6 and there was no "easy" way to add additional providers into the tracing pipeline from an ASP.NET/IIS application.

IIS 7.0 reduces the complexity in enabling and managing tracing data. Administrators can enable tracing from within the new IIS 7.0 administration console. Web developers can quickly and efficiently plug into the IIS 7.0 tracing pipeline (which uses ETW as the platform) with a few lines of additional code in their application.

For more information on Enterprise Tracing for Windows and the improvements to ETW in Windows Vista, you'll find a great article on the Microsoft Developer Network (MSDN) at http://msdn.microsoft.com/msdnmag/issues/07/04/ETW/.

Configuring IIS 7.0's Failed Request Tracing

By default, IIS 7.0's tracing isn't enabled on Windows Vista. It is available, though, if it's installed during the setup process. It is important to understand how to enable tracing and create rules to capture the events you are looking for.

A key aspect of failed request tracing is the understanding of how to scope rules to remove noise from the log files and help narrow down the problem. In such cases, you might only want to establish rules for a particular error or condition. Here we will walk you through how to best use this feature of tracing.

Enable Tracing for IIS 7.0

To use tracing in IIS 7.0, we first must add that in Windows Vista:

1. Click the **Windows** button and navigate to **Control Panel**.

2. From Control Panel Home (not Classic View, although you could take that route as well), click **Programs | Turn Windows features on or off**.

3. From within the Windows Features window, expand **Internet Information Services | World Wide Web Services | Health and Diagnostics**.

4. Check the **Tracing** check box and then click the **OK** button (see Figure 6.7).

Figure 6.7 Turning Windows Features on and off

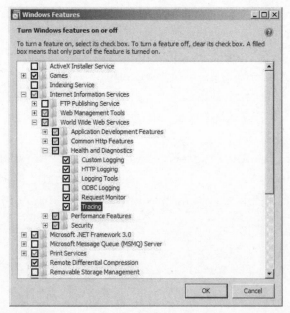

Using IIS Manager

To start the configuration Failed Request Tracing Rules, you use IIS Manager to enable Failed Request Tracing for a given Web application. Although you can define rules by virtual directory or by Web application level, the failed request tracing feature must be enabled at the site level first:

1. Using IIS Manager, navigate down to your target Web site.

2. Click **Failed Request Tracing Rules** and then click the **Open Feature** in the Actions pane.

3. Click **Edit Site Tracing…** from the Actions pane.

4. Check the **Enable** check box.

5. Define the directory location where all failed request files will be stored and the maximum number of log files you'd like maintained.

6. Click the **OK** button.

Centralized Tracing for ASP.NET and IIS 7.0

Following the theme of integrating ASP.NET and IIS 7.0, tracing information is now aggregated into the same pipeline. In addition to the integration is the theme of extensibility, which allows Web developers to add their own tracing information into that same pipeline. This gives administrators and developers a single file that defines all the tracing information for all components that interact within a given request. This capability is not only great for testing purposes during a development phase, but it also provides a wealth of information while you're working on issues in production.

Let's first take a look at a simple scenario where an ASP.NET developer can plug into the IIS 7.0 tracing infrastructure. Create a simple .aspx page with the following code and save it as simpletrace.aspx:

```
<%@ Page language="C#" trace="true" %>


<%
  Trace.Write("HowToCheatIIS7- Chapter 6: Interesting Info");
  Trace.Warn("HowToCheatIIS7- Chapter 6: Issue");
  Response.Write("hello, world");
%>
```

If you now browse to this page, you'll see a wealth of information at the bottom of the page (see Figures 6.8 and 6.9). It also includes the tracing information we defined within the Tracing Information section.

Figure 6.8 Hello, World's Trace Information

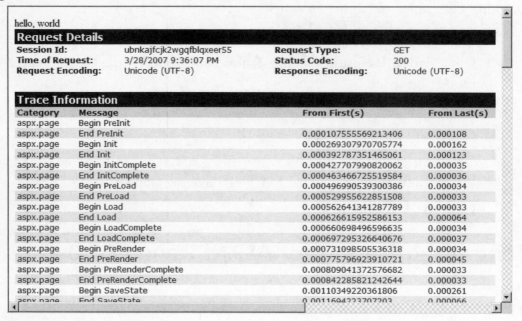

Figure 6.9 Hello Word Information

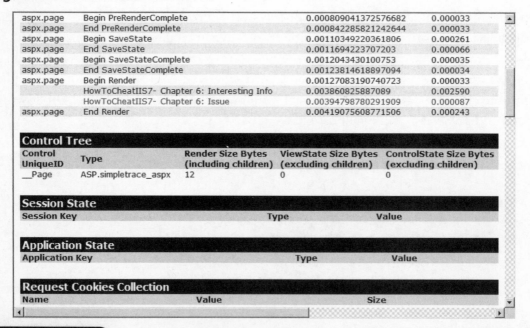

There is nothing new here to experienced ASP.NET developers. That's actually the cool part! Although this tool was available in ASP.NET before IIS 7.0, it only maintained information from ASP.NET. With the @Page declaration having the trace attribute set to *true*, we will still only see ASP.NET-based information on this page.

Now it's time to see the centralized view of ASP.NET and IIS information in action. To do this, you must define the kind of information you want the Failed Request Tracing Rules to capture and store for you:

1. Using IIS Manager, navigate down to your target Web application.

2. Click **Failed Request Tracing Rules** and then click the **Open Feature** in the Actions pane.

3. From the Actions pane, click the **Add…** link.

4. From the Specify Content to Trace page, select **ASP.NET (*.aspx)** and click **Next**.

5. From the Define Trace Conditions page, check the **Status Codes** check box and enter **200** as the status code.

6. From the Select Trace Providers page, select only the following options:

   ■ Providers: ASPNET

   ■ Verbosity: Verbose

   ■ Areas: Page

7. Click **Finish**.

You'll now see the rule shown in Figure 6.10 in the Failed Request Tracing Rules page.

Using your browser, navigate back to the simpletrace.aspx page. You should see the same result. But now we need to look at the trace file that was produced by IIS 7.0:

1. Click the **Windows** button and click **Computer**.

2. Navigate to the folder where the defined Failed Tracing Rules should be stored. The default location is %SystemDrive%\inetpub\logs\FailedReqLogFiles\W3SVC1\.

Figure 6.10 A Failed Request Rule

Here you should see all the failed request files for this site. The format is in FR######.xml, where ###### is a number which increments with each new failed request being created. If you use a program like Notepad to open the contents of one of the failed request files, you'll notice that the file is actually just XML (the file extension points that out as well). By having the results stored in an XML format, Microsoft has opened up the possibilities of what can be done with this data.—including pulling the data periodically from the local folder and storing it in a rich database such as SQL Server 2005!

There is also a file named freb.xsl that is an XML style sheet used to give the failed requests a nice look and feel when you open a failed request file using Internet Explorer. In fact, Figure 6.11 shows the failed request file for our previous request using Internet Explorer.

NOTE

Microsoft is continuing to invest in the IIS 7.0 platform and embedding those changes in the server version of IIS 7.0, which will ship as part of Windows Server 2008. One such improvement is an updated style sheet for the Failed Request Tracing files.

The past style sheet (Windows Vista) was great in terms of providing a more pleasant viewing experience of the FRT file versus a straight Notepad view of the XML, but it still required the user to hunt through the entire contents to find any warnings or failures. The new version of the style sheet (Windows Server 2008) will provide a simplified view of the trace file and focus on the warnings and failures within the contents. However, the user can still expand the views to see the entire contents. The goal was to reduce the amount of data users have to sift through each time they look at a Failed Request Trace.

As with the version of IIS 7.0 that ships with Windows Vista, the Windows Server 2008 version of IIS 7.0 will continue to provide all the rich tracing information in the same XML format.

With the release of Windows Server 2008, administrators will be able to store the FRT files on a remote share via a UNC path. At the time of this writing, Windows Server 2008 has yet to ship, so these features could change or could be cut in the final release of the product.

Figure 6.11 A Failed Request File

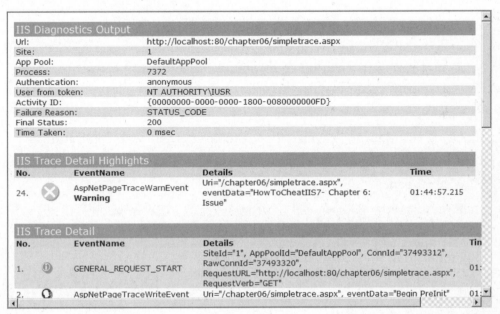

Toward the bottom of this Web page, you'll find the trace information as defined within the ASP.NET page (see Figure 6.12).

Figure 6.12 ASP.NET Trace Information

12.	☻	AspNetPageTraceWriteEvent	LoadComplete"	01:
13.	☻	AspNetPageTraceWriteEvent	Uri="/chapter06/simpletrace.aspx", eventData="End LoadComplete"	01:
14.	☻	AspNetPageTraceWriteEvent	Uri="/chapter06/simpletrace.aspx", eventData="Begin PreRender"	01:
15.	☻	AspNetPageTraceWriteEvent	Uri="/chapter06/simpletrace.aspx", eventData="End PreRender"	01:
16.	☻	AspNetPageTraceWriteEvent	Uri="/chapter06/simpletrace.aspx", eventData="Begin PreRenderComplete"	01:
17.	☻	AspNetPageTraceWriteEvent	Uri="/chapter06/simpletrace.aspx", eventData="End PreRenderComplete"	01:
18.	☻	AspNetPageTraceWriteEvent	Uri="/chapter06/simpletrace.aspx", eventData="Begin SaveState"	01:
19.	☻	AspNetPageTraceWriteEvent	Uri="/chapter06/simpletrace.aspx", eventData="End SaveState"	01:
20.	☻	AspNetPageTraceWriteEvent	Uri="/chapter06/simpletrace.aspx", eventData="Begin SaveStateComplete"	01:
21.	☻	AspNetPageTraceWriteEvent	Uri="/chapter06/simpletrace.aspx", eventData="End SaveStateComplete"	01:
22.	☻	AspNetPageTraceWriteEvent	Uri="/chapter06/simpletrace.aspx", eventData="Begin Render"	01:
23.	☻	AspNetPageTraceWriteEvent	Uri="/chapter06/simpletrace.aspx", eventData="HowToCheatIIS7- Chapter 6: Interesting Info"	01:
24.	✖	AspNetPageTraceWarnEvent **Warning**	Uri="/chapter06/simpletrace.aspx", eventData="HowToCheatIIS7- Chapter 6: Issue"	01:
25.	☻	AspNetPageTraceWriteEvent	Uri="/chapter06/simpletrace.aspx", eventData="End Render"	01:
26.	ⓘ	GENERAL_REQUEST_END	BytesSent="13894", BytesReceived="311", HttpStatus="200", HttpSubStatus="0"	01:

Now you're seeing the same basic results in this trace file as you saw on the actual page for ASP.NET. But what about the integration between ASP.NET and IIS 7.0? For that, we need to open up the scope of the information that we want to see in the failed request. To do that, we'll create a new rule and select all tracing providers:

1. Using IIS Manager, navigate down to your target Web application.

2. Click **Failed Request Tracing Rules** and then click **Open Feature** in the Actions pane.

3. First, select the *previous rule* and then click the **Remove** link in the Actions pane. We'll do this to keep things simple.

4. From the Actions pane, click the **Add...** link.

5. From the Specify Content to Trace page, select **ASP.NET (*.aspx)** and click **Next**.

6. From the Define Trace Conditions page, check the **Status Codes** check box and enter **200** as the status code.

7. From the Select Trace Providers page, we won't deselect anything. Thus, we'll watch for everything.

8. Click **Finish**.

9. Using a browser, navigate back to the **simpletrace.aspx** page and then open the latest failed request log file.

You should see an increase in the amount of information within the trace file. Although this is a bit "noisy," you get a good idea of the amount of information found within the trace, and you see how the ASP.NET, IIS 7.0, and developer-defined tracing information is centralized into a single file.

There is a known issue when trying to use the ASP.NET trace provider: It won't show up in the list of trace providers when you create a new rule.

Open %windir%\system32\inetsrv\config\applicationHost.config using Notepad and add the following to *<traceProviderDefinitions>*:

```
<traceProviderDefinitions>

    ...other providers defined...

            <add name="ASPNET" guid="{AFF081FE-0247-4275-9C4E-021F3DC1DA35}">
                <areas>
                    <add name="Infrastructure" value="1" />
                    <add name="Module" value="2" />
                    <add name="Page" value="4" />
                    <add name="AppServices" value="8" />
                </areas>
            </add>
        </traceProviderDefinitions>
```

The issue noted previously is relevant to the initial version of Windows Vista. This issue will be resolved in the final version of Windows Server 2008 and Windows Vista Service Pack 1 and the workaround will no longer be needed.

Modify the XML

The following XML is taken from the applicationHost.config file. It encapsulates all the changes we previously made. The *path* attribute in the *<location>* node points to the application path within the Default Web Site:

```xml
<location path="Default Web Site/Chapter06">
        <system.webServer>
            <tracing>
                <traceFailedRequests>
                    <add path="*">
                        <traceAreas>
                            <add provider="ASP" verbosity="Verbose" />
                            <add provider="ASPNET"
areas="Infrastructure,Module,Page,AppServices" verbosity="Verbose" />
                            <add provider="ISAPI Extension" verbosity="Verbose" />
                            <add provider="WWW Server"
areas="Authentication,Security,Filter,StaticFile,CGI,Compression,Cache,RequestNotifi
cations" verbosity="Verbose" />
                        </traceAreas>
                        <failureDefinitions statusCodes="200" />
                    </add>
                </traceFailedRequests>
            </tracing>
        </system.webServer>
    </location>
```

The default Failed Request Tracing setting in IIS 7.0 is to not allow the trace Failed Request settings to be configured beyond the server level. To change this, you'll need to modify the section found within the applicationHost.config file and change the overrideModeDefault setting from Deny to Allow:

```xml
<sectionGroup name="tracing">
            <section name="traceFailedRequests" overrideModeDefault="Deny" />
            <section name="traceProviderDefinitions" overrideModeDefault="Deny"
/>
 </sectionGroup>
```

Breakpoints: Extending IIS 7.0's Tracing

The theme of extensibility continues even into IIS 7.0's failed request tracing. The ability for a developer who develops custom modules using IIS 7.0's APIs to also push his or her module's errors into the same error log used by IIS is arguably the most powerful feature in all of IIS 7.0. A developer who raises events through the life of a module can emit these events in IIS 7.0's failed request logs in sequence with all other IIS events.

It is important for system administrators and developers alike is to understand how these custom events will be persisted to the log file. Beyond that, they need to know how to easily distinguish between these custom events and those emitted by the core IIS server.

How Developers Extend Their Module to Support Failed Request Tracing

A potential topic in and of itself, we can't turn a deaf ear to understanding how developers will take advantage of this feature. It is more important, though, to know how to find the custom events than to help narrow the problem to custom code rather than in IIS's core server. In this section, we will provide a sample of a module with events that are emitted to the trace log files in error conditions with the goal of showing how they live side by side with IIS's core server events. The core principles in this sample will show you how any Web application on IIS 7.0 can interject its own application information into the combined trace file generated by IIS 7.0.

Using Visual Studio C# Express Edition (which is a free download), let's develop a Custom Error Module that we'll use to override the default Error Module that ships with IIS 7.0. To develop an IIS 7 module or handler, we'll need to install all the required components for VS C# Express or VB.NET to work on Microsoft Windows Vista:

- Microsoft Visual Studio Express Editions (C#, VB.NET, J#)
- Visual Studio 2005 Service Pack 2
- Visual Studio 2005 Update for Windows Vista

You can download and install these components (and it should be done in the order defined previously) from http://msdn.microsoft.com/vstudio/express/down-loads/.

Visual Studio C# Express Edition (VSCSE) provides the ability to compile in both Release and Debug modes. The main difference between the two when compiling your code base is that the Debug version of the DLL is a bit larger and includes the symbols (.pdb) file.

VSCSE has a default setting of building (aka compiling) in the Release format. To enable Debug mode building, we'll need first expose the ability to make this change with Visual Studio:

1. With VSCSE running, click **Tools | Options** from the menu bar.

2. At the bottom-left corner of the Options window, check the **Show all settings** check box.

3. Expand **Projects and Solutions** and then click the **General node**.

4. Check the **Show advanced build configurations** check box.

5. Click the **OK** button (see Figure 6.13).

Figure 6.13 VSCSE Options

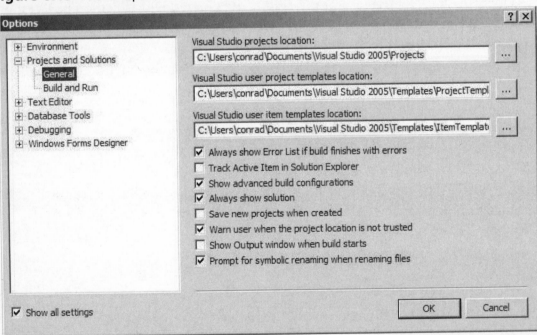

Now that we have this configured, we can select the build type we'd like to use in compiling our application or class.

Create and Compile

To get started, let's start the Microsoft Visual C# 2005 Express Edition development environment and create a new project:

1. Click the **Windows** button | **All Programs | Microsoft Visual C# 2005 Express Edition**.

2. From the top menu bar, click **File | New Project**.

3. Select **Class Library** and set the Name to **HowToCheatIIS7**.

4. Click **OK** (see Figure 6.14).

Figure 6.14 Creating a New Project with Visual C# 2005 Express Edition

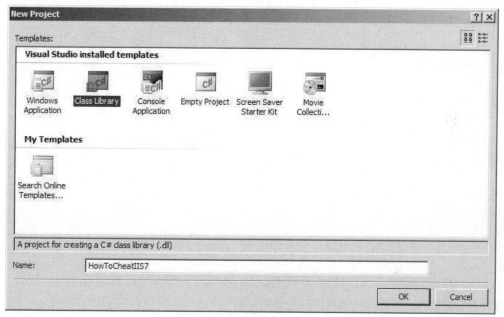

To leverage the Microsoft.Web.Administration object model and to connect into the IIS pipeline, we'll need to create a couple of references to our project:

1. Right-click the **References** folder and select **Add References...** from the context menu.

2. Within the **Browse** tab, navigate to the **%WINDIR%\System32\InetSrv** folder and select **Microsoft.Web.Administration.dll**, and then click the **OK** button.

Follow the same basic instructions, but this time we'll add the **System.Web** assembly from the **.NET** tab.

Ensure that the build is set to **Debug** by selecting it from the build drop-down menu (see Figure 6.15).

Figure 6.15 Setting the Build to Debug

```csharp
using System;
using System.Web;
using System.Collections;
using System.Diagnostics;


namespace HowToCheatIIS7
{


    public class TraceModule : IHttpModule
    {

        TraceSource tsStatus;


        // register callbacks as well as the trace source.
        public void Init(HttpApplication application)
        {
            application.EndRequest += (new
EventHandler(this.Application_EndRequest));
            tsStatus = new TraceSource("tsStatus");
        }


        private void Application_EndRequest(Object source, EventArgs e)
        {
            tsStatus.TraceEvent(TraceEventType.Start, 0, "[TraceModule] Start");

            tsStatus.TraceEvent(TraceEventType.Warning, 0, "[TraceModule]
Warning");
```

```
        tsStatus.TraceEvent(TraceEventType.Stop, 0, "[TraceModule] Stop");
    }


    public void Dispose()
    {
    }
  }
}
```

Compile the application by clicking the **Build | Build Solution** menu. Once our code has been compiled, we can find the HowToCheatIIS7.dll and HowToCheatIIS7.dll.

Add Managed Module to IIS 7.0

With our new module compiled, we'll now add it to IIS 7.0. Before we can add our new module into IIS, we'll need to copy our compiled components to the /bin directory of our Web application.

Using IIS Manager, we'll now add our new module into the IIS 7 pipeline. In this example, we're going to add our module to a specific application within the Default Web Site:

1. Click **Modules** and then click the **Open Feature** from within the Actions pane. Or you can simply double-click the **Modules** icon (see Figure 6.16).

Figure 6.16 Adding a New Module to IIS 7

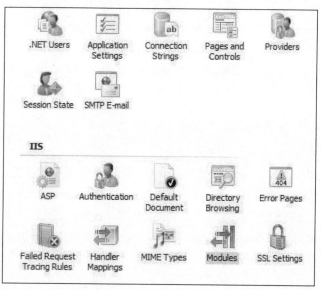

2. From the Actions pane, click **Add Managed Module**… (see Figure 6.17).

Figure 6.17 The Add Managed Module

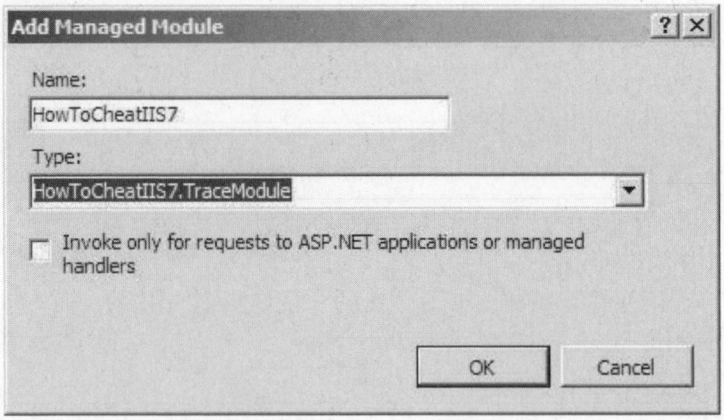

3. In the Add Managed Module window, provide the following information and then click the **OK** button:

- Name: HowToCheatIIS7
- Type: HowToCheatIIS7.TraceModule

This also could be done by directly updating the web.config file for the application. The following would be added within the <modules> XML node.

```
<add name="HowToCheatIIS7" type="HowToCheatIIS7.TraceModule" preCondition="" />
```

You'll now see HowToCheatIIS7 added to the list of modules. Clicking the **View Ordered List…** link in the Actions pane, you'll see the actual order in which IIS7 will process each module as a request is submitted to this application. Our new module will be at the bottom of this list. By moving it up in the list, you'll be able to capture and potentially modify data and actions before later modules. This is extremely useful when you want to trace certain types of information before another module handles the request.

Enabling Trace

Our module has now been developed, compiled, and configured in IIS 7, but we have to tell IIS 7 to listen for tracing information from our new component. The following web.config file defines the three configuration settings that need to be defined for our tracing information within our module to be captured and included in a Failed Request Tracing Log file:

```xml
<configuration>

    <system.webServer>

        <modules>

            <add name="TraceModule" type="HowToCheatIIS7.TraceModule" />

        </modules>

    </system.webServer>


    <system.diagnostics>

        <sharedListeners>

            <add name="IisTraceListener" type="System.Web.IisTraceListener,
System.Web, Version=2.0.0.0, Culture=neutral, PublicKeyToken=b03f5f7f11d50a3a" />

        </sharedListeners>


        <switches>

            <add name="DefaultSwitch" value="All" />

        </switches>


        <sources>

            <source name="tsStatus" switchName="DefaultSwitch">

                <listeners>

                    <add name="IisTraceListener" type="System.Web.IisTraceListener,
System.Web, Version=2.0.0.0, Culture=neutral, PublicKeyToken=b03f5f7f11d50a3a" />

                </listeners>

            </source>

        </sources>

    </system.diagnostics>

</configuration>
```

Now that all of the pieces are in place, navigate your browser back to the simple-trace.aspx page. Once that page has completed rendering, open the latest FR######.xml file using your browser (see Figure 6.18).

Any Web developer who is building either a Web application or IIS 7.0 modules can now plug into the Failed Request Trace pipeline. This will result in less time and code the Web developer must focus on creating a tracing mechanism for the application. It will also reduce the number of trace files that a Web administrator must use to triage and resolve a given issue relating to a Web application.

Figure 6.18 IIS Diagnostics Output and Trace Details

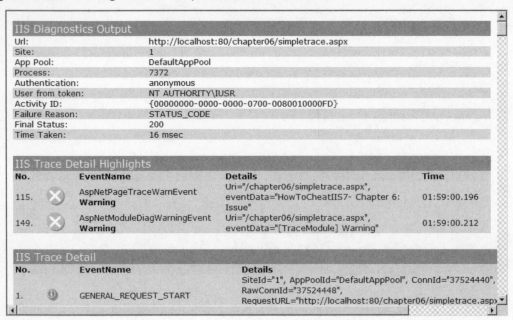

Although our example explains how to override the tracing mechanism that ships with IIS 7.0, the same type of logic and code could be leveraged within a custom application or another module that is not specifically focused on tracing. Take, for example, a developer who is creating a customer authentication module that will replace how IIS 7.0 does authentication. The developer can plug her tracing details within the same tracing pipeline as IIS 7.0. By doing so, the operations team or Web server administrator can get a single trace file with all applications participating within a troubled or failed request on a production machine.

Due to the ability to have a single trace file for all components to plug into for a given request, Web server administrators and IT operations managers will be demanding that Web developers and ISVs plug into that infrastructure. In the long term, this will result in faster turnaround in resolving production issues and reduced overhead on server resources.

Reality: Inside What Tracing Can't Do in IIS 7.0

There is one undeniable truth in technology: There is no "magic pixie dust." The same goes for this powerful feature in IIS 7.0; there are simply some things that it can't do, and this section exists for this very reason. In some situations, failures exist outside the boundaries of the runtime engine, such as service failures or bad configurations. For these cases, most will find the Event Viewer is their best friend, whereas some errors might occur in Web applications during runtime that tracing simply can't help. In these cases, it is important to understand how to effectively tackle these issues.

For example, a difficult yet realistic reality in Web applications is the deployment of code that presents memory leaks. Tracing doesn't offer any functionality to ascertain the currently used memory of your Web application. How does one tackle this difficult problem? There are several different paths of attack, but the first action is to determine that you have a true leak, as well as to figure out how to attack the problem once it exists. At this point, we will discuss the tools available for closing in on this problem in Debug Diagnostics.

Identifying That You Have a Memory Leak

The unfortunate truth is that many times you anticipate a memory leak when you actually don't have one. Instead, you have different behaviors of an application, such as long-term allocations for performance or short-term allocations that cause spikes. You should understand how to use the Event viewer to best understand whether you have a memory leak; only then do you take action.

When researching a potential memory leak, you must first understand that there is a difference between objects hanging around longer than you expected and losing the handle on an object, which actually constitutes a leak.

The .NET Framework provides a rich and extensible object-oriented programming platform that also removes the developer from having to handle his or her own memory management. Although this does make developers more productive, it can become a bit frustrating when scaling your application for production use and seeing the memory allocations run wild. There is no actual "fix" to resolve this issue, but it requires that a developer understand how memory management in the .NET Framework works.

It is not the intended scope of this chapter to provide the definitive resource for memory management and performance for the .NET Framework, ASP.NET, or IIS 7.0, but it would be a bit neglectful to not at least mention a few guidelines to get you going.

The Garbage Collector (GC) is responsible for managing the memory allocation for all objects used within a .NET application. The GC will maintain the state of an object in memory and will remove it from physical memory when it needs to make more space using a finalizing process, or it will keep an object around due to a parent object keeping a reference to it. A common issue in memory management for ASP.NET is unknowingly maintaining an object or even a collection of objects. A good example of this is when you bind to an event handler to a static or cached object.

Here is an example of a simple event handler within ASP.NET:

```
private void InitializeComponent()
        {
                this.Load += new System.EventHandler(this.Page_Load);
                staticObject.myEvent += new
myEventEventHandler(this.staticObject_myEvent);
        }
```

Each time the ASP.NET page that has this code in it is called, a new event handler and listeners will be created for it. The base object that the event handler is referencing is a static object and will live until it is explicitly finalized and destroyed or until the application is unloaded from the host application (i.e., restarting the IIS application pool). With the static object as an anchor, all the event handlers that were created per page request will continue to live on within the GC because there is a parent object that is still alive. One way to help clear this up is to manually unhook the event handler when it's no longer needed.

When using a COM object within your .NET code base, you'll have to ensure that you properly release the object and not simply set the object to null or *nothing*. The following method will instruct the .NET Framework to release a COM object. If you don't do this, the object may reside in memory for much longer that you expect:

```
System.Runtime.InteropServices.Marshal.ReleaseComObject(comObj)
```

Shortcut...

Native Code and Managed Code Is All the Same in IIS 7.0

In previous versions of IIS, the ability to control and override IIS functionality was limited to those that could code in native code (C and C++). With IIS 7.0, the playing field is a bit more level, although there are still areas where native code is the only option.

IIS 7.0 also provides a new native core server API for C++ developers that replaces ISAPI filters. To compile an IIS 7.0 module using native code, you'll need to use the latest Windows Vista Platform SDK, which contains the IIS header file (httpserv.h).

Microsoft provides a starter kit for IIS 7.0 module development for C++: www.iis.net/default.aspx?tabid=3&subtabid=31&g=5&i=1062.

Downloading Debug Diagnostics and Enable Leak Tracker

This section outlines how to obtain the download for Debug Diagnostics and enable a memory leak rule to track down a problem with memory allocation.

With all the great built-in tools and platform components for diagnostics that ship as part of IIS 7, Microsoft also provides some additional tools. One such tool is the IIS Debug Diagnostics Tool, which is available as a free download from www.microsoft.com/downloads/details.aspx?FamilyID=28bd5941-c458-46f1-b24d-f60151d875a3&DisplayLang=en.

Capturing Memory Links

With the Debug Diagnostics Tool (DDT) installed, do the following:

1. Open the tool by navigating to the **Windows** button | **All Programs** | **Debug Diagnostics Tool 1.1** | **DebugDiag 1.1 (x86)**.

2. From within the Rules tab, click the **Add Rule...** button (see Figure 6.19).

Figure 6.19 The Rules Tab

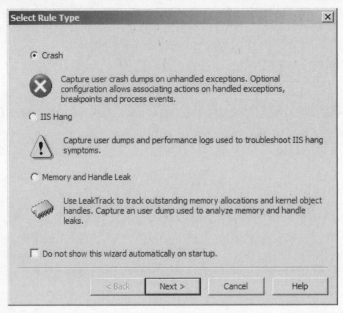

3. The Select Rule Type page provides three options:

    ■ Crash

    ■ IIS Hang

    ■ Memory and Handle Leak
       For the purpose of this exercise, select the **Memory and Handle Leak**
    option and click **Next**. From the Select Target page, find the IIS process
    (**w3wp.exe**) and click **Next** (see Figure 6.20).

Figure 6.20 The Select Target Page

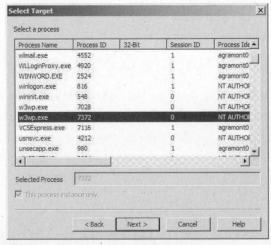

4. From the Configure Leak Rule page (see Figure 6.21), there re a number of options allow you to control the behavior of the new rule.

Figure 6.21 The Configure Leak Rule Page

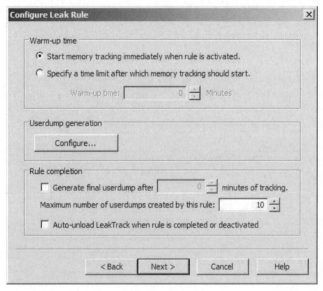

5. From the Select Dump Location and Rule Name (Optional) page (see Figure 6.22), this is where you give the rule a friendly name and a location where all the user dump information will be stored.

Figure 6.22 The Select Dump Location and Rule Name (Optional) Page

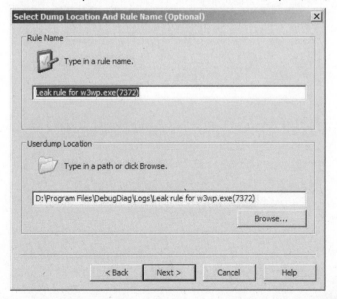

6. Finally, the Rule Completed page allows you to activate the rule for immediate use (see Figure 6.23).

Figure 6.23 The Rule Completed Page

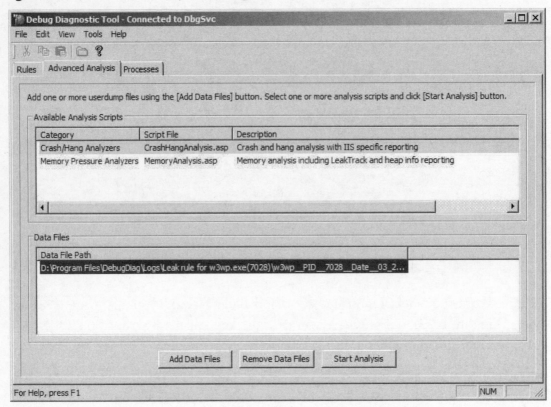

Summary

Unlike past IIS versions, the ability to troubleshoot your Web server and applications is a focal point for Microsoft. IIS 7.0 offers a strong troubleshooting approach using failed request tracing that is powerful and developer extensible and that easily pinpoints most of the common failures that occur in IIS 7.0. For the other lower percentage of problems, you can effectively understand the toolsets available to troubleshoot these problems when they occur. Finally, the key is to understand what failed request tracing can do for you—and what it can't.

Solutions Fast Track

Custom Error Messages

- ☑ Error messages can be configured by server, site, or application.

- ☑ Error messages are defined within the applicationHost.config file for the server or the web.config file for a given site or application/virtual directory.

- ☑ Error messages can be a static or dynamic file. You can also redirect to an external site when a specific error or status code is reached. .

- ☑ Detailed error messages provide a rich set of details about a specific error that assist in troubleshooting the issue.

- ☑ ASP.NET and IIS 7 are not integrated when it comes to error responses. The default setting is for IIS 7 to automatically decide how to handle errors.

Failed Request Tracing

- ☑ Failed Request Tracing can capture more than just errors. Tracing can be done on a given set of HTTP status codes or an amount of time.

- ☑ Developers should incorporate tracing details into their Web applications and components. This will help Web server administrators troubleshoot issues in a production environment.

Writing Tracing Information

☑ Tracing information from ASP.NET, IIS, and custom modules can be written to a single XML file.

☑ Tracing information can be done within ASP.NET:

```
Trace.Warn("HowToCheatIIS7- Chapter 6: Issue");
```

☑ Tracing information can be done within a .NET Module

```
tsStatus.TraceEvent(TraceEventType.Warning, 0, "[TraceModule] Warning");
```

Frequently Asked Questions

The following Frequently Asked Questions, answered by the authors of this book, are designed to both measure your understanding of the concepts presented in this chapter and to assist you with real-life implementation of these concepts. To have your questions about this chapter answered by the author, browse to **www.syngress.com/solutions** and click on the **"Ask the Author"** form.

Q: I'm a Web host and would like to be able to allow my customers to define their own tracing settings. Is this possible?

A: Yes, but doing so does require some thoughtful configuration. First, you'll need to change the <section name="traceFailedRequests" overrideModeDefault="Deny" /> in the applicationHost.config file and change the overrideModeDefault setting to Allow, but be careful because this will impact all the sites and applications on that server.

Q: Can I completely replace the ErrorModule that ships with IIS 7.0 with my own .NET code?

A: Absolutely! This is one of the great benefits of IIS 7.0 and the integration with ASP.NET. With some simple coding, a developer can create his or her own module that handles errors. Best of all, this can be done on a per-site level., so you don't have to impact the way all errors are going to be handled for other sites that want to use the default components.

Q: Can I use the Failed Request Tracing on production servers even if there aren't issues?

A: Sure, but there is always the I/O overhead when the log files are written to disk. Beyond that, you could have all File not Found (404) errors written out so you can see which URLs people are trying to navigate to and perhaps reroute those future requests. With the configuration setting that provides a maximum number of log files, you can be sure that you won't fill up your disk with log files.

Q: Can I enable/disable an existing Failed Request Tracing Rule?

A: No. At the moment, you have to delete a rule when you don't want it to "run" and then recreate it when you want those log files generated again.

Chapter 7

Putting It All Together

Solutions in this chapter:

- **Migrating to IIS 7.0**
- **Fitting and Finishing Work with IIS 7.0**
- **The Developer's Call-To-Arms**

☑ **Summary**

☑ **Solutions Fast Track**

☑ **Frequently Asked Questions**

Introduction

It has been said time and time again, there is no perfection in software. The entire planning process is focused on mitigating risks, avoiding pitfalls, and succeeding at all costs. In short, there is no "perfect" plan for moving from IIS 6.0 to 7.0. Guaranteed successes or failures in your planning or risk assessments just don't exist. At the end of the day, your success will be measured by how effective you leverage what is offered *in the box* for IIS 7.0. So study your current environment, understand your present dependencies on IIS features, and those non-IIS features your developer knows about. Using these as your building blocks, develop a step-by-step plan that takes the shortest yet most concise route to IIS 7.0. With the knowledge gained in this book, you will be well on your way to effectively deploying the most secure, powerful, and manageable Web server ever released by Microsoft.

BEST PRACTICES ACCORDING TO MICROSOFT

At the time of this writing, Microsoft was still actively working on IIS 7.0. The release of Windows Vista with IIS 7.0 offers a full Web server, though one that will change. It is because of this that Microsoft recommends IIS 7.0 on Windows Vista for development and learning purposes only—not for any true deployment scenarios. The release of Windows Server 2008 Beta 3 had primary changes in IIS 7.0 directed towards deployment. You should evaluate this version of IIS 7.0 to understand migrating to IIS 7.0 from IIS 6.0.

Migrating to IIS 7.0

The primary reason to migrate to IIS 7.0 is simple: flexibility. In previous chapters, you learned all the various moving parts that make up this profound release of IIS. Your migration strategy greatly depends on your ability to evaluate your IIS 6.0 environment, build a blueprint for your system on IIS 6.0, and cross-reference as you migrate to IIS 7.0. The end goal is to cause as little disruption as possible to your services, yet ensure you take advantage of the benefits IIS 7.0 has to offer.

Migration Considerations

Successful migrations to and from any platform are the end result of careful consideration, planning, and execution. Before you start upgrading servers willy-nilly, there are some questions you should ask to help identify how much of your network is eligible for the transition.

- Are any Web servers just serving up static content? For example, are you running several FTP servers, or sites that only store resources like images and JavaScript for other Web sites? If so, these are prime candidates for migration, and will probably provide the smoothest upgrade path. If these resource sites are spread out across your server farm, you should consider consolidating them onto one box.

- Are any of your sites using URLScan to filter requests? If yes, you'll need to consider moving to IIS 7.0's Request Filtering instead.

- Are you running ASP.NET 1.0, 1.1, or FPSE applications? If so, there will be additional configuration issues. You should consider the ramifications of converting your ASP.NET applications to ASP.NET 2.0 before undertaking the server migration.

- Are you running ISAPI filters from IIS 5.1 or earlier? You may have to check with the vendor for a newer version. There is a good possibility one might not be available, in which case a replacement must be built.

- Are you only running IIS on the boxes you're upgrading? Consider installing the Server Core version of Windows Server 2008 instead of a full-fledged version. Server Core is a command-line only flavor of Windows, a la Unix, that doesn't contain any GUI code. No shell means a smaller surface area than even the Web Edition. How can your Web server fall victim to an animated cursor flaw when the server is incapable of using animated cursors?

Upgrading Paths by OS Version

As I mentioned at the beginning of the chapter, if you're running anything older than Windows Server 2003 in a production environment, your migration experience will be slightly more complicated than if you had just bit the bullet and upgraded with the rest of the world.

The following direct upgrade paths are supported:

- IIS 6 | Windows Server 2003 => IIS 7 | Windows Server 2008
- IIS 5.1 | Windows XP => IIS 7 | Windows Vista

There are no guarantees that migration tools will be offered by Microsoft. As such, you will be tasked with building your own migration strategy. It goes without saying that if you are running previous versions of IIS before IIS 6.0, you should seriously consider moving to IIS 6.0 prior to jumping to IIS 7.0. The IIS 7.0 process model for the most part stole much of its design from the IIS 6.0 process model, so most applications running on IIS 6.0 will likely run fine on version 7. If you do choose to directly jump from IIS 4.0 or 5.0 to IIS 7.0, you should understand your migration strategy and how to execute it.

For example, in IIS 5.0 your process isolation was very different than in IIS 6. The process model in IIS 5.0 made assumptions that your ISAPI filters were always running as a local system, and in Inetinfo.exe, and that they had access to the raw HTTP request information. This isn't the case in IIS 6, nor is that changing in IIS 7.0. So the questions you should ask yourself include the following;

- How do you isolate your site and applications into application pools?
- Will your ISAPI filters work when used in multiple processes?
- Can your applications run with limited privileges such as Network Service?

This is the tip of the iceberg, but it gives you an idea of what to crunch when planning a migration from IIS 5 to 7.0. Nonetheless, it is completely possible to go from version 5 to version 7 of IIS.

Upgrade versus Clean Install

The time-tested rule-of-thumb regarding Windows is that it is always better to do a clean installation on existing hardware than it is to perform an in-place upgrade. That's because, in the past, Windows tried to install the newer version over the top of the older one, and it didn't always do the best job. Often, old files and settings were left behind, cluttering up the hard drive and making troubleshooting the system difficult. For some administrators, a new deployment of Windows provides a fresh start for servers that seem to get slower as time goes on.

But all that changed with Vista and Windows Server 2008. The new installer is image-based, not file-based. So during an upgrade, all the systems' programs and settings are backed up, a clean image is copied to the hard drive and expanded, and then the programs and settings are migrated to the new image. Thus, installations are just as painless as with a fresh partition.

That being said, a clean installation may still be the way to go for system administrators who need a cathartic release every five years or so. It also may be easier (and sometimes cheaper) for sysadmins to only deploy new OS releases on new hardware, in the same way they manage their desktops.

Upgrade Steps

As I mentioned earlier in the chapter, the installation process on Windows Vista and Windows Server 2008 is image-based, instead of file-based as in previous versions. This means upgrades are also handled differently than in earlier versions. Currently, the upgrade process happens in three stages:

- Detect and gather
- Image copy and unpacking
- Restore settings

Let's take a closer look at what occurs in these phases.

Detect and Gather

During an upgrade to Windows Vista or Windows Server 2008, the installer looks for all features and settings in the previous operating system. If IIS is detected on the existing Windows installation, all metabase and IIS state information will be gathered and persisted to a hidden folder on the main partition. Any file system content not created or owned by Windows will remain intact through the upgrade, so all Web content you have on the hard drive will still be there after first boot.

Image Copy and Unpacking

The installation phase consists of copying the installation image to the hard drive, and then activating optional features, such as IIS, if they were detected on the original OS. The IIS features activated are based on the IIS state information gathered from the original OS. Because IIS 6 was nowhere near as modular as IIS7, the installer will err on the side of caution when configuring IIS 7's new features. You won't be able to specify which features you want. Instead, if any of the main IIS-related Windows services are installed on the old OS, all of the related IIS 7 features will be installed for maximum compatibility.

The following series of tables illustrates the IIS 6 services that will be detected, and the IIS 7 features that will be installed as a result:

If World Wide Web Service (W3SVC) Is Installed

IIS-ASP	IIS-ISAPIFilter
IIS-BasicAuthentication	IIS-LegacyScripts
IIS-CGI	IIS-LoggingLibraries
IIS-ClientCertificateMapping-Authentication	IIS-ManagementScriptingTools
IIS-CustomLogging	IIS-ManagementService
IIS-DefaultDocument	IIS-ODBCLogging
IIS-DigestAuthentication	IIS-RequestFiltering
IIS-DirectoryBrowsing	IIS-RequestMonitor
IIS-HttpCompressionDynamic	IIS-ServerSideIncludes
IIS-HttpCompressionStatic	IIS-StaticContent
IIS-HttpErrors	IIS-URLAuthorization
IIS-HttpLogging	IIS-WindowsAuthentication
IIS-HttpRedirect	IIS-WMICompatibility
IIS-HttpTracing	WAS-ConfigurationAPI
IIS-IISCertificateMapping-Authentication	WAS-NetFxEnvironment
IIS-IPSecurity	WAS-ProcessModel
IIS-ISAPIExtensions	

If FTP Service (MSFTPSVC) Is Installed

IIS-FTPServer

If Internet Services Manager (INETMGR.EXE) Is Installed

IIS-FTPManagement	IIS-ManagementConsole
IIS-LegacySnapIn	

If IIS Administrative Service (IISADMIN) Is Installed

IIS-Metabase

This strategy gives you the greatest chance of booting up with a Web server that is fully functional for your applications. Unfortunately, you won't have any control over which services are installed as a result of the service detection process. You will have an opportunity later to fine-tune your Web server footprint after the upgrade is complete.

Restore Settings

After the image is unpacked and the optional features like IIS are configured, the settings that were gathered and set aside during the first phase are reapplied. At this point, the metabase settings from the original IIS (5 or 6) are translated into the new XML format and applied to the ApplicationHost.config file.

SOME INDEPENDENT ADVICE

IIS 7.0 on Windows Vista or Windows Server 2008 is still in beta as of this writing. Currently, some known issues with upgrades will impact your sites upon completion. These will obviously be resolved prior to final release, despite their current presence, even with Microsoft offering you a Go Live license for IIS 7.0 customers.

After the Upgrade

The speed of your upgrade depends on a number of variables like hardware, the number of installed features, and so on. Afterwards, you're booted into Windows for the first time. Now what? Well, chances are that your server is probably not ready to start shelling out Web pages to the masses quite yet. So, let's look at some of the things you can do to optimize IIS 7.0.

Fitting and Finishing Work in IIS 7.0

No upgrade or clean install is complete without some action items. The first thing to understand is that often on clean installs many people will install the entire product. It is a well-known tactic that guarantees less troubleshooting since everyone knows they can always strip after the fact. This approach makes sense given that most administrators, like you, aren't deeply involved with just one technology or even a couple. Instead, you have to manage many servers, all running various applications from Microsoft and elsewhere. The least amount of toil entails making sure that with everything installed your Web applications actually do work. So cool, do that…When you're finished, then come back.

Afterward, you must diligently clean up to ensure you're running the most optimized, smallest footprint Web server possible. A great number of individuals doing server administration don't know what their Web applications are built on or what their dependencies are. Thus, the question is often asked, "How can I figure this out on my IIS 5.0 or 6.0 servers?"

This wasn't as easy on previous versions, but it certainly is on IIS 7.0. With the new tracing infrastructure in IIS 7.0, you can literally step through your Web applications and determine from the trace log what features are used.

Furthermore, you can spend much time and energy troubleshooting if you don't have the tools set up right off the bat. You can enable failed request tracing for only 500 errors to ensure that when they occur, you have access to the files. To strengthen that approach, set up a scheduled task to copy the old files to another location and increase the number of trace logs to keep.

The last step is to protect yourself in case of problems with your server. Unfortunately, IIS 7.0 does not make an initial configuration backup of application-host.config. Therefore, you need to. So let's make sure this is done.

Using Tracing to Isolate Your Server Features

In IIS 7.0, the Failed Request Tracing is misleading. Yes, it is used to locate potential failure points and causes but at the same time many don't realize it's just fine for requests that work like HTTP 200. It is so easy to learn what modules are used by your Web applications, yet it is so tricky to so many because they get caught up in the term "failed."

The first step is to build some sort of mechanism to allow you to emulate your client's use of your Web applications. This is often referred to as load testing, but in our case load isn't the goal of just using the application a good start? So many ways exist to do this that it is outside the scope of this book. However, let's assume you do have some sort of ability to make requests to your IIS 7.0 server.

SOME INDEPENDENT ADVICE

A number of solutions are available in the marketplace, varying from free to expensive, for automating requests to your Web server. In fact, if you are a developer, you can probably just build your own. If you struggle with not having a solution, take a look at tools like tinyget from Microsoft.

The second step is to enable tracing for all HTTP status codes equaling 200 and 300 for all content. This is important to ensure you grab all requests that do not equal an error—what many of us refer to as your application's "happy path." To set up this rule, do the following:

1. In IIS Manager, click the Web site name—for example, Default Web Site.

2. On the home page, click **Failed Request Tracing**.

3. In the task pane, click **Add**.

4. Select **All Content** when asked to select what to trace.

5. For conditions, check Status Codes and type **200, 301, 302**.

6. Click **Finish**.

To validate that your rule was successful, it should now appear in the list view on the failed request tracing page, as shown in Figure 7.1.

Figure 7.1 Failed Request Tracing Rule

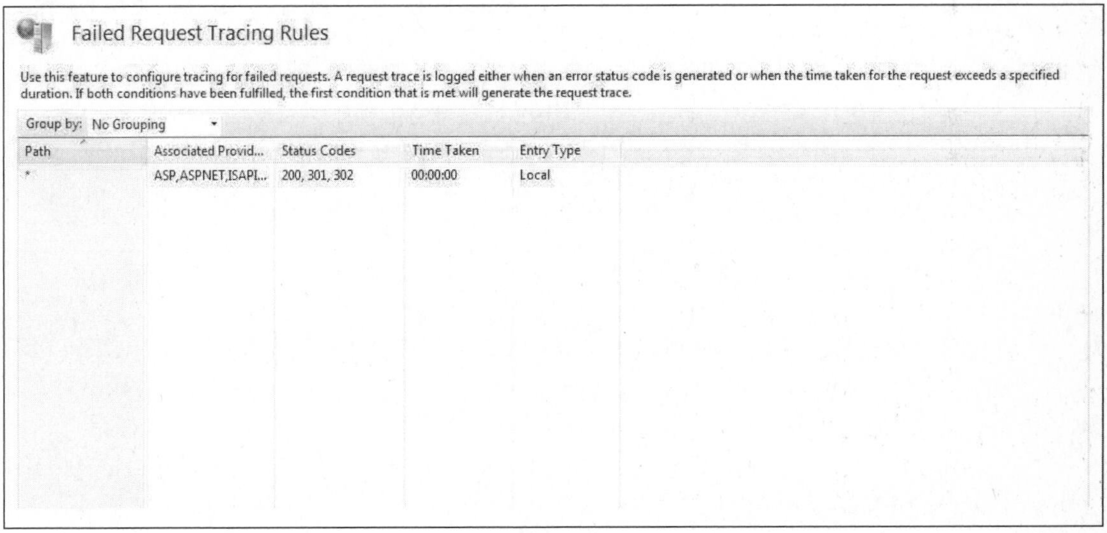

The next step is to enable tracing for the site and set the path. This will put the rule previously defined into action and start the tracing. This is an important concept covered in Chapter 6: that failed request tracing is always a two-step process. It requires that rules are defined and then tracing is enabled.

To enable tracing for your Web site, do the following:

1. In IIS Manager, click your Web site (for example, Default Web Site).

2. On the Default Web Site home, in the task pane click **Failed Request Tracing** under **Configure**.

3. Click **Enable** and set the path value and number of trace files to retain. Click **OK**.

Your rule is now enabled and new requests to the server that have the HTTP status 200, 301, 302 will have a trace file created.

Our last step is to create simulated requests that are similar to those sent to your production server. This, as mentioned earlier, is accomplished in a multitude of ways using load simulators or automated HTTP clients.

SOME INDEPENDENT ADVICE

This topic of simulating your client's usage is often confusing to many administrators. They are not aware that they have a blueprint of their clients' usage patterns for their Web applications in the IIS log files. The key goal is to extract those usage patterns out of the log files and put them into usage scenario scripts that will simulate the same traffic against your Web server.

Your IIS log files can be parsed in a multitude of ways, but we highly recommend using the Log Parser toolset. It can extract the necessary data from the log files and provide you with the HTTP requests to use in your automated HTTP scripts. For more information on Log Parser, see this online Webcast at http://www.iis.net/default.aspx?tabid=2&subtabid=26&i=36, as well as the Syngress book Log Parser Toolkit (ISBN: 1-932266-52-6).

After completing your simulated test, the evaluation stage takes place where you will analyze the failed request tracing logs. This is where the pattern of the requests will tell you what binaries are used.

For example, let's talk about those modules that are removable for a particular type of Web application. This includes sites and applications using static HTML requests, classic Active Server Pages (ASP), an ISAPI extension request, and, lastly, an ASP.NET request.

Static HTML Requests

These are fairly simple to recognize, but it's important you know what authentication types are used for the requests. This will tell you whether you need the static module (most will), as well as any authentication modules.

If you are using images, Cascading Style Sheets (CSS), or any text-based type of files on your server, you will likely need the default handler for static content. It is very unlikely you will need to remove this.

Module Name	Default IIS 7.0 Install Status
StaticFileModule	Default
AnonymousAuthenticationModule	Default
BasicAuthenticationModule	Not Installed
WindowsAuthenticationModule	Not Installed
DigestAuthenticationModule	Not Installed

As you can see, after upgrading from IIS 6.0 to IIS 7.0, the default state is to install all functionality IIS 7.0 offers. This could potentially result in having 1 to 4 modules installed that are not necessary, or installed by default on IIS 7.0 clean installs.

For example, using the preceding table, you could ascertain that after upgrading you do not need basic or digest authentication. To remove them, you can stop them from being loaded in any of the worker processes, as we showed in Chapter 3. To review, here is how you can remove modules easily from IIS 7.0.

You can use any one of the tools available, but for the sake of simplicity let's use the IIS Manager to remove the AuthDigest module since this is a seldom-used module. The same steps can be done to remove any of the preceding modules.

1. Go to **Start | Administrative Tools | Internet Information Services (IIS) Manager**.

2. At the server level, click **Modules**.

3. Click **DigestAuthenticationModule**. Then, in the **Actions** pane, click **Remove**.

4. Click **Yes** to confirm the removal.

Classic ASP Requests

ASP requests are slightly tricky in IIS 7.0 since they require two modules installed for one feature. However, if you aren't using ASP pages, you can remove at least one module, and possibly a second (IsapiModule). To determine if your Web application is using ASP, search your content directory (or directories) or use Failed Request

Tracing to determine if you have files with the extension .asp. Also, if you have access to your IIS 6.0 server, you can view the ScriptMaps, as shown in Figure 7.2.

Figure 7.2 IIS 6.0 Default Install ScriptMaps

```
File  Edit  Format  View  Help
ScriptMaps               : (LIST)  (51 Items)
".asp,C:\WINDOWS\system32\inetsrv\asp.dll,5,GET,HEAD,POST,TRACE"
".cer,C:\WINDOWS\system32\inetsrv\asp.dll,5,GET,HEAD,POST,TRACE"
".cdx,C:\WINDOWS\system32\inetsrv\asp.dll,5,GET,HEAD,POST,TRACE"
".asa,C:\WINDOWS\system32\inetsrv\asp.dll,5,GET,HEAD,POST,TRACE"
".idc,C:\WINDOWS\system32\inetsrv\httpodbc.dll,5,GET,POST"
".shtm,C:\WINDOWS\system32\inetsrv\ssinc.dll,5,GET,POST"
".shtml,C:\WINDOWS\system32\inetsrv\ssinc.dll,5,GET,POST"
".stm,C:\WINDOWS\system32\inetsrv\ssinc.dll,5,GET,POST"
".asax,C:\WINDOWS\Microsoft.NET\Framework\v2.0.50727\aspnet_isapi.dll,5,GET,HEAD,POST,DEBUG"
".ascx,C:\WINDOWS\Microsoft.NET\Framework\v2.0.50727\aspnet_isapi.dll,5,GET,HEAD,POST,DEBUG"
".ashx,C:\WINDOWS\Microsoft.NET\Framework\v2.0.50727\aspnet_isapi.dll,1,GET,HEAD,POST,DEBUG"
".asmx,C:\WINDOWS\Microsoft.NET\Framework\v2.0.50727\aspnet_isapi.dll,1,GET,HEAD,POST,DEBUG"
".aspx,C:\WINDOWS\Microsoft.NET\Framework\v2.0.50727\aspnet_isapi.dll,1,GET,HEAD,POST,DEBUG"
".axd,C:\WINDOWS\Microsoft.NET\Framework\v2.0.50727\aspnet_isapi.dll,1,GET,HEAD,POST,DEBUG"
".vsdisco,C:\WINDOWS\Microsoft.NET\Framework\v2.0.50727\aspnet_isapi.dll,1,GET,HEAD,POST,DEBUG"
".rem,C:\WINDOWS\Microsoft.NET\Framework\v2.0.50727\aspnet_isapi.dll,1,GET,HEAD,POST,DEBUG"
".soap,C:\WINDOWS\Microsoft.NET\Framework\v2.0.50727\aspnet_isapi.dll,1,GET,HEAD,POST,DEBUG"
".config,C:\WINDOWS\Microsoft.NET\Framework\v2.0.50727\aspnet_isapi.dll,5,GET,HEAD,POST,DEBUG"
".cs,C:\WINDOWS\Microsoft.NET\Framework\v2.0.50727\aspnet_isapi.dll,5,GET,HEAD,POST,DEBUG"
".csproj,C:\WINDOWS\Microsoft.NET\Framework\v2.0.50727\aspnet_isapi.dll,5,GET,HEAD,POST,DEBUG"
".vb,C:\WINDOWS\Microsoft.NET\Framework\v2.0.50727\aspnet_isapi.dll,5,GET,HEAD,POST,DEBUG"
".vbproj,C:\WINDOWS\Microsoft.NET\Framework\v2.0.50727\aspnet_isapi.dll,5,GET,HEAD,POST,DEBUG"
".webinfo,C:\WINDOWS\Microsoft.NET\Framework\v2.0.50727\aspnet_isapi.dll,5,GET,HEAD,POST,DEBUG"
".licx,C:\WINDOWS\Microsoft.NET\Framework\v2.0.50727\aspnet_isapi.dll,5,GET,HEAD,POST,DEBUG"
".resx,C:\WINDOWS\Microsoft.NET\Framework\v2.0.50727\aspnet_isapi.dll,5,GET,HEAD,POST,DEBUG"
".resources,C:\WINDOWS\Microsoft.NET\Framework\v2.0.50727\aspnet_isapi.dll,5,GET,HEAD,POST,DEBUG"
".master,C:\WINDOWS\Microsoft.NET\Framework\v2.0.50727\aspnet_isapi.dll,5,GET,HEAD,POST,DEBUG"
".skin,C:\WINDOWS\Microsoft.NET\Framework\v2.0.50727\aspnet_isapi.dll,5,GET,HEAD,POST,DEBUG"
".compiled,C:\WINDOWS\Microsoft.NET\Framework\v2.0.50727\aspnet_isapi.dll,5,GET,HEAD,POST,DEBUG"
".browser,C:\WINDOWS\Microsoft.NET\Framework\v2.0.50727\aspnet_isapi.dll,5,GET,HEAD,POST,DEBUG"
".mdb,C:\WINDOWS\Microsoft.NET\Framework\v2.0.50727\aspnet_isapi.dll,5,GET,HEAD,POST,DEBUG"
".jsl,C:\WINDOWS\Microsoft.NET\Framework\v2.0.50727\aspnet_isapi.dll,5,GET,HEAD,POST,DEBUG"
".vjsproj,C:\WINDOWS\Microsoft.NET\Framework\v2.0.50727\aspnet_isapi.dll,5,GET,HEAD,POST,DEBUG"
".sitemap,C:\WINDOWS\Microsoft.NET\Framework\v2.0.50727\aspnet_isapi.dll,5,GET,HEAD,POST,DEBUG"
".msgx,C:\WINDOWS\Microsoft.NET\Framework\v2.0.50727\aspnet_isapi.dll,1,GET,HEAD,POST,DEBUG"
".ad,C:\WINDOWS\Microsoft.NET\Framework\v2.0.50727\aspnet_isapi.dll,5,GET,HEAD,POST,DEBUG"
".dd,C:\WINDOWS\Microsoft.NET\Framework\v2.0.50727\aspnet_isapi.dll,5,GET,HEAD,POST,DEBUG"
".ldd,C:\WINDOWS\Microsoft.NET\Framework\v2.0.50727\aspnet_isapi.dll,5,GET,HEAD,POST,DEBUG"
".sd,C:\WINDOWS\Microsoft.NET\Framework\v2.0.50727\aspnet_isapi.dll,5,GET,HEAD,POST,DEBUG"
".cd,C:\WINDOWS\Microsoft.NET\Framework\v2.0.50727\aspnet_isapi.dll,5,GET,HEAD,POST,DEBUG"
".adprototype,C:\WINDOWS\Microsoft.NET\Framework\v2.0.50727\aspnet_isapi.dll,5,GET,HEAD,POST,DEBUG"
".lddprototype,C:\WINDOWS\Microsoft.NET\Framework\v2.0.50727\aspnet_isapi.dll,5,GET,HEAD,POST,DEBUG"
".sdm,C:\WINDOWS\Microsoft.NET\Framework\v2.0.50727\aspnet_isapi.dll,5,GET,HEAD,POST,DEBUG"
".sdmDocument,C:\WINDOWS\Microsoft.NET\Framework\v2.0.50727\aspnet_isapi.dll,5,GET,HEAD,POST,DEBUG"
".ldb,C:\WINDOWS\Microsoft.NET\Framework\v2.0.50727\aspnet_isapi.dll,5,GET,HEAD,POST,DEBUG"
".svc,C:\WINDOWS\Microsoft.NET\Framework\v2.0.50727\aspnet_isapi.dll,1,GET,HEAD,POST,DEBUG"
".mdf,C:\WINDOWS\Microsoft.NET\Framework\v2.0.50727\aspnet_isapi.dll,5,GET,HEAD,POST,DEBUG"
".ldf,C:\WINDOWS\Microsoft.NET\Framework\v2.0.50727\aspnet_isapi.dll,5,GET,HEAD,POST,DEBUG"
".java,C:\WINDOWS\Microsoft.NET\Framework\v2.0.50727\aspnet_isapi.dll,5,GET,HEAD,POST,DEBUG"
".exclude,C:\WINDOWS\Microsoft.NET\Framework\v2.0.50727\aspnet_isapi.dll,5,GET,HEAD,POST,DEBUG"
".refresh,C:\WINDOWS\Microsoft.NET\Framework\v2.0.50727\aspnet_isapi.dll,5,GET,HEAD,POST,DEBUG"
```

Unlike previous versions of IIS, IIS 7.0 exposes the ISAPI development platform in a single module. Any ISAPI extension built against the ISAPI platform will require that this module be installed to work. ASP.dll is an ISAPI extension that will take advantage of this module and, if not used, can safely remove the module.

Module Name	Handler Name	Default IIS 7.0 Install Status
IsapiModule	N\A	Not Installed
	ASPClassic	Not Installed
	Isapi-dll	Not Installed

You can remove the Classic ASP module by doing the following:

1. Click **Start | Administrative Tools | Internet Information Services (IIS) Manager**.

2. At the server level, click **Handler Mappings**.

3. Click **ASPClassic**, and in the **Actions** pane, click **Remove**.

4. Click **Yes** to confirm the removal.

To remove IsapiModule as well, do the following:

1. Click **Start | Administrative Tools | Internet Information Services (IIS) Manager**.

2. At the server level, click **Modules**.

3. Click **IsapiModule**, then in the **Actions** pane, click **Remove**.

4. Click **Yes** to confirm the removal.

SOME INDEPENDENT ADVICE

You should cautiously move forward when deciding whether to remove IsapiModule from IIS 7.0. It is safer to understand the ISAPI extensions (for example, handler) that are safe to remove, rather than removing this module. If you choose to remove this module, keep in mind that doing so will disable any ISAPI extension on the system and cause a configuration error.

ISAPI-based Extension Requests

ISAPI-based extension requests are usually more difficult to ascertain since these requests are easily confused with ISAPI filters. It is important to understand how to locate these requests in trace files to ensure you understand how to effectively enable or disable this functionality on your IIS 7.0 server.

The easiest method prior to upgrading to IIS 7.0 is to use your IIS 6.0 system as a reference point. All ISAPI-based extensions are stored in the metabase and are available to you in one of two ways. The first is by reviewing the ISAPI\CGI restriction list, as shown in Figure 7.3. Otherwise, you can directly access the metabase and review your ScriptMaps to understand the ISAPIs currently installed. The safest method is to use the restriction list since it indicates which handler is actually installed and allowed to execute.

Figure 7.3 IIS 6.0 Web Service Extensions in IIS Manager

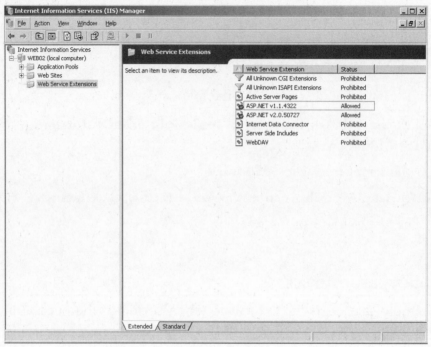

After already upgrading, you will need to use Failed Request Tracing or some other tool that will indicate what binaries are loaded in your worker process. A tool commonly used by many at Microsoft is Microsoft TechNet's SysInternals tool, Process Explorer. This tool (available for free from Microsoft at www.microsoft.com/technet/sysinternals/utilities/ProcessExplorer.mspx) gives you direct access to your worker process while executing to indicate what binaries are loaded in the worker process. It offers insight into the potential ISAPIs or CGIs loaded (if any) in your worker process.

To remove an ISAPI or CGI, perform the exact same steps used to remove ASP.dll earlier in this chapter.

ASP.NET Requests

ASP.NET requests are the more traditional type, such as ASPx pages. ASP.NET requests also are Web services, handlers, and so on, though the goal remains the same.

The end plan is to determine whether ASP.NET is used, and furthermore, what version or versions are present.

ASP.NET is a platform–agnostic development platform that, as discussed earlier, is heavily used by many in the IIS community. Because it is agnostic, ASP.NET is made available for multiple platforms and originally started with ASP.NET 1.0 running on Windows 2000. The most common used today on IIS servers is ASP.NET 1.1 and 2.0.

ASP.NET 1.1 was released independently from IIS 6.0, yet it is available on the Windows Server 2003 CD-ROM. Furthermore, ASP.NET 1.1 and 2.0 are available on the disc starting with Windows Server 2003 R2. The goal of this exercise is to determine if you are in fact using ASP.NET 1.1 or 2.0 and ensuring you can enable, or better yet, disable the functionality on your server.

ASP.NET 1.1 in IIS 7.0 will require IsapiModule much like classic ASP (for example, asp.dll). To disable ASP.NET 1.1, simply remove the <handlers> section mapping for ASP.NET's ISAPI. Unlike ASP.NET 2.0, 1.1 does not participate nor support the new integrated pipeline.

For ASP.NET 2.0, it gets slightly trickier because of the new integrated pipeline. As we discussed in our core server chapter, IIS 7.0 supports two modes of operation for the application pool: Classic and Integrated. This makes it important to know what application versions your system needs in order to understand what is potentially removable.

For ASP.NET 2.0, the following table lists the modules or handlers used:

Module Name	Handler Name	Default IIS 7.0 Install Status
IsapiModule	N\A	Not Installed
WebEngine	N\A	Not Installed
	TraceHandler-Integrated	Not Installed
	WebAdminHandler-Integrated	Not Installed
	AssemblyResourceLoader-Integrated	Not Installed
	PageHandlerFactory-Integrated	Not Installed
	SimpleHandlerFactory-Integrated	Not Installed
	WebServiceHandlerFactory-Integrated	Not Installed

Continued

Module Name	Handler Name	Default IIS 7.0 Install Status
	HttpRemotingHandlerFactory-rem-Integrated	Not Installed
	HttpRemotingHandlerFactory-soap-Integrated	Not Installed
	AXD-ISAPI-2.0	Not Installed
	PageHandlerFactory-ISAPI-2.0	Not Installed
	SimpleHandlerFactory-ISAPI-2.0	Not Installed
	WebServiceHandlerFactory-ISAPI-2.0	Not Installed
	HttpRemotingHandlerFactory-rem-ISAPI-2.0	Not Installed
	HttpRemotingHandlerFactory-soap-ISAPI-2.0	Not Installed
	AXD-ISAPI-2.0-64	Not Installed
	PageHandlerFactory-ISAPI-2.0-64	Not Installed
	SimpleHandlerFactory-ISAPI-2.0-64	Not Installed
	WebServiceHandlerFactory-ISAPI-2.0-64	Not Installed
	HttpRemotingHandlerFactory-rem-ISAPI-2.0-64	Not Installed
	HttpRemotingHandlerFactory-soap-ISAPI-2.0-64	Not Installed
	ISAPI-dll	Not Installed

As you can see, there are many decisions to make when determining what is not needed. Keep in mind during the upgrade process that IIS 7.0 must be configured to ensure that Web applications still work. However, for compatibility reasons, the goal is to ensure that what was installed on previous versions is also installed and available. This makes for a happy cleanup for these upgrades, so enjoy it as you reduce your environment and management tasks.

Centralizing Your Log File to Reduce Clutter

Centralizing your log file isn't required, nor is it always the recommended approach for all environments. However, centralized logging (better known as server-wide logging) reduces disk clutter and simplifies access to log data. It also enhances performance by reducing the number of log file handles open on large servers. Obviously, on servers that host only one or two Web sites, centralized logging is potential overkill.

Centralized logging comes in two flavors—Centralized binary logging and Centralized W3C logging—and each has their upside. For 95 percent of the cases, Centralized W3C logging is the most effective and simplest approach.

Start off by ensuring you enable some extended properties so you can locate data for each individual site. This property, s-sitename, will log the site name the request is associated with, such as Default Web Site. For example, Default Web Site is logged as W3SVC1, indicating this request belongs to this site. It makes it easy to then extract it from the log files requests for the individual site.

BEST PRACTICES ACCORDING TO MICROSOFT

For more information on Centralized logging, Microsoft has a Webcast aimed at understanding each type, as well as discussions about how each works, their advantages and disadvantages, and lastly how to set them up on IIS 6.0. This Webcast will apply to IIS 7.0 for the most part, minus how to enable it. These log types were only enabled in the metabase in IIS 6.0 and had no IIS Manager–supported method. In IIS 7.0 on Windows Server 2008, logging changes are made in the IIS Manager, as well as directly in the configuration.

SOME INDEPENDENT ADVICE

In Windows Vista, there are no logging capabilities in the IIS Manager. The only way to change the logging type was directly through configuration or via one of the other administration tools discussed in Chapter 5. This was supplemented with community support on Microsoft's IIS.NET DownloadCENTER located at www.iis.net/downloads/default.aspx?tabid=34&g=6&i=1328 with a logging module.

Windows Server 2008 has full user interface support for logging.

To enable centralized W3C logging, do the following:

1. Open an elevated command-prompt.
2. Change to the **%windir%\system32\inetsrv** directory.
3. Using **Appcmd.exe**, issue the following command:

```
C:\Windows\System32\inetsrv>appcmd set config -section:log
/CentralLogFileMode:CentralW3C
```

After setting this value, you will must restart HTTP to have it change the logging type since HTTP.sys does all of the IIS logging. To do this, issue the following command:

```
Net stop http /y & net start w3svc
```

To view your consolidated log file, navigate to the %systemdrive%\inetpub\logs\ w3svc directory.

Getting a Backup of Your Configuration

The last step is to ensure that you get a working, accurate backup of your primary configuration file. If you have enabled delegation allowing Web.config files to store IIS configuration then this is not a holistic backup, instead just the server configuration. It is, nonetheless, the most important aspect of IIS 7.0 so having a good backup is essential in case of a disaster or mistakes.

There are two methods to obtaining a backup of which you choose what you feel is most appropriate and comfortable for you. The first is to make a copy of the file and save it in another directory, such as appHostBackup directory. The second approach is to use appcmd.exe like we showed in chapter 5.

To use AppCmd.exe, issue the following command:

```
Appcmd add backup MyFirstBackupInIIS7
```

In either case, it's paramount that you have a backup of applicationhost.config. As an administrator, you're doubtless aware that backups can rescue you from some very sticky situations.

The Developer's Call to Arms

IIS7 represents the most exciting developer opportunity since ASP.NET 1.0 was released five years ago. Never has Microsoft had an application platform so flexible.

Plus, integrating the .NET Framework as a first-class citizen in the request pipeline opens the door to potentially fascinating new capabilities. Microsoft continues with the inclusion of FastCGI in IIS 7.0 to better support other languages such as PHP or Ruby on Rails delivered on top of this amazing platform.

If you are interested in understanding the multitude of ways to build custom functionality in IIS 7.0, start by understanding how to satisfy the business needs of the world. If they need caching servers, reverse proxies, or highly scalable front-end authentication servers, then IIS 7.0 is the Web platform to start with.

Downloading the Native C\C++ Starter Kit

If your responsibilities today include building ISAPI filters, you should start learning about the new, improved powers of the Native API for C\C++ developers. You can download this starter kit on www.iis.net (www.iis.net/downloads/default.aspx?tabid=34&g=6&i=1301) and learn how to get started building your first IIS 7.0 native module.

Downloading the Managed Code Starter Kit

With IIS 7.0's strong support for ASP.NET 2.0's managed interfaces, you can begin developing tomorrow's applications today. You can start converting your existing modules to IIS 7.0, or if new to the API, learn more by starting with the IIS 7.0 Managed Code starter kit at www.iis.net/downloads/default.aspx?tabid=34&i=1302&g=6.

Building IIS Manager Extensions for Your Modules

You should no longer spend cycles building software for IIS that adds functionality but at the same time spend hundreds of design hours building user interfaces for that software. Instead, give the power to your customers by adding IIS Manager modules to your software package so your customers can configure your software using the same familiar tool they use for IIS 7.0: the IIS Manager.

SOME INDEPENDENT ADVICE

Microsoft has gone to great lengths to help developers get started building IIS Manager modules. Using managed code, you can quickly add functionality directly to the IIS Manager. To get started, use Microsoft's IIS.NET site at www.iis.net/devcenter.

Adding Tracing to Your Modules

In the software realm, a perfect world centers around shipping fascinating software to millions of users. In the not-so-perfect world, your software will have bugs and you have to support those millions of users, which gets very expensive. In this book, you learned how powerful the diagnostics stack is in IIS 7.0, and as a developer you need to use it. You should add eventing to your modules to allow error conditions to get caught right alongside IIS 7.0's. With this powerful functionality, you can cut your time to resolution by almost 50 percent, if not more.

Get started learning about tracing your modules by using Microsoft's IIS.NET Developer Center at www.iis.net/devcenter.

Summary

Microsoft has given you a great deal of power with IIS 7.0. You are now tasked with harnessing that power and building a secure, robust, scalable Web solution. In this section, we provided you with the questions to ask yourself and strategies to consider. Beyond that, you learned about some of the changes that could potentially impact your environment that are considered one-off changes in IIS 7.0.

IIS 7.0 is as unique as the mathematical function pi (π) and offers numerous options. It is the LEGO Web server with enterprise-class features built in and developer-ready APIs to help make your mission possible. All you have to do is build it. With the guidance given in this book, administrators can effectively deploy Web servers that reap the rewards of building a highly secure, customized, performance-driven Web server.

As for you developers out there, don't miss the incredible opportunity to build what was never possible using IIS.

Solutions Fast Track

Migrating to IIS 7.0

☑ Upgrading to Windows Vista or Windows Server 2008 is nearly as clean as a fresh install with the new Image-based setup.

☑ Understanding how IIS 5.0, or IIS 6.0, features will be migrated to IIS 7.0 is the first step toward allowing you to be successful in your fit-n-finish work.

Fitting and Finishing Work with IIS 7.0

☑ Remove unnecessary components to avoid patching unnecessary binaries loaded in your IIS 7.0 worker process.

☑ Enable Centralized logging to reduce log file clutter.

☑ Create a configuration backup to ensure you're safe in case of catastrophic failures.

The Developer's Call to Arms

☑ Stop using the difficult ISAPI extension APIs and start using the APIs Microsoft used to build their 40+ modules.

☑ Start using the productivity given by manage code and apply it to the powerful IIS 7.0 Web request pipeline.

☑ Microsoft built it, so now all you have to do is add your modules to the IIS Manager and administration for your features to sit right with IIS's features.

☑ Reduce your support costs, add beneficial tracing to your modules and pages, and save countless support hours.

Frequently Asked Questions

The following Frequently Asked Questions, answered by the authors of this book, are designed to both measure your understanding of the concepts presented in this chapter and to assist you with real-life implementation of these concepts. To have your questions about this chapter answered by the author, browse to **www. syngress.com/solutions** and click on the **"Ask the Author"** form.

Q: Are FrontPage Extensions (FPSE) supported on IIS 7.0?

A: Yes, but they aren't available as part of the IIS 7.0 installation. FPSE can be downloaded separately, with more information available at www.iis.net/downloads/default.aspx?tabid=34&g=6&i=1460.

Q: What will happen if FPSE is installed on the server before it is upgraded to Windows Server 2008?

A: None of your FPSE settings will be migrated, and the W3SVC service will be disabled after the upgrade has been completed. This is because Microsoft assumes that, since FPSE was required and in use, the server was insecure.

Q: Will I be able to upgrade from Windows 2000 Server to Windows Server 2008?

A: No, unfortunately not. If you're on anything other than Windows Server 2003, you will need to build a new IIS 7.0 box and manually migrate your sites.

Q: Will any IIS services be disabled after the upgrade?

A: Possibly, if the upgrade process detected settings that could make your server insecure. For example, if FPSE was installed on the server, the W3SVC service will be explicitly disabled.

Monitoring IIS 6.0 with Microsoft Log Parser

Scripts and Samples in this Appendix:

- **Analyzing Request Details**
- **Analyzing Error Requests**
- **Analyzing Illegal Requests**

You can download the scripts in this Appendix from www.syngress.com/solutions.

Introduction

IIS 6.0 is the previous version of the Internet Information Services (IIS) offered by Microsoft. And, it is still very widely deployed. This special appendix teaches you to monitor log files from IIS 6.0 using Microsoft Log Parser. The Log Parser tool was born around 2000 as a utility to test the logging mechanisms of Microsoft's Internet Information Services (IIS). The first inception of the tool allowed users to retrieve and display all the fields from a single log file in any of the three text-logging formats supported by IIS.

As tests became more complicated, the need arose for more specialized tasks, including the possibility to filter log entries matching specific criteria and to sort the resulting entries according to values of specific fields. To provide a succinct and well-established way to specify these operations from a command-line shell, the tool underwent its first major makeover and began to support a very limited dialect of the SQL language. Log Parser 1.0 was born, and its use began spreading among internal Microsoft users and product support analysts.

After some time, the SQL language dialect processor was completely redesigned, enriched with functions, aggregate functions, and the *GROUP BY* clause, and with improved performance characteristics; at the same time, the tool underwent a second major architectural makeover, which separated the log file parsers and the console output formatter from the core SQL engine, making it possible for generic "input formats" and "output formats" to easily plug in with the architecture. Just for fun, the first non-IIS input formats made their appearance, including the Event Log (EVT) input format and the File System (FS) input format, together with the first nonconsole output format, the SQL output format. It didn't take long for IIS program managers to notice that the tool's capabilities could be leveraged by end users as well, greatly simplifying most of the tasks related to processing of log files. In fact, in November 2001 Log Parser 2.0 made its public debut as a freely downloadable tool from the pages of www.microsoft.com.

The user response was so favorable that version 2.1 of the tool, which included many new input and output formats, was included in the IIS 6.0 Resource Kit Tools, published in April 2002.

The tool has been continuously improved since then, thanks especially to the feedback and suggestions of its many users; new input and output formats have been added, and the core SQL engine has been improved with new functions and better-performing algorithms.

This 2.2 version marks the latest release of the Log Parser tool, designed and engineered with the vision of helping users achieve their data-processing goals in a simple, fast, and powerful way.

It includes a variety of well-known services including Hyper Text Transfer Protocol (HTTP), File Transfer Protocol (FTP), Simple Mail Transfer Protocol (SMTP), and Network News Transfer Protocol (NNTP). Although each of these services handles its own site access activity logging, there are no built-in tools that are able to parse from these plain text log files in order to extract useful information.

With additional log sources such as the HTTP error log (HTTPERR) and URL filtering log (URLSCAN, if installed), it is a tedious task to analyze these different log sources and try to understand the activities taking place in the IIS server. This Appendix will showcase the magic of Microsoft's Log parser tool in trying to make any system administrator's life easier with many creative parsing queries.

Monitoring Performance and Usages

One of the major advantages of monitoring the site access activity logging is that the log file helps you to keep track of all the details when a particular request is sent to your IIS server. It provides you with who, when, where, and how contents are being accessed.

Site access details are vital to understanding the usage and health performance of your IIS server. Information that is logged includes a visitor's IP address, user account accessing the contents, timestamp of when requests were made, server status reply about the request, the requested resource location, the amount of bytes used in the request, and more. Table A.1 shows the types of IIS services and supported log formats.

Table A.1 IIS Services and Logging Formats

Type of Service	IIS	NCSA	ODBC	W3C Extended	Centralized Binary
FTP	Yes	No	Yes	Yes	No
Web	Yes	Yes	Yes	Yes	Yes
SMTP	Yes	Yes	Yes	Yes	No
NNTP	Yes	Yes	Yes	Yes	No

> **NOTE**
>
> It is recommended that you configure logs using the World Wide Web Consortium (W3C) extended format. This is the most comprehensive log format in IIS and it allows you to customize different logging property fields. The queries shown in this Appendix are based on W3C extended format.

Analyzing Request Details

Let's start with some basic information about the IIS site logging feature. By default, the World Wide Web service (w3svc) and Microsoft FTP service (msftpsvc) are configured with W3C extended format. However, not all fields are enabled. SMTP service (smtpsvc) uses the same W3C extended format, but is not enabled by default. For the NNTP service (nntpsvc), logging is not enabled with Microsoft IIS log format as the default.

It is recommended that you use the W3C extended format and enable all extended log fields for the maximum amount of access details. With such details, you are able to analyze the requests pattern in a more precise manner. Table A.2 exhibits the available log fields supported in W3C extended format.

Table A.2 W3C Extended Log Fields

Property	Field	Description
Client IP Address	c-ip	Client IP address that accessed the IIS server
User Name	cs-username	User name that accessed the IIS server
Service Name	s-sitename	Site name serving the request, for example, W3Svc1
Server Name	s-computername	IIS server name
Server IP Address	s-ip	IIS server IP address serving the request
Server Port	s-port	IIS server port number serving the request
Method	cs-method	Client action request, for example, GET, POST

Continued

Table A.2 W3C Extended Log Fields

Property	Field	Description
URI Stem	cs-uri-stem	Request content name, for example, html, asp page
URI Query	cs-uri-query	Query action along with client request
Protocol Status	sc-status	Status code of the request
Protocol Substatus	sc-substatus	Substatus code of the request
Win32 Status	sc-win32-status	Status code in Windows terms
Bytes Sent	sc-bytes	Number of bytes sent by server
Bytes Received	cs-bytes	Number of bytes received by server
Time Taken	time-taken	Amount of time to process the request
Protocol Version	cs-version	Client protocol version, for example, HTTP, FTP
Host	cs-host	Client computer name
User Agent	cs(User-Agent)	Application used by client, for example, browser
Cookie	cs(Cookie)	Content of cookies send or received
Referer	cs(Referer)	Previous URL that directed client to current site

NOTE

Even though W3C extended log format provides many extended log fields, some fields do not provide useful meaning to certain IIS services. For example, *cs-host, cs(User-Agent) cs(Cookie) cs(Referer)* will be a *NULL* value and show as '-' in the Microsoft FTP service log file, as those fields are not related to the service.

The default log path for IIS is located at %Windir%/system32/Logfiles/. Each service has its own logging directory using the service name (w3svc, msftpsvc) followed by site ID X. The following lists the default log folder names of IIS services:

- **FTP** MSFTPSVCX

- **W3C** W3SVCX

- **SMTP** SMTPSVCX

- **NNTP** NNTPSVCX

The X represents the service site ID. For example, a default website site ID is 1, and the w3svc1 will be the default log path. This site ID is the identification number generated by IIS when you create a new service site. In previous versions of IIS, the identification numbers are incremental, but with IIS 6.0, the site ID is randomly created by IIS based on the website's name. It is recommended that you relocate this default log path to a dedicated disk volume and secure it with proper NTFS permissions listed here:

- **Administrators** Full Control

- **System** Full Control

- **Backup Operator** Read

If you need to grant access to a user or user's application to access the log file, you should only grant *read* permission, as the log file should not be modified at all. When relocating the default log path, you can either place it on a dedicated disk partition or you can configure remote logging; this is another way to help you secure the log file from being modified by attackers.

> **NOTE**
>
> It is important to note that time logged in W3C extended format uses Greenwich Mean Time (GMT) per W3C specification. For more information on how to enable W3C extended log fields, please refer to www.microsoft.com/resources/documentation/WindowsServ/2003/standard/proddocs/en-us/log_customw3c.asp.

In this section, we will focus on the following log fields used to diagnose performance information for different IIS requests:

- **Bytes Sent and Received (sc-bytes, cs-bytes)** The number of bytes IIS uses to accept and reply to a request. This can give you bandwidth usage information about IIS server, allowing you to plan for future network bandwidth upgrades. It can also tell you when something is wrong with your server. For example, if there is a sudden increase in bytes sent or received by the FTP server, you might want to check if there are users uploading or downloading a huge file that could be compromising disk and bandwidth resources.

- **Status Code (sc-status)** IIS reply status code tells you whether the request was successfully fulfilled by IIS or why the request failed. Again, this not only helps you in troubleshooting IIS server, but it also give you clues as to whether someone is trying to gain unauthorized access to your IIS server.

- **Time Taken (time-taken)** The amount of time IIS took to fulfill the request. This is helpful in determining how long a request was served. For example, if an active server page (ASP) query took more than 2 minutes to complete, you might want to review the coding to determine if there is a problem with the logic flow.

- **Request Content (cs-uri-stem)** The requested resource filename, particularly useful in locating most and least popular content in your IIS server. Coupled with other fields, you will be able to identify what content page take a long time to process and the bandwidth occupied by the content.

Obtaining Long Running Web Requests

The Ch02Top10WebRequests.sql query returns the top 10 long-running web requests from a particular web log source. It includes details about the requested filename, the number of times it was called, the maximum time spent for the request, and the average bytes sent. The output result is grouped by the requested filename in order of the maximum time taken followed by the number of hits.

```
---Ch02Top10WebRequests.sql---
SELECT
    TOP 10
    STRCAT(EXTRACT_PATH(cs-uri-stem),'/') AS RequestPath,
    EXTRACT_FILENAME(cs-uri-stem) AS RequestedFile,
    COUNT(*) AS Hits,
    MAX(time-taken) AS MaxTime,
    AVG(time-taken) AS AvgTime,
    AVG(sc-bytes) AS AvgBytesSent
```

```
FROM %source% TO %destination%
GROUP BY cs-uri-stem
ORDER BY MaxTime, TotalHits DESC
---Ch02Top10WebRequests.sql---
```

This query is particularly useful in identifying problematic web requests. For example, if there is an ASP query listed in the result, you need to check the code and figure out why it took such a long time to process. A long running request might affect the server's entire performance, as the application is taking CPU processing cycles from other requests.

The *%source%* at *FROM* clause is the log source parameter. It could be '*ex*.log*', meaning the query will traverse down from the current query directory looking for W3C extended log files, You can also specify the website ID as *<//localhost/w3svc/1>* to parse the log files located in w3svc1 log directory.

The *%destination%* at *TO* clause lets you specify the output filename for storing the result. In order to get the correct output you need to specify *-o:(output)* format when running the query. If omitted, *NATIVE* mode or *−o:NAT* will be the default output format.

To run the query, access a command prompt, navigate to the directory where you installed the query samples, and enter the following:

```
C:\Log parser>LogParser.exe
file:Ch02Top10WebRequests.sql?source="<//localhost/w3svc/1>"
+destination="Top10WebRequests.txt" -o:NAT
```

TIP

Since IIS 6.0 does not apply incremental site ID as it did in previous versions, to quickly identify which site ID associated with different websites, you can use the built-in Active Directory Services Interfaces (ADSI) query, **iisweb.vbs /query**, at the command prompt. This will list all websites registered locally with site name, site id, status, IP, port, and host header name.

The query instructs Log parser to read Ch02Top10WebRequests.sql with the log source (local machine website ID 1) and generate output in *NATIVE* format to the Top10WebRequests.txt text file. If you do not want to see the process statistics, you can specify *-stats:OFF* at the end of the command syntax. The following shows the sample output of Top10WebRequests.txt:

RequestedPath	RequestedFile	Hits	MaxTime	AvgTime	AvgBytesSent
/reg/	reg.asp	821	80212	40212	1200
/expand/	incoming.asp	4095	39322	29322	20322
/processing/	cust_up.asp	3900	33293	30233	2932
/kiv/	stock.html	8032	32002	31922	370921
/expand/	detail.asp	6293	30092	29392	39223
/processing/	cust_add.asp	200	15082	13978	2011
/processing/	inv_tune.asp	2099	13021	12911	8232
/kiv/	elite.aspx	5822	11929	9218	932
/	news.asp	10003	8922	6832	2111
/html/	abs.html	4022	7990	5820	29201

The output shows that the potential problematic query includes reg.asp, which took a maximum of 80 seconds to process with an average of 1.2 kilobytes sent. This information indicates that you should ask the developer to revise the query and try to optimize the code. Another example, stock.html, which took a maximum of 32 seconds processing time for IIS to serve the 370 kilobytes static content, should be reorganized to a smaller content page.

This useful query helps to identify long-running web requests in your IIS server. You are advised to run this query routinely or customize it to your needs in order to get the latest health status of the applications running on IIS server.

WARNING

It is important to note that the queries presented in this Appendix are assumed to be running on a healthy IIS server. This means that there are no hardware bottlenecks such as CPU, memory, network bandwidth, etc.

Swiss Army Knife...

Scanning Big Images

Huge image file will incur longer processing time and consume additional network bandwidth. By applying the following example query, you will be able to identify the top 10 largest image files:

```
---Ch02Top10Images.sql---
SELECT
    TOP 10
    STRCAT(EXTRACT_PATH(TO_LOWERCASE(cs-uri-stem)),'/') AS RequestedPath,
    EXTRACT_FILENAME(TO_LOWERCASE(cs-uri-stem)) AS RequestedFile,
    COUNT(*) AS Hits,
    MAX(time-taken) AS MaxTime,
    AVG(time-taken) AS AvgTime,
    MAX(sc-bytes) AS BytesSent
FROM %source% TO %destination%
WHERE
    (EXTRACT_EXTENSION(TO_LOWERCASE(cs-uri-stem)) IN ('gif';'jpg'))
    AND
    (sc-status = 200)
GROUP BY TO_LOWERCASE(cs-uri-stem)
ORDER BY BytesSent, Hits, MaxTime DESC
---Ch02Top10Images.sql---
```

The modified query will look for the top 10 image files based on size of bytes transferred; the output also includes the maximum and average time taken by IIS to send the images to the client end. As shown in the query, it will scan images with the file extensions .gif and .jpg and a 200 *sc-status*, which indicates a successful request. *TO_LOWERCASE* is use to ensure request filenames are converted to lowercase before being compared with the query parameter and the *GROUP BY* clause. For example, if requests were made to an image file with the names of ipp0002.gif and ipp0002.Gif, though both are the same file, Log parser will output two different names.

Again, you can freely modify the query to suit your needs. For example, if your website contains bitmap files (BMP) or Portable Network Graphic (PNG) files, you can simply add in bmp or png in the *WHERE* clause.

Obtaining The Most Popular FTP Downloads

The Ch02Top10FtpDownloads.sql query returns the most popular FTP downloads from a particular FTP log source. It includes details of the requested filename, the number of times it was downloaded, the average time spent for the request, and the average kilobytes sent. The output is grouped by requested filename total downloads.

```
---Ch02Top10FtpDownloads.sql---
SELECT
    TOP 10
    TO_LOWERCASE(cs-uri-stem) AS RequestedFile,
    COUNT(*) AS TotalDownloads,
    DIV(AVG(sc-bytes),1024) AS AvgBytesSent(k)
FROM %source% TO %destination%
WHERE
    (cs-method LIKE '%sent')
    AND
    (sc-status = 226)
GROUP BY RequestedFile
ORDER BY TotalDownloads, AvgBytesSent(k) DESC
---Ch02Top10FtpDownloads.sql---
```

This query is particularly useful in identifying the most popular FTP downloads. As shown in the query, you will notice how we can apply built-in functions of Log parser to convert the number of bytes sent by the server to kilobytes format. First, the query averages out the *sc-bytes*; this derives the actual file size of the content. This value is then divided by 1024, which returns the kilobytes of the file size.

The *WHERE* clause is the key in this query. It determines the download request by comparing *cs-method* to the command *sent*. Typical IIS FTP log file shows *[232]sent* followed by the filename in the *cs-uri-stem* field. The [223] indicates the 223rd connection to the FTP service since it was started, where '*sent*' represent the server sent the file to client. The status code 226 indicates the request has been successfully fulfilled.

To run the query, access a command prompt, navigate to the directory where you installed the query samples, and enter the following:

```
C:\Log parser>LogParser.exe file:Ch02Top10FtpDownloads.sql?source="ex*.log"
+destination="Top10FtpDownloads.txt" -stats:OFF -o:NAT
```

This instructs Log parser to read *Ch02Top10FtpDownloads.sql* with the log source ex*.log, meaning all extended log files in the current directory matching input mask.

Output is generated in *NATIVE* format to the *Top10FtpDownloads.txt* text file, This query also uses *-stats:OFF* to hide Log parser processing statistics. The following shows the sample result of the query:

```
RequestedFile              TotalDownloads        AvgBytesSent(K)
-------------------        --------------        -----------------
/download/avreport.zip     2822                  20656
/download/pro2k.exe        2193                  9832
/susan/holiday.zip         1902                  13230
/download/basic.zip        802                   8781
/faq.pdf                   792                   1292
/download/released.zip     502                   2003
/susan/games.zip           390                   1829
/arron/networkv2.vsd       102                   5921
/location/map.gif          99                    121
/download/update.txt       23                    188
```

TIP

You can easily change the query to find the Top 10 least popular downloads by removing the *DESC* syntax. In other words, *DESC* instructs Log parser to list in descending order, where the highest number of downloads will be at the top. By removing the *DESC*, the default order is ascending, which will display the results from the lowest number to highest number of downloads.

Another simple modification is to find the top 10 uploads. To do so, change the selection criteria to *cs-method LIKE '%created'*, and replace the *sc-bytes* (server sent bytes) to *cs-bytes* (client sent bytes). The method name *created* represents upload and *cs-bytes* indicates file size sent from client side.

Monitoring Entry Points

The Ch02Top10EntryPoints.sql query returns the entry points of your website. An entry point is defined as the first content requested by clients. A hyphen '–' in the *cs(Refer)* field can be treated as an entry point, as the request was made without any referrer information. The query generates results that include the entry point path, requested content, average time taken, and total number of hits. The output is grouped by requested content details in the order of total hits.

```
---Ch02Top10EntryPoints.sql---
SELECT
    Top 10
    STRCAT(EXTRACT_PATH(TO_LOWERCASE(cs-uri-stem)),'/') AS RequestedPath,
    EXTRACT_FILENAME(TO_LOWERCASE(cs-uri-stem)) AS EntryPoint,
    AVG(time-taken) AS AvgTime,
    COUNT(*) AS Hits
FROM %source% TO %destination%
WHERE
    (cs(Referer) IS NULL)
    AND
    (sc-status BETWEEN 200 AND 307)
GROUP BY cs-uri-stem, cs(Referer)
ORDER BY Hits DESC
---Ch02Top10EntryPoints.sql---
```

Running this query enables you to understand the most popular entry Uniform Resource Locator (URL) from a particular website. This information is useful in website design planning; when you notice the average time taken for a particular entry point is high, you will need to look at the requested content, and fine-tune it to provide better user experience.

To run the query, access a command prompt, navigate to the directory where you installed the query samples, and enter the following:

```
C:\Log parser>LogParser.exe
file:Ch02Top10EntryPoints.sql?source="<//webhost/w3svc/example.com>"
+destination="Ch02Top10EntryPoints.txt" -stats:OFF -o:NAT
```

The query starts off by extracting the requested content path and the content name, and then calculates the average time spent by IIS on fulfilling the request. Notice that the log source is reading from a Web server called *Webhost* with the website description *example.com*.

The *WHERE* clause in the query instructs Log parser to check if the *cs(Referer)* value is equal to *NULL*. Although you will notice the '–' in the W3C extended log file, during actual parsing the Log parser will treat it as a *NULL* value. Hence, checking this *NULL* value will indicate that this is the first request the client is requesting. In short, this is an entry point. The last part of the query checks for *sc-status* code, which indicates whether the request made has been successful or not. A nonerror status code falls between 200 to 307 according to HTTP Request For

Comment (RFC) specification. 200 indicates a successful reply, while 3XX indicates a redirection. For example, if the request is made to */mydir/*, by default IIS will redirect to the configured default page, hence a 301 response is made. The reason for 307 as the last in the range is because that is the last valid HTTP status code per RFC specification.

TIP

For more information about HTTP status code definitions, please refer to the Microsoft Knowledge article: IIS Status Codes at support.microsoft.com/?id=318380 or visit www.w3.org/Protocols/rfc2616/rfc2616-sec10.html#sec10 for the RFC specification.

The following shows the sample result of the query:

RequestedPath	EntryPoint	AvgTime	Hits
/	index.aspx	1843	92142
/main/		4329	79210
/main/	index.aspx	2983	67092
/support/	mainkb.aspx	3984	47382
/support/	kbsearch.aspx	19320	37798
/support/	faq.aspx	8920	29012
/customer/	login.aspx	3981	13944
/customer/	lastchanged.html	2930	9382
/	topnews.aspx	8221	8321
/main/	newsfeed.aspx	7292	3023

From the query results, you will get a better picture about how often IIS content is being accessed. This information also illustrates user behavior and preferences. For example, certain users like to access the latest news directly (*topnews.aspx*). Take note on the second listing that the *EntryPoint* is blank. In this case, the entry points were made on the specific path only, whereby IIS will return the default document page.

TIP

Now, you can find valid entry points with *Ch02Top10EntryPoints.sql*, but how about invalid or error entry points? You can change the *WHERE* clause *sc-status* checking from successful replies to unsuccessful. Changing it to *sc-*

status BETWEEN 400 AND 505 will allow you to track down invalid or error entry points.

Monitoring Web Referrers

The Ch02Top10Referrer.sql query returns the top 10 referrers to your website. We define a referrer as requests that do not originate from the website. It is easy to identify, as the cs(Referer) field should contains URLs other than the current website. The query generates results including: the successful requested content, total number of hits, remote host name, and referrer's URL. The output is grouped by requested content, remote host name, referrer's URL and is ordered by total hits.

NOTE

The following query assumes a request was made by a client browser and will include referrer field information. However, certain browsers can be configured not to send this detail, hence, IIS may log '-' as the data for the *cs(Refer)* field.

```
---Ch02Top10WebReferrer.sql---
SELECT
    Top 10
    EXTRACT_FILENAME(TO_LOWERCASE(cs-uri-stem)) AS RequestedFile,
    count(*) AS Hits,
    REVERSEDNS(EXTRACT_TOKEN(cs(Referer), 2, '/')) AS HostName,
    TO_LOWERCASE(EXTRACT_TOKEN(cs(Referer), 0, '?')) AS ReferrerURL
FROM %selection%
WHERE
    (HostName <> '%domainname%')
    AND
    (cs(Referer) IS NOT NULL)
    AND
    (EXTRACT_EXTENSION(TO_LOWERCASE(cs-uri-stem)) IN ('asp';'aspx';'html';'html'))
    AND
    (sc-status BETWEEN 200 AND 307)
GROUP BY RequestedFile, HostName, ReferrerURL
```

```
ORDER BY Hits DESC
---Ch02Top10WebReferrer.sql---
```

This query is particularly useful in understanding referrers that are bringing traffic to your website. It is also a good starting point to understand how well your affiliate partners are doing if you are running affiliated programs to attract traffic.

Let's look at the some of the actions performed in the query. First, it extracts the content filename, then resolves the remote host IP address to a host name using the *REVERSEDNS* function, and finally extracts the full request path without any query string from the referrer's URL.

> **NOTE**
>
> It is important to note that *REVERSEDNS* requires Domain Name Service (DNS) server access. It will take a longer processing time if there are many IP addresses to be resolved. When Log parser is unable to resolve the host name, remote IP address will be shown instead.

Notice that in the *FROM* clause, we specify *%selection%* rather than *%source%* and *%destination%*, as in the previous query. This a more flexible query, as we can control the output directive at the command-line level. For example, when executing the query at a command line, you could enter the following:

```
LogParser.exe
file:Ch02Top10WebReferrer.sql?selection="<1> TO
output.csv"+domainname="www.mysite.com" -o:CSV
```

This syntax will pass in the value *<1> TO output.csv* into the query, while the -*o:CSV* instructs Log parser to generate the result in Comma Separated Values (CSV) format

Or, you can do it the following way:

```
LogParser.exe
file:Ch02Top10WebReferrer.sql?selection="<1>"+domainname="www.mysite.com"
```

This syntax will pass in the value *<1>* into the query, and use the default *NATIVE* format to generate output, since we did not specify the -*o* directive.

The *WHERE* clause in the query instructs Log parser to check if the referrer is from its own site. This is done by checking the *%domainname%* parameter. It then makes sure that the referrer field is not empty. The current query focuses on the filenames that have .asp, .aspx, .html or .htm in the file extension, and successful responses with status codes between 200 and 307.

To run the query, access a command prompt, navigate to the directory where you installed the query samples, and enter the following:

```
C:\Log parser>LogParser.exe file:Ch02Top10WebReferrer.sql?selection="<1> TO
output.csv"+domainname="www.mysite.com" -o:CSV
```

With this, Log parser parses the log files from website ID 1, with *www.mysite.com* as the *%domainname%*, since we want to filter the local referrer. The query will generate the result in a file named *output.csv* using comma–separated value (CSV) format.

The following shows the sample result of the query:

```
RequestedFile,Hits,HostName,ReferrerURL
default.aspx,18323,,www.google.com, http://www.google.com/search
11966.aspx,13299,search.yahoo.com,http:// http://search.yahoo.com/search
rss.aspx,9921,blog.joycode.com,http://blog.joycode.com/sync/refresh.asp
faq.html,7212,netsvr,http://netsvr/printers/ipp_0001.asp
testtree.aspx,5723,192.168.10.2,http://192.168.10.2/loadtest.aspx
hostheader.asp,2332,www.baidu.com, http://www.baidu.com/baidu
nlbsetup.htm,1993,www.networkfaq.com,http://www.networkfaq.com/nlb/link.html
8213.aspx,921,rd.3exp.com,http://rd.3exp.com/news.asp
redirect.asp,722,freelink.com,http://freelink.com/42/923/921/link
redirect.asp,125,link.mysite.com,http://link.mysite.com/cust/3023/track.asp
```

TIP

This example query looks for successful requests. You can simply modify the *sc-status* parameter in the *WHERE* clause to look for 404 errors, which indicate "page not found". With this information, if you are looking for broken URLs referred by the remote host, you can inform related parties to correct the error and reflect the latest URL for the desired content.

Master Craftsman...

Identify Image Leaching

Image leaching is defined as hot-linking or borrowing images directly from your Web server. This causes additional bandwidth due to these unwanted requests. By modifying the example query, you will be able to identify these leaching activities.

```
---Ch02Top10ImageLeaching.sql---
SELECT
    Top 10
    TO_LOWERCASE(cs-uri-stem) AS RequestedFile,
    count(*) AS Hits,
    STRCAT(TO_STRING(DIV(SUM(sc-bytes),1024)),'k') AS TotalBytesSent,
    TO_LOWERCASE(EXTRACT_TOKEN(cs(Referer), 0, '?')) AS ReferrerURL
FROM %selection%
WHERE
    (EXTRACT_TOKEN(cs(Referer), 2, '/') <> '%domainname%')
    AND
    (cs(Referer) IS NOT NULL)
    AND
    (EXTRACT_EXTENSION(TO_LOWERCASE(cs-uri-stem)) IN ('gif';'jpg';'bmp'))
    AND
    (sc-status IN (200;304))
GROUP BY RequestedFile, ReferrerURL
ORDER BY Hits, TotalBytesSent DESC
---Ch02Top10ImageLeaching.sql---
```

The modified query will list the top 10 image leaching activities outside the website's Fully Qualify Domain Name (FQDN), specifically looking for images with .gif, .jpg and .bmp extensions. The result will include requested image names, total hits with total number of kilobytes of those illegal requests, and the referrer's URL.

In this particular query, we only check for a HTTP status code of either 200 or 304. Status code 304 represents that the data was not modified; meaning a previous request was made on the same image, but there were no changes since that request. However, you will see minor bandwidth usage in *sc-bytes*; this is due to the status code and HTTP headers sent to remote machines.

Using the results, you will be able to take further action in dealing with these illegal requests. For example, you can either block access or report the activity to the referrer host webmaster.

Monitoring Bandwidth Usage

The Ch02DailyBandwidth.sql query produces a daily report from a particular log source. The calculation of bandwidth usage is based on total incoming and outgoing bytes from IIS server. Since this query only utilizes *cs-bytes* for incoming traffic and *sc-bytes* for outgoing traffic, this query can be apply to any IIS service, such as SMTP or NNTP. The query summarizes bandwidth on a daily basis together with the total incoming and outgoing bandwidth usage in kilobyte format.

```
---Ch02DailyBandwidth.sql---
SELECT
    TO_STRING(TO_TIMESTAMP(date, time), 'MM-dd') AS Day,
    DIV(Sum(cs-bytes),1024) AS Incoming(K),
    DIV(Sum(sc-bytes),1024) AS Outgoing(K)
INTO %chartname%
FROM %source%
GROUP BY Day
---Ch02DailyBandwidth.sql---
```

It is important to collect bandwidth usage information, as it provides the overall performance of traffic occurring in your IIS service. For example, if there is a sudden surge in FTP bandwidth usage, you might want to parse the log file to see the recent activities that caused the sudden increase in bandwidth usage. It could be that your FTP server has been *tagged*, and become a public host for illegal software and movie file distribution. You could also utilize these usage details to plan for your network bandwidth requirements.

This query is simple and neat; first it uses the *TO_TIMESTAMP* function to consolidate the *date* and *time* field into month/month – day/day format. After that, it totals up the daily usage from bytes received by the server (*cs-bytes*) and bytes sent from the server (*sc-bytes*). The figures are then divided by 1024 to generate a kilobytes unit.

The *SELECT* part of the query produces the following output:

```
Day    Incoming(K) Outgoing(K)

----   ----------- ---------------

08-11 33243       203923

08-12 69023       582830

08-13 58328       458391

......
```

This type of output is perfect for a chart display. Notice the *INTO* clause in the query; we will use this clause and specify the output image file using the *%chartname%* parameter. Next, as you might already be aware, the *%source%* is where you specific the log source.

> **NOTE**
>
> The example shown in this section only uses one chart type (ColumnStacked3d). To learn more about different chart types supported, you can refer to Appendix B in the back of this book, or access the help document using the following command:
>
>   C:\ Log parser>LogParser.exe -h -o:chart | more
>
> This will show you available chart type details as well as parameters you can specify when using the o:chart method. However, it is important to take note that chart diagram outputs require Microsoft Office XP or later to be installed. This is because chart diagram outputs use the Office application library when generating the output.

To run the query, access a command prompt, navigate to the directory where you installed the query samples, and enter the following:

```
C:\Log parser>LogParser.exe

file:Ch02DailyBandwidth.sql?chartname="daily.gif"+source="<

//localhost/smtpsvc/1>" -o:chart -chartType:ColumnStacked3d    -chartTitle:"Daily
SMTP Bandwidth Report"

-view -groupSize:800x600
```

First, *daily.gif* is specified as the output filename, and since we are interested in visualizing bandwidth usage for the SMTP service, we point the log source to the default SMTP site. To output as a chart, use the *o:chart* option. Specify the chart type using *-chartType*; this example uses a Column Stacked chart with 3D effect. The -

chartTitle specifies the chart title, and finally, the *-view* instructs Log parser view the image file at the end of the process and *-groupSize* specifies the image resolution size. See Figure A.1 for the sample chart diagram.

Figure A.1 Sample Chart Diagram – Daily SMTP Bandwidth Report

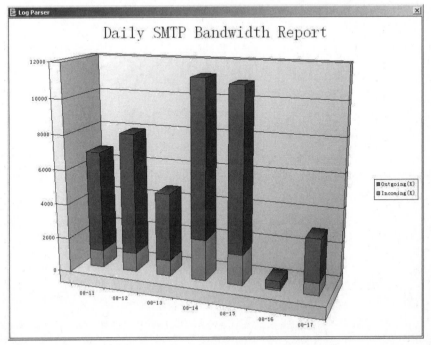

TIP

Removing the *-view* parameter saves the chart diagram image directly to disk without viewing it after parsing. Combine this with a simple batch file and task scheduler, and you can create an HTML file to display an automatically updated chart image.

Master Craftsman...

More Bandwidth Usage Analysis

With a few small changes to the existing query, you can monitor hourly or monthly bandwidth usage for a specific range of dates. The key is in the *SELECT* clause. For example, to obtain hourly bandwidth usage, instead of selecting per day grouping, change it to hourly.

```
---Ch02HourlyBandwidth.sql---
SELECT
    QUANTIZE(TO_TIMESTAMP(date, time), 3600) AS Hour,
    DIV(Sum(cs-bytes),1024) AS Incoming(K),
    DIV(Sum(sc-bytes),1024) AS Outgoing(K)
INTO %chartname%
FROM %source%
GROUP BY Hour
---Ch02HourlyBandwidth.sql---
```

The query first quantizes the date and time to the nearest hour, which results in an hourly grouping of the results. Take note that now the log source should be a daily log file, such as ex080104.log

To make it more interesting, what if you would like to know the bandwidth usage for a specific date range? The answer:

```
---Ch02DateBandwidth.sql---
SELECT
    TO_STRING(TO_TIMESTAMP(date, time), 'MM-dd') AS Day,
    DIV(Sum(cs-bytes),1024) AS Incoming(K),
    DIV(Sum(sc-bytes),1024) AS Outgoing(K)
INTO %chartname%
FROM %source%
Where (Day BETWEEN '%from%' AND '%to%')
GROUP BY Day
---Ch02DateBandwidth.sql---
```

Notice that a *WHERE* clause is added to apply the date range condition, and two additional variables are used. To run the query, you will enter:

Continued

```
C:\Log parser>LogParser.exe
file:Ch02DateBandwidth.sql?chartname="daterange.gif"+source="<//localhost/msf
tpsvc/1>"
+from="08-01"+to="08-07" -o:chart -chartTitle:"FTP Bandwidth Usage" -view
-chartType:ColumnStacked3d
```

This command instructs Log parser to parse default FTP website log files from August 1st to August 7th.

Next, to gather monthly information, simply change it to the following:

```
---Ch02MonthlyBandwidth.sql---
SELECT
    TO_STRING(TO_TIMESTAMP(date, time), 'MMMM') AS Month,
    DIV(Sum(cs-bytes),1024) AS Incoming(K),
    DIV(Sum(sc-bytes),1024) AS Outgoing(K)
INTO %chartname%
FROM %source%
GROUP BY Month
---Ch02MonthlyBandwidth.sql---
```

As you may have noticed, simple modifications to the SELECT statement and adding a WHERE clause will help you to obtain useful information. This makes Log parser a very powerful and flexible parsing tool.

Ensuring Stability

Besides providing performance and usage information, periodically analyzing W3C extended log files gives you the inside view of server health status. HTTPERR and URLSCAN log files provide further details that are not captured in the W3C extended log file. Analyzing these different log files helps to ensure the stability of your IIS server. Key capabilities include identifying ASP errors with the request details, error codes, and messages; understanding the difference between client side versus service side errors; translating HTTP status code to meaningful error messages; and analyzing URLSCAN log files.

Analyzing Error Requests

By analyzing error requests, you can determine the health of your IIS applications, find clues for troubleshooting, and identify potential risks associated with the request.

Besides the key IIS log fields introduced in previous section, you will learn more about the following useful log fields:

- **User name (cs–username)** This field captures the username making the request. If anonymous access is allowed, the default IUSR_<COMPUTER-NAME> account will be the request identity and it is logged as '-' in the IIS log file. If the site is configured to use user authentication, users will be required to provide a valid username and password, and IIS will log the user-name in the log file.

- **Procotol Substatus (sc–substatus)** This is a property field for W3C extended log format that was introduced in IIS 6.0. In previous versions of IIS, only status codes are captured in IIS logs, making troubleshooting more troublesome, as some general status codes contain substatuses. For example, 404.2 and 404.3 both are generic "file not found" errors. However, in IIS 6.0, 404.2 indicates that the dynamic content extension was not allowed, while 404.3 tell you that the required Multipurpose Internet Mail Exchange (MIME) type is not registered with IIS server.

- **Win32 Status (sc–win32–status)** This field holds the Win32 programming error code. This status code gives you more information about the request status, and helps you troubleshoot further when the HTTP status and sub-status do not provide enough information.

In addition, HTTPERR and URLSCAN log files can assist you in analyzing error requests. IIS 6.0 uses the HTTP.SYS kernel mode driver. This driver keeps its own log files and it is an important source for identifying error requests and understanding server health status. The default log path for HTTPERR is *%windir%/system32/Logfiles/HTTPERR* . Table A.3 exhibits the available log fields supported in HTTPERR.

Table A.3 HTTP Error Log Fields

Property	Field	Description
Date	Date	The date when the request was made
Time	Time	The time when the request was made
Server Name	s-computername	IIS server name
Client IP Address	c-ip	Client IP address that accessed the IIS server

Continued

Table A.3 continued HTTP Error Log Fields

Property	Field	Description
Client Port	c-port	Client source port number
Server IP Address	s-ip	IIS server IP address serving the request
Server Port	s-port	IIS server port number serving the request
Protocol Version	cs-version	Client protocol version, for example, HTTP 1.0 / 1.1
Method	cs-method	Client action request, for example GET, POST
URI	cs-uri	Requested content and query string (if any)
User Agent	cs(User-Agent)	Application used by client, for example, browser
Referer	cs(Referer)	Previous URL that directed client to current site
Cookie	cs(Cookie)	Content of cookies send or received
Host	cs-host	Client computer name
Protocol Status	sc-status	Status code of the request
Bytes Sent	sc-bytes	Number of bytes sent by server
Bytes Received	cs-bytes	Number of bytes received by server
Time Taken	time-taken	Amount of time to process the request
Service Name	s-siteid	Site ID serving the request, for example, W3Svc1
Reason Phrase	s-reason	Short error description
Queue Name	s-queuename	Name of the application pool

TIP

To learn more about HTTPERR logging, please refer to: *INF: Http.sys Registry Settings for IIS* at http://support.microsoft.com/?id=820129 and *INFO: Error Logging in HTTP API* at http://support.microsoft.com/?id=820729.

Although IIS 6.0 has advanced security features that are part of Windows Server 2003, you can deploy the URLSCAN Internet Server API (ISAPI) filter to further restrict HTTP requests. URLSCAN monitors incoming HTTP requests based on a set of rules. If requests do not comply with the URLSCAN rule sets, IIS replies with a "404 File Not Found" error to the client and writes an entry in the URLSCAN log file.

By default, URLScan creates daily log files for each worker process. These log files are created in the *%windir%/system32/inetsrv/urlscan/logs/* folder. Table A.4 exhibits the available log fields supported in URLSCAN.

Table A.4 URLSCAN Log Fields

Property	Field	Description
Date	Date	The date when the request was blocked
Time	Time	The time when the request was blocked
Client IP Address	Clientip	Client IP address that accessed the IIS server
Reason	Comment	Reason detail of blocked request
Service Name	siteinstance	Site ID serving the request, for example, W3Svc1
URL	url	Requested content name and query string

NOTE

Most of the features included in URLSCAN are built into IIS 6.0. Hence, you need to analyze your particular environment to determine whether you actually need to deploy URLScan. For more information about IIS 6.0 built-in security features and differences with URLScan, please refer to www.microsoft.com/technet/security/tools/urlscan.mspx?#XSLTsection1231211 20120.

Identifying Error Requests

The Ch02ClientErrors.sql query provides a list of the error requests that occurred due to invalid client requests. For example, if the client IP address is prohibited from visiting the content, IIS returns a 403.6 HTTP status code. The result generated includes the requested content filename, the error code, and the actual interpreted error message.

```
---Ch02ClientErrors.sql---
SELECT
    RequestedFile, ErrCode, Total, ClientDesc, ErrDesc, Win32Desc
    USING sc-win32-status AS WinCode,
    REPLACE_IF_NULL(TO_LOWERCASE(cs-username),'Anonymous') AS UserName,
    STRCAT(STRCAT(' (',REVERSEDNS(c-ip)),')') AS ClientIP,
    TO_LOWERCASE(cs-uri-stem) AS RequestedFile,
    STRCAT(TO_STRING(sc-status), STRCAT('.',TO_STRING(sc-substatus))) AS ErrCode,
    Count(*) AS Total,
    STRCAT(Username,ClientIP) AS ClientDesc,
    CASE ErrCode
        WHEN '400.0' THEN 'Bad Request.'
        --Access Error--
        WHEN '401.1' THEN 'Access Denied - Login failed.'
        WHEN '401.2' THEN 'Access Denied - Logon failed due to server config.'
        WHEN '401.3' THEN 'Access Denied - ACL checking failed.'
        WHEN '401.4' THEN 'Access Denied - Authorization failed by filter.'
        WHEN '401.5' THEN 'Access Denied - Authorization failed by ISAPI/CGI
application.'
        WHEN '401.7' THEN 'Access Denied - Access denied by URL authorization
policy on the Web server.'
        --Forbidden Error--
        WHEN '403.1' THEN 'Forbidden - Execute access.'
        WHEN '403.2' THEN 'Forbidden - Read access.'
        WHEN '403.3' THEN 'Forbidden - Write access.'
        WHEN '403.4' THEN 'Forbidden - SSL required.'
        WHEN '403.5' THEN 'Forbidden - SSL 128 required.'
        WHEN '403.6' THEN 'Forbidden - IP address rejected.'
        WHEN '403.7' THEN 'Forbidden - Client certificate required.'
        WHEN '403.8' THEN 'Forbidden - Site access denied.'
        WHEN '403.9' THEN 'Forbidden - Too many users.'
        WHEN '403.10' THEN 'Forbidden - Invalid configuration.'
        WHEN '403.11' THEN 'Forbidden - Password change.'
        WHEN '403.12' THEN 'Forbidden - Mapper denied access.'
        WHEN '403.13' THEN 'Forbidden - Client certificate revoked.'
        WHEN '403.14' THEN 'Forbidden - Directory listing denied.'
        WHEN '403.15' THEN 'Forbidden - Client Access Licenses exceeded.'
        WHEN '403.16' THEN 'Forbidden - Client certificate is untrusted or
invalid.'
        WHEN '403.17' THEN 'Forbidden - Client certificate has expired or is
not yet valid.'
```

```
        WHEN '403.18' THEN 'Forbidden - Cannot execute requested URL in the current
application pool.'
        WHEN '403.19' THEN 'Forbidden - Cannot execute CGIs for the client in this
application pool.'
        WHEN '403.20' THEN 'Forbidden - Passport logon failed.'
        --Not Found Error--
        WHEN '404.0' THEN 'Not Found - File or directory not found.'
        WHEN '404.1' THEN 'Not Found - Web site not accessible on the
requested port.'
        WHEN '404.2' THEN 'Not Found - Web service extension lockdown policy
prevents this request.'
        WHEN '404.3' THEN 'Not Found - MIME map policy prevents this request.'
        --Non-Common Error--
        WHEN '405.0' THEN 'HTTP verb used to access this page is not allowed.'
        WHEN '406.0' THEN 'Client browser does not accept the MIME type of the
requested page.'
        WHEN '407.0' THEN 'Proxy authentication required.'
        WHEN '412.0' THEN 'Precondition failed.'
        WHEN '413.0' THEN 'Request entity too large.'
        WHEN '414.0' THEN 'Request-URI too long.'
        WHEN '415.0' THEN 'Unsupported media type.'
        WHEN '416.0' THEN 'Requested range not satisfiable.'
        WHEN '417.0' THEN 'Execution failed.'
        WHEN '423.0' THEN 'Locked error.'
        WHEN '424.0' THEN 'Failed Dependency.'
        ELSE 'Unknown error'
    END AS ErrDesc,
    WIN32_ERROR_DESCRIPTION(WinCode) AS Win32Desc
FROM %source%
WHERE (sc-status BETWEEN 400 AND 424)
GROUP BY RequestedFile, ErrCode, ClientDesc, ErrDesc, Win32Desc
ORDER BY Total DESC
---Ch02ClientErrors.sql---
```

Though it looks complicated, this query is actually straight-forward. The *USING* clause defines three variables referenced by other columns in the query. The SQL statement first declares the *sc-win32-status* as *WinCode*, then it gathers the user name for the requests, placing the content *Anonymous* in that field if an anonymous user makes the request. The SQL statement then formats the *c-ip* field as a standard IP address. Finally, the *STRCAT* function concatenates *UserName* and *ClientIP* variables to *ClientDesc*.

The *CASE* clause is used to determine the actual message from the *ErrCode*. The *WHERE* clause filters the request to only include those status codes related to client side requests, which, according to RFC specification, ranges from 400 to 424. Additional substatus codes are defined per IIS status code documentation. One of the output fields, *Win32Desc,* is actually the Win32 error message obtained using the *WIN32_ERROR_DESCRIPTION* function.

To run the query, access a command prompt, navigate to the directory where you installed the query samples, and enter the following:

```
C:\Log parser>LogParser.exe
file:Ch02ClientErrors.sql?source="<1>" -o:NAT -rtp:-1 > ClientErrors.txt
```

This command instructs Log parser to read the default website log files, output all rows in *NATIVE* format, and redirect output to the *ClientErrors.txt* text file.

```
RequestedFile                    ErrCode   Total    ClientDesc
------------------------------   -------   -----    ------------------------
/printers/ipp_0002.asp           401.1     322      Anonymous (192.168.10.18)
/printers/ipp_0002.asp           401.2     322      Anonymous (192.168.10.18)
/printers/hplaser/.printer/      404.0     61       indev\susan (susan.indev)
/certsrv/default.asp             404.2     28       indev\administrator (indev)
/secure/syscheck.aspx            401.3     24       indev\viewer (192.168.10.21)
/certenroll/                     403.14    3        indev\susan (susan.indev)
/printers/ipp_0004.asp           401.5     2        Anonymous (192.168.10.93)


ErrDesc
--------------
Access Denied - Login failed.
Access Denied - Logon failed due to server config.
Not Found - File or directory not found.
Not Found - Web service extension lockdown policy prevents this request.
Access Denied - ACL checking failed.
Forbidden - Directory listing denied.
Access Denied - Authorization failed by ISAPI/CGI application.


Win32Desc
------------------------
The operation completed successfully.
No credentials are available in the security package.
The system cannot find the file specified.
Windows cannot open this program because it has been prevented by a software
restriction policy.
```

```
For more information, open Event Viewer or contact your system administrator.
Logon failure: unknown user name or bad password.
Access is denied.
The operation completed successfully.



Statistics:
-----------
Elements processed: 32121
Elements output:    15
Execution time:     8.18 seconds
```

TIP

When you experience huge amounts of client side errors, you can modify the *WHERE* clause condition to isolate errors base on more specific code ranges. For example, if you would like to focus on access related errors, simply change the ending status code to 401.

To quickly summarize client side errors, you can simplify the query to the following:

```
---Ch02ClientErrorsSummary.sql---
SELECT
     STRCAT(TO_STRING(sc-status), STRCAT('.',TO_STRING(sc-substatus)))
AS ErrCode,
     Count(*) AS Total
FROM %source%
WHERE
     (sc-status BETWEEN 400 AND 424)
GROUP BY ErrCode
ORDER BY Total DESC
---Ch02ClientErrorsSummary.sql---
```

Swiss Army Knife...

Analyzing Server Side Errors

Modifying the last query to the following will provide you with details of server-side errors:

```
---Ch02ServerErrors.sql---
SELECT
    RequestedFile, ErrCode, Total, ErrDesc, Win32Desc
    USING sc-win32-status AS WinCode,
    TO_LOWERCASE(cs-uri-stem) AS RequestedFile,
    STRCAT(TO_STRING(sc-status), STRCAT('.',TO_STRING(sc-substatus))) AS
ErrCode,
    Count(*) AS Total,
    CASE ErrCode
        WHEN '500.0' THEN 'Internal server error.'
        WHEN '500.12' THEN 'Server Error - Application is busy restarting on
the Web server.'
        WHEN '500.13' THEN 'Server Error - Web server is too busy.'
        WHEN '500.15' THEN 'Server Error - Direct requests for Global.asa
are not allowed.'
        WHEN '500.16' THEN 'Server Error - UNC authorization credentials
incorrect.'
        WHEN '500.18' THEN 'Server Error - URL authorization store cannot be
opened.'
        WHEN '500.100' THEN 'Server Error - Internal ASP error.'
        WHEN '501.0' THEN 'Header values specify a configuration that is not
implemented.'
        WHEN '502.1' THEN 'Web server received an invalid response while
acting as a gateway or proxy.'
        WHEN '502.2' THEN 'Error in CGI application.'
        WHEN '503.0' THEN 'Service unavailable'
        WHEN '504.0' THEN 'Gateway timeout.'
        WHEN '505.0' THEN 'HTTP version not supported.'
        ELSE 'Unknown error'
    END AS ErrDesc,
```

Continued

```
        WIN32_ERROR_DESCRIPTION(WinCode) AS Win32Desc
    FROM %source%
    WHERE (sc-status BETWEEN 500 AND 505)
    GROUP BY RequestedFile, ErrCode, ErrDesc, Win32Desc
    ORDER BY Total DESC
    ---Ch02ServerErrors.sql---
```

The modified query only parses error requests with HTTP status codes ranging from 500 to 505, which are server side error codes.

Understanding ASP Errors

To further understand what is causing server side errors, the Ch02AspErrors.sql query generates a list of the server side errors that occurred in your ASP application. Under normal circumstances, these type of errors are often caused by coding errors in the server side query, for example, |12|800a0009| Subquery_out_of_range:_'arrayA(...)'. This error indicates that the *arrayA* defined in a server side query is out of range. The format normally starts with a pipe character followed by a line number, another pipe separator, the error code, and finally one last pipe separator with an ASP error message.

In some special error instances, IIS may only capture the first two separator values, such as |32|8004005| This type of error might not be caused by an ASP query, but rather another problem such as an incorrect IIS configuration. The query results include the error ASP page name, the query string submitted if any, the error detail, message, and the line number in the ASP page that caused the error. This query lists the most frequent to least frequent ASP pages that had errors.

```
---Ch02AspErrors.sql---
SELECT
    Uri, Errorcode, ErrorMsg, LineNo, Total
    USING STRCAT(cs-uri-stem, REPLACE_IF_NOT_NULL(cs-uri-query, STRCAT('?', cs-uri-
query))) AS QryStr,
    TO_LOWERCASE(EXTRACT_TOKEN(QryStr, 0, '|')) AS Uri,
    EXTRACT_TOKEN(cs-uri-query, 2, '|') AS ErrorCode,
    EXTRACT_TOKEN(cs-uri-query, -1, '|') AS ErrorMsg,
    EXTRACT_TOKEN(cs-uri-query, 1, '|') AS LineNo,
    COUNT(*) AS Total
FROM %source%
WHERE
```

```
    (cs-uri-stem LIKE '%.asp')
    AND
    (sc-status = 500)
GROUP BY Uri, ErrorCode, ErrorMsg, LineNo
ORDER BY Total DESC
---Ch02AspErrors.sql---
```

With the result, you can quickly identify which ASP query is experiencing the most errors during processing and the type of errors. The line number comes in handy when you need to pinpoint which line of the code breaks.

This query is simplified in Log parser version 2.2, as the new *EXTRACT_TOKEN* function makes it easier to obtain the desired value in the *cs-uri-query* field. First, the query extracts the ASP content requested along with the query string, if any. The *USING* clause declares aliased field-expressions that are not part of the output columns, but can be referenced anywhere in the query. This is particularly useful for improving readability of the query. After that, the error string in the field is extracted into 3 different columns, namely, error code, message, and the query line number.

The condition in the *WHERE* clause looks for ASP requests using the *LIKE* operator to locate any requests containing the string *.asp*. The request HTTP status must be equal to 500. Log parser will only return requests matching both conditions. To run the query, access a command prompt, navigate to the directory where you installed the query samples, and enter the following:

```
C:\Log parser>LogParser.exe
file:Ch02AspErrors.sql?source="ex*.log" -o:NAT -rtp:-1 > AspErrors.txt
```

The command syntax tells Log parser to parse all extended log files in the current directory, and output it in *NATIVE* format, which is a default screen listing. The *-rtp* stands for rows to print. The default rows to print are 10, hence after 10 rows, the query pauses for user interaction. To avoid this, we specify *-1* to instruct Log parser to output all rows without any pause. The result is then redirected to a text file named *AspErrors.txt:*

```
Uri                                                  ErrorCode
---------------------------------------------------  ---------
/asp/doorwaytop.asp?                                 800a01a8
/asp/depositcheck.asp?                               800a0401
/asp/leftmenu.asp?                                   ASP_0147
/asp/login.asp?                                      80004005
```

```
/certenroll/nsrev_netsvr2.asp                        80070005
/asp/cust_postupdate.asp?custid=134&sel_id=454647    800a0009
/asp/reportsearch.asp?id=29&format=2&style=lightdesc ASP_0113
/print/pdfview.asp                                   800a01a8
/submit.asp                                          800a01b6

. . . . . . . . . . . . . .
```

```
ErrorMsg                                                  LineNo Total
-------------------------------------------------------- ------ ----
-
Object_required:_'objRst'                                  326    320
Expected_end_of_statement                                   7     182
500_Server_Error                                            -     153
Keyword_xsl:call-template_may_not_be_used_here.__          99     93
CCertAdmin::IsValidCertificate_Access_is_denied._0x80070005_(WIN32:_5) 6  33
Subscript_out_of_range:_'arrayA(...)'                      820    29
Script_timed_out                                            -     16
Object_required:_'ACEpdfObj'                                7      8
Object_doesn't_support_this_property_or_method:_'SetAccountID' 29   4
```

```
Statistics:
-----------
Elements processed: 27649
Elements output:    20
Execution time:     12.32 seconds
```

In the sample output, *leftmenu.asp* is producing a general 500_Server_Error, hence no *LineNo* was given. This type of error might be caused by the code itself and no full error message is being captured by IIS; it could also be that the ASP engine crashed. Normally, you need to check the Windows Event Viewer to see if there is an additional event log entry that provides more information.

Analyzing HTTPERR Errors

The HTTP Application Programming Interface (API) error logs are generated by HTTP.SYS. This kernel mode driver handles HTTP requests and routes them to the related application pool. Errors that occur in this driver will trigger a log entry in the HTTP API error logs. By default, HTTP API error logging is enabled; you can monitor this log file to troubleshoot client HTTP request errors. For example, a 503 status code indicates that the application is not available. This log file also captures illegal requests sent to IIS including bad request, forbidden access, and more.

NOTE

Brief descriptions of HTTP.SYS roles:

- Keeping track of client connections established to the server.
- Accept HTTP requests and route it to respective application pool request queue.
- Facilitate Quality of Service (QoS) features, including connection limits, timeouts, request queue length, and throttling bandwidth usage.
- Send responses back to client and implement kernel mode caching.

New log fields are supported when software updates are installed. Additional properties are now available for logging in the Httperr#.log file in IIS 6.0. Visit support.microsoft.com/?id=832975 for additional information.

The Ch02AppPoolErrors.sql query scans the HTTP API error log and produces a list of failed requests related to application pool errors. The query focuses on the famous 503 service unavailable error that results from a variety of conditions. Output includes the server and the client IP address, website detail, the number of errors, the name of the application pool, and the error message.

```
---Ch02AppPoolErrors.sql---
SELECT
    REVERSEDNS(c-ip) AS ClientIP,
    TO_LOWERCASE(cs-uri) AS ClientRequest,
    STRCAT(STRCAT('SiteID:',To_STRING(s-siteid)),STRCAT(STRCAT('(',s-ip),')')) AS
WebSite,
    COUNT(*) AS Total,
    s-queuename AS AppPool,
```

```
        CASE s-reason
            WHEN 'AppOffline' THEN 'Application error, AppPool taken offline.'
            WHEN 'AppPoolTimer' THEN 'AppPool too busy.'
            WHEN 'AppShutdown' THEN 'AppPool being shutdown.'
            WHEN 'ConnLimit' THEN 'Site level connection limit reached.'
            WHEN 'Disabled' THEN 'AppPool disabled and offline.'
            WHEN 'N/A' THEN 'Internal error. E.g. memory allocation failed.'
            WHEN 'QueueFull' THEN 'AppPool request queue is full.'
            ELSE 'Unknown error'
        END AS ErrDesc
FROM HTTPERR
WHERE (sc-status = 503)
GROUP BY ClientIP, ClientRequest, WebSite, AppPool, ErrDesc
ORDER BY Total DESC
---Ch02AppPoolErrors.sql---
```

This query is particularly useful when performing a full scan of the entire history of web application errors. If you notice many errors such as those indicating an application shuts down, you might want to do a filter on specific websites depending on the application pool to minimize the impact of downtime.

The *STRCAT* function for the *WebSite* column is defined as '*Site ID:YY (X.X.X.X)*' format, where *YY* represents the website ID and *X.X.X.X* is the site IP address. Notice that in the *FROM* clause, the *HTTPERR* directive instructs Log parser to parse all *HTTPERR#* log files. You can change it to *httperr2.log* if you wish to only scan the log file. Take note that you must specify the *httperr2.log* path or it must located at the same path as the query.

To run the query, access a command prompt, navigate to the directory where you installed the query samples, and enter the following:

```
C:\Log parser>LogParser.exe
file:Ch02AppPoolErrors.sql -o:NAT -rtp:-1 > AppPoolErrors.txt
```

This instructs Log parser to output the result as *NATIVE* format with all rows at once, and redirect it to the *AppPoolErrors.txt* text file:

```
ClientIP          ClientRequest        WebSite                     Total
--------------    ------------------   -------------------         -----
192.168.10.112    /                    SiteID:2(192.168.10.18)     24
192.168.10.99     /crm/index.aspx      SiteID:832483(192.168.10.18) 18
susan.indev       /deploy/upload.asp   SiteID:2912(192.168.10.19)  9
wastest           /loadtest.aspx       SiteID:2(192.168.10.18)     3
```

```
AppPool              ErrDesc
-------------        -----------------------------
DefaultAppPool       AppPool disabled and offline.
CRMv2                AppPool too busy.
InHousePool          Internal error. E.g. memory allocation failed.
TestPool             Site level connection limit reached.


Statistics:
-----------
Elements processed: 1135
Elements output:    4
Execution time:     0.09 seconds
```

Swiss Army Knife...

Understanding Invalid Requests

While the sample query focuses on application pool-related errors, the following modified query scans for invalid requests. These error requests are not yet reaching the actual website and application pool, rather, they are dropped at the HTTP.SYS driver level; hence there is no website ID or application pool name. Typical causes will be unknown host name, access forbidden due to restriction rules, and others.

```
---Ch02HTTPErrors.sql---
SELECT
    TO_STRING(TO_TIMESTAMP(date, time), 'MM-dd') AS Day,
    REVERSEDNS(c-ip) AS ClientIP,
    TO_LOWERCASE(cs-uri) AS ClientRequest,
    s-ip AS WebServerIP,
    COUNT(*) AS Total,
    s-reason AS ErrDesc
FROM HTTPERR
WHERE
    (sc-status <> 503)
```

Continued

```
      AND
      (sc-status IS NOT NULL)
   GROUP BY Day, ClientIP, ClientRequest, WebServerIP, ErrDesc
   ORDER BY Day DESC
   ---Ch02HTTPErrors.sql---
```

This query groups results by day, starting from the most recent errors. It searches for invalid requests with sc-status not equal to 503 or NULL. The *s-reason* field provides the error detail of the request. For detailed information on these messages, please refer to *INFO: Error Logging in HTTP API* at http://support.microsoft.com/?id=820729.

Analyzing URLSCAN Errors

Monitoring URLSCAN log files allows you to detect rejected requests or malicious attacks against your server. If you suspect your application requests were blocked by URLSCAN, you can analyze the log entries to fine-tune URLSCAN.ini to suit your application needs.

NOTE

Before analyzing URLSCAN errors, you must install URLSCAN. For information on how to install URLSCAN, please refer to:
Using URLSCAN on IIS at http://support.microsoft.com/?id=307608.

The Ch02UrlscanErrors.sql query scans the URLSCAN logs and produces a list of rejected requests that failed to comply with URLSCAN.ini rule sets. This query extracts critical information from the log files, summarizes it, and makes it easier to understand. The result includes the client IP address, the targeted requests, the website ID, the number of time requests got rejected, and the reason for rejection.

```
---Ch02UrlscanErrors.sql---
SELECT
    REVERSEDNS(clientip) AS ClientIP,
    TO_LOWERCASE(url) AS ClientRequest,
    siteinstance AS WebSiteID,
    COUNT(*) AS Total,
    EXTRACT_TOKEN(EXTRACT_TOKEN(comment,0,', '),0, 'Request') AS ErrDesc
FROM URLSCAN
GROUP BY ClientIP, ClientRequest, WebSiteID, ErrDesc
```

```
ORDER BY Total DESC
---Ch02UrlscanErrors.sql---
```

The query scans every URLSCAN log files in the default path *%windir%/system32/inetsrv/urlscan/logs/*. Notice that the URLSCAN log format field name is quite different from the rest of IIS-related logs. For more information, please refer to in Appendix C for URLSCAN input format. The error message from the log files is simplified and extracted as the *ErrDesc* column. The result is ordered by the number of rejected requests.

To run the query, access a command prompt, navigate to the directory where you installed the query samples, and enter the following:

```
C:\Log parser>LogParser.exe
file:Ch02UrlscanErrors.sql -o:NAT -rtp:-1 > UrlscanErrors.txt
```

This instructs Log parser to output the result in *NATIVE* format with all rows at once, and redirect it to the *UrlscanErrors.txt* text file:

```
ClientIP        ClientRequest
--------------  -----------------------------------------------------------
----------
192.168.10.43   /printers/hplaser/.printer/
192.168.10.43   /rettest.idq
192.168.10.243  /asp/doorway.asplanguageid=2&gmtoffset=480
192.168.10.212  //cgi-bin/..%255c..%255c..%255c..%255cwinnt/system32/cmd.exe
192.168.10.212
//adsamples/..%c0%af..%c0%af..%c0%af..%c0%af../winnt/system32/cmd.exe
192.168.10.212  /iisadmpwd/aexp2b.htr
192.168.10.249  -
192.168.10.249  -
192.168.10.212
//iisadmpwd/..%f0%80%80%af..//..%f0%80%80%af../winnt/system32/cmd.exe
192.168.10.212
//_vti_adm/..%252f..%252f..%252f..%252fwinnt/system32/cmd.exe
192.168.10.243  /asp/eventindex.files/eventselection.htm
192.168.10.243  /asp/..\images\neteller.gif
192.168.10.212  /scripts/iisadmin/bdir.htr
192.168.10.249  -
192.168.10.249  -
192.168.10.249  -
192.168.10.40   /printers/hplaser/.printer/
```

```
WebSiteID      Total     ErrDesc
---------      -----     -------------------------------------------------
1              354       URL contains '.' in the path.
1              332       URL contains extension '.idq'
1923490        294       URL contains sequence '&'
73223          103       URL normalization was not complete after one pass.
73223          102       URL contains extension '.exe'
1              85        URL contains extension '.htr'
-              78        Sent verb '/GET'
-              78        Sent verb 'TRACE'
73223          69        URL contains high bit character.
73223          56        URL contains disallowed header 'transfer-encoding:'
1923490        53        URL contains '.' in the path.
1923490        31        URL contains sequence '\'
73223          12        URL contains extension '.htr'
-              9         Sent verb 'OPTIONS'
-              4         Sent verb 'pGET'
-              1         Sent verb '=POST'
1              3         URL contains '.' in the path.


Statistics:
-----------

Elements processed: 924
Elements output:     19
Execution time:      23.08 seconds
```

From the sample output, the request rejected the most is */printers/hplaser/.printer/*. To solve this error, simply change the value for *AllowDotInPath* from 0 to 1 in URLSCAN.ini, and restart IIS services for the changes to take effect. Next in the sample, you will notice a number of rejected requests with weird characters in the request column. These are general attempts to exploit IIS server, and of course none of those requests are successful, as they are blocked by URLSCAN. In the next section we will explore these exploits more.

Scanning for Security Breaches

Log files are an important and useful troubleshooting channel to resolve failure or error requests, as well as the usage status of the IIS server. The other key factor in why log files are so important is that they are also a valuable source of information for identifying potential attack behavior and intrusion patterns.

By understanding these attack requests, not only are you able to tell whether the attacks have been successful or not, you also can plan the next course of action against these failed requests. These requests could be anything, including information disclosure, unauthorized access, and more.

Analyzing Illegal Requests

An illegal request is any request that a user should not send to the server under normal circumstances, but would send in the case of an attack. For example, a hacker trying to gain remote access might try exploiting a known vulnerability via IIS. Hence, it is vital to be aware of illegal requests made to the server and ensure the server is running with the latest service packs and hot fixes.

This section analyzes all IIS-related log sources, ranging from W3C extended logs to HTTPERR and URLSCAN log files. For more information, please refer to:

- Table A.2 W3C Extended Log Fields
- Table A.3 HTTPERR Log Fields
- Table A.4 URLSCAN Log Fields

Scanning For Failed Authentication and Unauthorized Access

Failed authentication occurs when a user accessing protected content fails to properly authenticate with the server, while unauthorized access indicates that a user failed the Access Control List (ACL) checking on the requested content. Such information provides you with detail about users or attackers who are trying to access certain content that they should not access.

The Ch02AuthAclFailure.sql query scans the W3C extended log files, searching for requests that fail authentication or are denied due to NTFS permissions. This query is similar to the Identify Error Requests sample query presented earlier in this Appendix, however, this focuses only on authentication and authorization failures.

```
---Ch02AuthAclFailures.sql---
SELECT
    RequestedFile, ClientDesc, Total, ErrDesc, ErrDate
    USING TO_LOWERCASE(cs-username) AS UserName,
    STRCAT(STRCAT(' (',REVERSEDNS(c-ip)),')') AS ClientIP,
    STRCAT(TO_STRING(sc-status), STRCAT('.',TO_STRING(sc-substatus))) AS ErrCode,
```

```
    TO_LOWERCASE(cs-uri-stem) AS RequestedFile,
    STRCAT(Username,ClientIP) AS ClientDesc,
    Count(*) AS Total,
    CASE ErrCode
        --Access Error--
        WHEN '401.1' THEN 'Access Denied - Login failed.'
        WHEN '401.2' THEN 'Access Denied - Logon failed due to server config.'
        WHEN '401.3' THEN 'Access Denied - ACL checking failed.'
        WHEN '401.4' THEN 'Access Denied - Authorization failed by filter.'
        WHEN '401.5' THEN 'Access Denied - Authorization failed by ISAPI/CGI
application.'
        WHEN '401.7' THEN 'Access Denied - Access denied by URL authorization
policy on the Web server.'
        --Forbidden Error--
        WHEN '403.1' THEN 'Forbidden - Execute access.'
        WHEN '403.2' THEN 'Forbidden - Read access.'
        WHEN '403.3' THEN 'Forbidden - Write access.'
        WHEN '403.4' THEN 'Forbidden - SSL required.'
        WHEN '403.5' THEN 'Forbidden - SSL 128 required.'
        WHEN '403.6' THEN 'Forbidden - IP address rejected.'
        WHEN '403.7' THEN 'Forbidden - Client certificate required.'
        WHEN '403.8' THEN 'Forbidden - Site access denied.'
        WHEN '403.9' THEN 'Forbidden - Too many users.'
        WHEN '403.10' THEN 'Forbidden - Invalid configuration.'
        WHEN '403.11' THEN 'Forbidden - Password change.'
        WHEN '403.12' THEN 'Forbidden - Mapper denied access.'
        WHEN '403.13' THEN 'Forbidden - Client certificate revoked.'
        WHEN '403.14' THEN 'Forbidden - Directory listing denied.'
        WHEN '403.15' THEN 'Forbidden - Client Access Licenses exceeded.'
        WHEN '403.16' THEN 'Forbidden - Client certificate is untrusted or invalid.'
        WHEN '403.17' THEN 'Forbidden - Client certificate has expired or is not yet
valid.'
        WHEN '403.18' THEN 'Forbidden - Cannot execute requested URL in the current
application pool.'
        WHEN '403.19' THEN 'Forbidden - Cannot execute CGIs for the client in this
application pool.'
        WHEN '403.20' THEN 'Forbidden - Passport logon failed.'
        ELSE STRCAT('Unknown error, status:',ErrCode)
    END AS ErrDesc,
    date AS ErrDate,
FROM %source%
```

```
WHERE
    (sc-status BETWEEN 401 AND 403)
    AND
    (cs-username IS NOT NULL)
    AND
    (date >= SUB(SYSTEM_TIMESTAMP(), TIMESTAMP('%day%', 'd')))
GROUP BY RequestedFile, ClientDesc, ErrDesc, ErrDate
ORDER BY Total DESC
---Ch02AuthAclFailures.sql---
```

The *USING* clause defines the *UserName* and *ClientIP* variables referenced by the *ClientDesc* column in the query. We use the *CASE* clause to derive the actual message based on the *ErrCode*. The *WHERE* clause specifies the status code related to either authentication or access errors, which, according to RFC specification, ranges from 401 to 403. The second condition checks for non-anonymous login, and the last condition determines the number of days of log files to scan.

To run the query, access a command prompt, navigate to the directory where you installed the query samples, and enter the following:

```
C:\Log parser>LogParser.exe
file:Ch02AuthAclFailures.sql?source="<1>"+day="1" -o:NAT -rtp:1 >
AuthAclFailures.txt
```

The syntax instructs Log parser to read the current day of the default website log files, output it in *NATIVE* format with all rows at once, and redirect it to *AuthAclFailures.txt*. The *+day* parameter specifies the number of days. The number *1* indicates today. To specify ten days before, use the value *11*, for example, *+day="11"*. Note that the maximum number of days that you can specify is 31, which is equivalent to one month. To facilitate scanning of all log files, simply remove the last checking condition.

RequestedFile	ClientDesc	Total
/secure/syscheck.aspx	indev\viewer (192.168.10.21)	84
/secure/	indev\administrator (netsvr)	72
/printers/ipp_0004.asp	indev\bernard (192.168.10.43)	50
/printers	indev\ali (netsvr)	21
/internal/	indev\administrator (192.168.18.19)	14
/devfolder/	myadmin	7
/passport/	guest (192.168.10.122)	3

```
ErrDesc                                                     ErrDate
-------------------------------------------------------     ----------
Access Denied - ACL checking failed.                        2004-09-01
Forbidden - Directory listing denied.                       2004-09-01
Access Denied - Authorization failed by ISAPI/CGI application. 2004-09-01
Access Denied - Login failed.                               2004-09-01
Forbidden - IP address rejected.                            2004-09-01
Access Denied - ACL checking failed.                        2004-09-01
Forbidden - Site access denied.                             2004-09-01


Statistics:
-----------
Elements processed: 27655
Elements output:    21
Execution time:     10.62 seconds
```

Master Craftsman...

Monitoring Other IIS services

Analyzing authentication failures in FTP services are as follows:

```
---Ch02FtpSecurity.sql---
SELECT
    TO_LOWERCASE(cs-username) AS UserName,
    REVERSEDNS(c-ip) AS ClientIP,
    date AS LogDate,
    COUNT(*) AS Total
FROM %source%
WHERE
    (cs-method LIKE '%PASS')
    AND
    (sc-status = 530)
GROUP BY UserName, ClientIP, LogDate
ORDER BY Total DESC
---Ch02FtpSecurity.sql---
```

Continued

To identify authentication failures in the FTP service, the query analyzes requests with the client method *PASS*, which represents the authentication process. Status code 503 indicates that the authentication failed due to invalid user credentials or that the security policy prohibited such logon requests. For more information about FTP status codes, please refer to: www.w3.org/Protocols/rfc959/4_FileTransfer.html.

For FTP access-related errors, the following query focuses on error code 550, which indicates requested action not taken, either due to the file requested not being available, insufficient permissions, or some other reason.

```
---Ch02FtpAccess.sql---
SELECT
    TO_LOWERCASE(cs-username) AS UserName,
    REVERSEDNS(c-ip) AS ClientIP,
    date AS LogDate,
    STRCAT(EXTRACT_TOKEN(cs-method,-1,']'),STRCAT(' ',cs-uri-stem)) AS
FtpRequest,
    COUNT(*) AS Total
FROM %source%
WHERE sc-status = 550
GROUP BY UserName, ClientIP, LogDate, FtpRequest
ORDER BY Total DESC
---Ch02FtpAccess.sql---
```

The core part of this query is the *FtpRequest field*, where Log parser extracts the actual actions performed that FTP services could not fulfill. A typical example of this would be *RMD mydir*, which indicates a failed attempt to remove the *mydir* directory, or *sent mydata.zip*, which tells you that client failed to download the file *mydata.zip.*

Analyzing SMTP authentication and relay failures:

```
---Ch02SmtpSecurity.sql---
SELECT
    REVERSEDNS(c-ip) AS ClientIP,
    date AS LogDate,
    CASE cs-method
        WHEN 'AUTH' THEN 'Authentication failed'
        WHEN 'RCPT' THEN STRCAT('Unable to Relay - ', cs-uri-query)
        ELSE STRCAT('Unknown error, method:',cs-method)
    END AS ErrDesc,
    COUNT(*) AS Total
```

Continued

```
From %source%
WHERE (sc-status IN (535;550))
GROUP BY ClientIP, LogDate, ErrDesc
ORDER BY Total DESC
---Ch02SmtpSecurity.sql---
```

Notice that this query is similar to the Ch02Ftpsecurity.sql query. The difference is the condition checking in the *WHERE* clause. In the IIS SMTP protocol, status code 535 defines authentication failures, where the *AUTH* is the authentication action requested by clients. For relay error, the status code is defined as 550 and *RCPT* is the action requested by clients. The *RCPT* action represents *'Received to'* the recipient of the e-mail, and it is captured in this format +*TO:+<username@domain-name.com>*. Notice that the query did not capture *cs-username* as in IIS SMTP. This field normally contains the client computer name when authentication fails. For more information about SMTP verbs and reply codes, please refer to: www.w3.org/Protocols/rfc822/rfc822.txt.

Analyzing NNTP error requests:

```
---Ch02NntpSecurity.sql---
SELECT
    CASE TO_LOWERCASE(cs-username)
        WHEN '<user>' THEN 'Anonymous'
        ELSE TO_LOWERCASE(cs-username)
    END AS UserName,
    REVERSEDNS(c-ip) AS ClientIP,
    STRCAT(cs-method,STRCAT(' ',cs-uri-stem)) AS NNTPRequest,
    Count(*) AS Total,
    CASE sc-status
        WHEN 400 THEN 'NNTP service discontinue.'
        WHEN 411 THEN 'Newsgroup not found.'
        WHEN 412 THEN 'No newsgroups selected.'
        WHEN 420 THEN 'No current article selected.'
        WHEN 421 THEN 'No next article in newsgroup.'
        WHEN 422 THEN 'No previous article in newsgroup.'
        WHEN 423 THEN 'No such article number in newsgroup.'
        WHEN 430 THEN 'No such article in newsgroup.'
        WHEN 435 THEN 'Article not wanted - do not send it.'
        WHEN 436 THEN 'Transfer failed - try again later.'
        WHEN 437 THEN 'Article rejected - do not try again.'
        WHEN 440 THEN 'Article posting not allowed.'
```

Continued

```
                WHEN 441 THEN 'Article posting failed'
                WHEN 480 THEN 'Logon required.'
                ELSE STRCAT('Unknown error - Request:', NNTPRequest)
         END AS ErrDesc
    FROM %source%
    WHERE (sc-status BETWEEN 400 AND 480)
    GROUP BY Username, ClientIP, NNTPRequest, ErrDesc
    ORDER BY Total DESC
    ---Ch02NntpSecurity.sql---
```

This query focuses on errors occurring during retrieval and posting of news articles. When a newsgroup allows anonymous posting, NNTP writes *<user>* as the anonymous *cs-username*, hence the *CASE* clause at the beginning of the query instructs Log parser to replace this string with the value *Anonymous*. The error code range 400 to 480 indicates negative responses by IIS NNTP. For more information about NNTP reply status code, please refer to: www.w3.org/Protocols/rfc977/rfc977.html.

Scanning Malformed HTTP Requests

As discussed earlier, HTTP.SYS is the kernel mode driver that handles HTTP requests, placing them into each application pool's request queue. This kernel mode driver captures invalid and malformed requests to the HTTPERR log file. If a request fails at this level, request detail will not get logged in the W3C extended log file, as the request never reaches the website. On the other hand, if a request gets past this HTTP.SYS checking, URLSCAN, if installed, will check the request again to see if it matches the URLSCAN rule sets. Finally, the request then reaches the application processing filter hosted on the IIS server.

The Ch02MalformedHTTP.sql query parses the HTTPERR log file searching for invalid requests. This query focuses on requests with status codes of 400, 403, and 411. Note that the HTTPERR log does not record a substatus code. Error 400 is categorized as "Bad Request", which may include requests with an invalid verb, host header name, or some other malformed HTTP header. 403 errors mean the request was forbidden, which may include attempts to access protected content or invalid URL references. 411 errors are mainly related to HTTP PUT requests where content length is not specified.

The query groups result on a daily basis and sorts by the number of invalid requests. Columns generated include the client IP address, the HTTP verb used, the targeted web server IP address, the number of invalid requests, and the detailed error message.

```
---Ch02MalformedHttp.sql---
SELECT
    TO_STRING(TO_TIMESTAMP(date, time), 'MM-dd') AS Day,
    REVERSEDNS(c-ip) AS ClientIP,
    cs-method AS ClientMethod,
    s-ip AS WebServerIP,
    COUNT(*) AS Total,
    CASE s-reason
        WHEN 'BadRequest' THEN 'Bad and Invalid Request.'
        WHEN 'Verb' THEN 'Invalid HTTP verb.'
        WHEN 'Hostname' THEN 'Hostname not found.'
        WHEN 'Header' THEN 'Invalid Header during parsing.'
        WHEN 'URL' THEN 'Invalid URL detected.'
        WHEN 'Forbidden' THEN 'Request denied'
        WHEN 'LengthRequired' THEN 'HTTP PUT length missing.'
        ELSE STRCAT('Unknown error, Err:',cs-uri)
    END AS ErrDesc
FROM HTTPERR
WHERE (sc-status IN (400;403;411))
GROUP BY Day, ClientIP, ClientMethod, WebServerIP, ErrDesc
ORDER BY Day, Total DESC
---Ch02MalformedHttp.sql---
```

This query is very useful for identifying potential attacks, though it also provides you with important details for troubleshooting. For example, a forbidden access captured by HTTP.SYS might indicate that a user is trying to access certain content that is not allowed. To further protect IIS, system administrators can further restrict access by blocking the client IP address at the firewall level, preventing such malformed requests from hitting the IIS server.

To run the query, access a command prompt, navigate to the directory where you installed the query samples, and enter the following:

```
C:\Log parser>LogParser.exe
file:Ch02MalformedHttp.sql -o:NAT -rtp:-1 > MalformedHttp.txt
```

This instructs Log parser to output the results in *NATIVE* format with all rows at once, and redirect it to *MalformedHttp.txt*. The following shows the sample result of the query:

Day	ClientIP	ClientMethod	WebServerIP	Total	ErrDesc
08-31	susan	PUT	192.168.10.18	15	HTTP PUT length missing.
08-31	devsvr2	GET	192.168.10.18	9	Request denied
08-29	testlabpc2	GET	192.168.10.18	21	Hostname not found
08-29	192.168.10.21	GET	192.168.10.43	16	Bad and Invalid Request.
08-29	testlabpc2	POST	192.168.10.43	7	Request denied
08-29 parsing.	susan	GET	192.168.10.18	1	Invalid Header during
08-27	192.168.10.21	GET	192.168.10.43	25	Invalid URL detected.
08-27	192.168.10.22	GET	192.168.10.43	8	Bad and Invalid Request.
08-27	192.168.10.23	Unparsed	192.168.10.43	7	Bad and Invalid Request.
08-27 parsing.	192.168.10.21	GET	192.168.10.43	2	Invalid Header during
08-18	devsvr2	Invalid	192.168.10.18	4	Invalid HTTP verb.

```
Statistics:

-----------

Elements processed: 232

Elements output:    18

Execution time:       21.61 seconds
```

Swiss Army Knife...

Detecting Code Red and Nimda

Back in 2001, the famous Code Red worm bombarded the IIS world. It exploited vulnerabilities in IIS 5.0 and IIS 4.0. Though IIS 6.0 is not vulnerable to this particular attack, it is sometimes helpful to know more about this notorious worm to learn how to deal with future worms. Code Red uses a known buffer overflow vulnerability that exists in Microsoft Indexing Service. By default, this service is enabled on an IIS 4.0 or IIS 5.0 server. It replicates itself by attacking more IIS servers from the infected machine.

Nimda, another IIS 'killer' worm, was first released back in 2000 utilizing a Web server folder traversal vulnerability. It allows malicious users to execute arbitrary code on the affected server, and spreads by using the same techniques as the Code Red variants, whereby it scan vulnerable machines and try to inject its code.

Continued

Although Microsoft had released patches for the vulnerability long before these worms were released, sadly, many un-patched infected IIS servers existed that began attacking other servers on the Internet.

By modifying the sample query to the following, you can view details regarding symptoms of these worms' attacks.

```
---Ch02Nimda.sql---
SELECT
    REVERSEDNS(c-ip) AS ClientIP,
    s-ip AS WebServerIP,
    COUNT(*) AS Total
FROM HTTPERR
WHERE
    (sc-status = 400)
    AND
    ((s-reason = 'URL') OR (s-reason = 'BadRequest'))
    AND
((cs-uri LIKE '%cmd.exe%') OR (cs-uri LIKE '%root.exe%'))
GROUP BY ClientIP, WebServerIP
ORDER BY Total DESC
---Ch02Nimda.sql---
```

For the Nimda worm, the footprint can be identified by checking the *cs-uri* field, where it is trying to access *cmd.exe* or *root.exe*. IIS 6.0 is not vulnerable to this web folder traversal attack and requests to certain command-line executables are strictly restricted to admin users only. Notice that the query checks for two different reasons: *URL* or *BadRequest*, as attackers might use different request queries and HTTP verbs when trying to exploit the server.

Next, to detect Code Red worm, try the following:

```
---Ch02CodeRed.sql---
SELECT
    REVERSEDNS(c-ip) AS ClientIP,
    s-ip AS WebServerIP,
    COUNT(*) AS Total
FROM HTTPERR
WHERE
    ((s-reason = 'URL') OR (s-reason = 'BadRequest'))
    AND
((cs-uri LIKE '%default.id_%') OR (cs-uri LIKE '%null.id_%'))
```

Continued

```
GROUP BY ClientIP, WebServerIP

ORDER BY Total DESC

---Ch02CodeRed.sql---
```

This query assumes that requests against *default.id_* and *null.id_* with s-reason belong to *URL* or *BadRequest* are mostly due to Code Red worm attacks. The *LIKE* clause checking the *.id_* represents the file extension, which can be *ida*, or *idq*. The underscore '_' matches any single character. Notice that the condition checking does not check for status code 400, as the buffer overflow request strings might mess up the status code field in HTTPERR log.

By running both queries, you can detect Code Red and Nimda worms, though these exploits do not harm IIS 6.0 server. However, using the results and filtering those attacking IP addresses at firewall level will reduce unwanted requests reaching the IIS server.

Scanning HTTP Verbs in Client Requests

Under most conditions, the common HTTP verbs used to make web requests are POST and GET. However, there are scenarios when other verbs are used. For example, Web Distributed Authoring and Versioning (WebDav) uses other verbs including OPTIONS, PROFIND, and others. The presence of these uncommon verbs in different log sources might indicate potential attacks if such services or components are not installed on IIS.

NOTE

To learn about WebDav, please refer to:
- HOW TO: Create a Secure WebDAV Publishing Directory at support.microsoft.com/?id=323470
- HTTP Extensions for Distributed Authoring – WEBDAV at ftp.isi.edu/in-notes/rfc2518.txt

The Ch02Httpverbs.sql query scans for uncommon verbs in W3C extended log files. The result includes the client IP address, the HTTP verbs used, the requested content, and status code, as well as the total number of requests.

```
---Ch02HttpVerbs.sql---
SELECT
    REVERSEDNS(c-ip) AS ClientIP,
    cs-method AS Verb,
```

```
   cs-uri-stem AS RequestedFile,
   STRCAT(TO_STRING(sc-status), STRCAT('.',TO_STRING(sc-substatus))) AS
StatusCode,
   COUNT(*) AS Total
FROM %source%
WHERE (cs-method NOT IN ('POST';'GET'))
GROUP BY ClientIP, Verb, RequestedFile, StatusCode
ORDER BY Total DESC
---Ch02HttpVerbs.sql---
```

This query scans for HTTP verbs other than *POST* or *GET*. Any requests using HTTP verbs other than POST or GET might be suspicious and might require further investigation.

To run the query, access a command prompt, navigate to the directory where you installed the query samples, and enter the following:

```
C:\Log parser>LogParser.exe
file:Ch02HttpVerbs.sql -o:NAT -rtp:-1 > HttpVerbs.txt
```

This instructs Log parser to output the results in *NATIVE* format with all rows at once, and redirect it to *HttpVerbs.txt*. The following shows the sample result of the query:

```
ClientIP        Verb     RequestedFile StatusCode Total
-------------   -------- ------------- ---------- -----
washost2        HEAD     /index.aspx   200.0      192
192.168.10.21   OPTIONS  /devtest/     404.0      93
192.168.10.36   PROPFIND /Download/    404.0      69
192.168.10.36   OPTIONS  /devtest/     404.0      21
testlabpc2      TRACE    /             501.0      11
```

From the sample output, it is clear that WebDav-related requests failed with 404 replies, and the *TRACE* verb is not implemented based on the 501 status code. The result is not only helpful to assist in troubleshooting, but it also provides clues as to which HTTP verbs clients use in their requests. For example, if you do not need the *TRACE* verb for the functionality of your website, you can install URLSCAN to restrict the HTTP verb.

Swiss Army Knife...

More HTTP Verbs Scanning

Let's recap the flow when a client makes an HTTP request. The request first reaches the HTTP kernel mode driver and, after limited parsing, the request is placed in an application pool request queue (assuming the application pool is healthy). Before the application process (ISAPI) takes over, URLSCAN (if installed) verifies the request against its configured rule sets. If the request passes the URLSCAN checking, the application ISAPI filter receives and processes the request.

Hence, there are two additional log sources that might contain suspicious HTTP verbs. The HTTPERR captures non-supported HTTP verbs:

```
---Ch02HttpErrVerbs.sql---
SELECT
    REVERSEDNS(c-ip) AS ClientIP,
    cs-method AS Verb,
    COUNT(*) AS Total
FROM HTTPERR
WHERE
    (sc-status = 400)
    AND
    (s-reason = 'Verb')
GROUP BY ClientIP, Verb
ORDER BY Total DESC
---Ch02HttpErrVerbs.sql---
```

This query looks for requests with status code 400 and with the *reason phrase* containing the string "verb." Normally, the verb will be "Invalid", as HTTP.SYS failed to parse the request.

Next, if URLSCAN is installed, the URLSCAN log files will capture all illegal HTTP verbs. By default, *GET*, *HEAD*, and *POST* are the only allowed HTTP verbs defined in URLSCAN.ini. To scan for rejected HTTP verbs in URLSCAN, try the following:

```
---Ch02UrlscanVerbs.sql---
SELECT
```

Continued

```
          REVERSEDNS(clientip) AS ClientIP,
          EXTRACT_TOKEN(comment,1,'\'') AS Verb,
          COUNT(*) AS Total
   FROM URLSCAN
   WHERE (comment LIKE '%Sent Verb%')
   GROUP BY ClientIP, Verb
   ORDER BY Total DESC
   ---Ch02UrlscanVerbs.sql---
```

Essentially, this query checks for URLSCAN comments that contain of the string "Sent Verb". The *EXTRACT_TOKEN* function extracts the value of the HTTP verb; the separator used in this example is a single quote ', the backslash \ is used to escape the single quote.

Scanning ASP Attacks

There many possible forms of ASP application attacks, including continuous requests that put a heavy process load on the server and SQL injections for abusing ASP forms. While there are no fixed patterns to detect actual attack procedures, it is possible to parse the W3C extended log files to determine possible attacks that might have taken place.

The Ch02AspAttacks.sql query is similar to Ch02AspErrors.sql. While the ASP error query focuses on generic ASP application errors caused by the query, this query detects possible attack behavior, for example if the error occurred many times in a day and originated from the same client IP address.

```
---Ch02AspAttacks.sql---
SELECT
    DISTINCT
    REVERSEDNS(c-ip) AS ClientIP,
    TO_LOWERCASE(cs-uri-stem) AS RequestedFile,
    TO_LOWERCASE(cs-uri-query) AS QryStr,
    COUNT(*) AS Total
FROM %source%
WHERE
    (TO_LOWERCASE(EXTRACT_EXTENSION(cs-uri-stem)) = 'asp')
    AND
    (sc-status = 500)
GROUP BY ClientIP, RequestedFile, QryStr
```

```
HAVING (Total > 100)
ORDER BY Total DESC
---Ch02AspAttacks.sql---
```

By looking at the requested content and query string (if any), you might be able to determine if those requests were legitimate or part of a malicious attack. The next course of action will be to verify the actual ASP script itself, correct code flaws, if discovered, and further protect the server by filtering out the requested client's IP address.

The condition checking in the *WHERE* clause looks for requests with status code 500 and the asp file that encountered the errors more than 100 times.

> **NOTE**
>
> The different between *HAVING* and *WHERE* is that *HAVING* is able to apply condition checks on aggregate functions. Adding a *HAVING clause* between the *GROUP BY* and *ORDER BY* clause allows you to specify additional checking.

To run the query, access a command prompt, navigate to the directory where you installed the query samples, and enter the following:

```
C:\Log parser>LogParser.exe
file:Ch02AspAttacks.sql?source="<2>" -o:NAT -rtp:-1 > AspAttacks.txt
```

The command syntax tells Log parser to parse all extended log files for website ID 2, output it in *NATIVE* format, and redirect the output to a text file named *AspAttacks.tx:*

```
ClientIP       RequestedFile           QryStr
Total
------------- ----------------------- ---------------------------------
----- -----
susan.indev    /cust_update.asp
|28|800a01a8|Object_required:_'objRst'  364
192.168.10.30  /asp/db_process.asp     -
213
testlabpc2     /default.asp            view=q&id=921&section=230
209
devsvr2        /asp/sport.asp          ASP_0147|500_Server_Error
166
```

```
192.168.10.21  /db/remove.asp          |6|80004005|
138


Statistics:
-----------
Elements processed: 47531
Elements output:    5
Execution time:     19.94 seconds
```

Summary

In this Appendix we have covered different IIS 6.0 log sources for understanding performance, reliability, and security in IIS server. Besides understanding the IIS logging structure, the general request processing flows, and running the sample queries, the core values delivered here are to help you realize what data is available in different log files and inspire creative thinking to derive meaningful information from this data. Microsoft Log parser is a free-form tool; it is up to system administrators like you to create useful queries and discover its true value.

SQL Grammar Reference

Topics in this Appendix:

- Complete Syntax
- Field-Expressions
- Query Syntax
- SELECT Clause
- USING Clause
- INTO Clause
- FROM Clause
- WHERE Clause
- GROUP BY Clause
- HAVING Clause
- ORDER BY Clause

In This Toolbox

Log Parser works on queries written using a dialect of the Structured Query Language (SQL). Even though the Log Parser SQL dialect draws much from the standard ANSI SQL language, there are some differences whose understanding will help users make the most out of the Log Parser tool.

Complete Syntax

```
<query> -> <select_clause> [ <using_clause>] [ <into_clause> ]
           <from_clause> [ <where_clause> ] [ <group_by_clause> ]
           [ <having_clause> ] [ <order_by_clause> ]


<select_clause> -> SELECT [ TOP <integer> ] [ DISTINCT | ALL ]
                        <selection_list>


<selection_list> -> <selection_list_el> [ , <selection_list> ]


<selection_list_el>    -> <field_expr> [ AS <alias> ] |
                        *


<using_clause>         -> USING <selection_list>


<into_clause>         -> INTO <into_entity>


<from_clause>         -> FROM <from_entity>


<where_clause>        -> WHERE <expression>


<expression>         -> <term1> [ OR <expression> ]


<term1>              -> <term2> [ AND <term1> ]


<term2>   -> <field_expr> <rel_op> <field_expr>                      |
              <field_expr> [ NOT ] LIKE <like_value>                |
              <field_expr> [ NOT ] BETWEEN <field_expr> AND
                  <field_expr>                                       |
              <field_expr> <unary_op>                                |
              <field_expr> <incl_op> <content>                       |
              <field_expr> <rel_op> [ALL|ANY] <content>              |
              ( <field_expr_list> ) <incl_op> <content>              |
              ( <field_expr_list> ) <rel_op> [ALL|ANY] <content>     |
              NOT <term2>                                            |
              ( <expression> )


<content>   -> ( <value_list> ) |
```

```
                    (  <query>  )

<group_by_clause>        -> GROUP BY <field_expr_list> [ WITH ROLLUP ]

<having_clause>          -> HAVING <expression>

<order_by_clause>        -> ORDER BY <field_expr_list> [ ASC | DESC ] |
                            ORDER BY * [ ASC | DESC ]

<field_expr_list>        -> <field_expr> [ , <field_expr_list> ]

<field_expr>             -> <sqlfunction_expr>       |
                            <function_expr>          |
                            <value>                  |
                            <alias>                  |
                            <field>

<sqlfunction_expr> -> <sqlfunction> ( [ DISTINCT | ALL ] <field_expr> )    |
                      <prop_sqlfunction> ( <field_expr> ) [ <on_fields> ] |
                      COUNT ( [ DISTINCT | ALL ] * )                       |
                      COUNT ( [ DISTINCT | ALL ] <field_expr_list> )       |
                      PROPCOUNT ( * ) [ <on_fields> ]                      |
                      PROPCOUNT ( <field_expr_list> ) [ <on_fields> ]

<function_expr>          -> <function> ( <field_expr_list> ) |
                            <case_statement>

<value_list>             -> <value_list_row> [ ; <value_list> ]

<value_list_row>         -> <value> [ , <value_list_row> ]

<sqlfunction>            -> SUM | AVG | MAX | MIN | GROUPING

<prop_sqlfunction>       -> PROPSUM
```

```
<on_fields>              -> ON ( <field_expr_list> )


<function>  -> ADD | BIT_AND | BIT_NOT | BIT_OR | BIT_SHL        |
               BIT_SHR | BIT_XOR | COALESCE | COMPUTER_NAME | DIV  |
               EXP | EXP10 | EXTRACT_EXTENSION | EXTRACT_FILENAME  |
               EXTRACT_PATH | EXTRACT_PREFIX | EXTRACT_SUFFIX      |
               EXTRACT_TOKEN | EXTRACT_VALUE | FLOOR               |
               HASHMD5_FILE | HASHSEQ | HEX_TO_ASC | HEX_TO_HEX16  |
               HEX_TO_HEX32 | HEX_TO_HEX8 | HEX_TO_INT             |
               HEX_TO_PRINT | IN_ROW_NUMBER | INDEX_OF             |
               INT_TO_IPV4 | IPV4_TO_INT | LAST_INDEX_OF | LOG     |
               LOG10 | LTRIM | MOD | MUL | OUT_ROW_NUMBER          |
               QNTFLOOR_TO_DIGIT | QNTROUND_TO_DIGIT | QUANTIZE    |
               REPLACE_CHR | REPLACE_IF_NOT_NULL | REPLACE_STR     |
               RESOLVE_SID | REVERSEDNS | ROT13 | ROUND | RTRIM    |
               SEQUENCE | SQR | SQRROOT | STRCAT | STRCNT | STRLEN |
               STRREPEAT | STRREV | SUB | SUBSTR | SYSTEM_DATE     |
               SYSTEM_TIME | SYSTEM_TIMESTAMP | SYSTEM_UTCOFFSET   |
               TO_DATE | TO_HEX | TO_INT | TO_LOCALTIME            |
               TO_LOWERCASE | TO_REAL | TO_STRING | TO_TIME        |
               TO_TIMESTAMP | TO_UPPERCASE | TO_UTCTIME | TRIM     |
               URLESCAPE | URLUNESCAPE | WIN32_ERROR_DESCRIPTION


<case_statement>     -> CASE <field_expression> <when_statement_list>

                        [ <else_statement> ] END


<when_statement_list> -> <when_statement> [ , <when_statement_list> ]

<when_statement>      -> WHEN <field_expression> THEN <field_expression>
```

```
<else_statement>        -> ELSE <field_expression>


<value>                 -> <string_value> |
                           <real>         |
                           <integer>      |
                           <timestamp>    |
                           NULL



<rel_op>                -> < | > | <> | = | <= | >=

<incl_op>               -> IN | NOT IN

<unary_op>              -> IS NULL | IS NOT NULL

<timestamp>             -> TIMESTAMP ( <string_value> , <timestamp_format> )

<timestamp_format>      -> ' *( <timestamp_separator> ) *( <timestamp_element>
                           *( <timestamp_separator> ) )'


<timestamp_element>     -> 1*4 y          |
                           1*4 M          |
                           MX | MP        |
                           1*4 d          |
                           dx | dp        |
                           1*2 h          |
                           hx | hp        |
                           1*2 m          |
                           mx | mp        |
                           1*2 s          |
                           sx | sp        |
                           1*2 l          |
                           lx | lp        |
                           1*2 n          |
                           nx | np        |
                           tt

<timestamp_separator> -> <any_char_except_timestamp_element> |
                         '?'
```

```
<field>                 -> '[' <field_name> ']'     |
                           <field_name>

<like_value>            -> ' *( <any_char> | % | _ ) '

<string_value>          -> ' *( <any_char> ) '

<comment>               -> '/*' <text> '*/'     |
                           '//' <text> CRLF
```

Field-Expressions

Field-expressions are the basic elements of any Log Parser SQL query; they define the values on which the various query clauses operate.

A field-expression is one of five possible elements:

- The name of a field.
- The alias of a field-expression.
- A function, taking zero or more field-expressions as arguments.
- An aggregate function, taking zero or more field-expressions as arguments.
- A constant.

Field Names

Field names are names of input record fields. The field-expression in the SELECT clause of the following query is one of the field names in the input records of the IISW3C input format:

```
SELECT cs-uri-stem
FROM extend1.log
```

Aliases

Aliases are alternative names that can be assigned to field-expressions for better readability. The field-expression in the WHERE clause of the following query is the alias of a field-expression in the SELECT clause:

```
SELECT cs-uri-stem AS Url
FROM extend1.log
WHERE Url LIKE '%.asp'
```

Functions

Functions are powerful elements of the Log Parser SQL language; virtually all queries written with the Log Parser SQL language make use of at least one function. Functions take zero or more field-expressions as arguments, process their values, and return a new value. The Log Parser SQL language supports more than 80 functions, ranging from string manipulation functions (for example, SUBSTR, STRCAT) to arithmetical functions (for example, ADD, EXP). The field-expression in the SELECT clause of the following query is a function, which takes two other field-expressions (in this case, field names) as arguments:

```
SELECT ADD(sc-bytes, cs-bytes)
FROM extend1.log
```

For each input record, this function calculates and returns the sum of the values of the two fields. For information on the functions supported by the Log Parser SQL language, refer to Appendix C.

Aggregate Functions

Aggregate functions are *special* functions in the SQL language. Similar to functions, aggregate functions take zero or more field-expressions as arguments, process their values, and return a new value. However, while functions operate on a single input record at a time, aggregate functions operate on *groups* of input records, returning a single value as the result of a calculation on all the input records belonging to a group. When a query does not use the GROUP BY clause, aggregate functions operate on the single group that includes all the input records. For this reason, queries whose SELECT clause contains aggregate functions return a single output record, whose values are the results of the aggregate functions calculated on all the input records. However, when a query uses the GROUP BY clause to define how input records should be grouped together, aggregate functions operate on each individual group. In this case, the query returns an output record for each group, containing the results of the aggregate functions calculated on the input records belonging to the group.

The Log Parser SQL language supports the following aggregate functions:

- COUNT
- SUM
- AVG
- MIN
- MAX
- PROPCOUNT
- PROPSUM
- GROUPING

COUNT Aggregate Function

The COUNT aggregate function calculates the number of items in a group.

This function has two distinct forms. The first form is:

```
COUNT( [ DISTINCT | ALL ] * )
```

When used with the * wildcard, the COUNT aggregate function returns the total number of input records belonging to a group. Using the DISTINCT keyword causes this function to calculate the number of *unique* input records only; using the ALL keyword (or not specifying a keyword) causes this function to calculate the number of *all* the input records, regardless of duplicates.

The second form of the COUNT aggregate function is:

```
COUNT( [ DISTINCT | ALL ] field-expression [ , field-expression … ] )
```

When used with a list of field-expressions as arguments, the COUNT aggregate function returns the total number of input records in which at least one of the specified field-expressions is non-NULL. The DISTINCT and ALL keywords have the same meaning as in the first form. In the Log Parser SQL language, the DISTINCT keyword is not allowed in aggregate functions when queries have a GROUP BY clause.

SUM and AVG Aggregate Functions

The SUM and AVG aggregate functions calculate the sum and the average of their arguments, respectively.

The syntax of these functions is:

```
SUM( [ DISTINCT | ALL ] field-expression )
AVG( [ DISTINCT | ALL ] field-expression )
```

Using the DISTINCT keyword causes these functions to calculate the sum or the average of the *unique* values of the specified field-expression; using the ALL keyword (or not specifying a keyword) causes these functions to calculate the sum or the average of *all* the values of the specified field-expression, regardless of duplicates. In the Log Parser SQL language, the DISTINCT keyword is not allowed in aggregate functions when queries have a GROUP BY clause.

MIN and MAX Aggregate Functions

The MIN and MAX aggregate functions calculate the minimum and the maximum values of their arguments, respectively.

The syntax of these functions is:

```
MIN( [ DISTINCT | ALL ] field-expression )
MAX( [ DISTINCT | ALL ] field-expression )
```

The DISTINCT keyword is supported only for compatibility with SQL standards, and it is meaningless with the MAX and MIN aggregate functions. In the Log Parser SQL language, the DISTINCT keyword is not allowed in aggregate functions when queries have a GROUP BY clause.

PROPCOUNT Aggregate Function

The PROPCOUNT aggregate function calculates the ratio of the number of records in the current group to the total number of records in the query or to the total number of records in a *larger* group containing the current group, thus yielding a *percentage* value.

The syntax of this function is:

```
PROPCOUNT( * ) [ ON field-expression [ , field-expression … ] ]
PROPCOUNT( field-expression [ , field-expression … ] ) [ ON field-expression [ , field-
expression … ] ]
```

The arguments of the PROPCOUNT aggregate function have the same meaning as the arguments of the COUNT aggregate function.

When the ON keyword is not specified, the PROPCOUNT aggregate function operates by calculating a COUNT aggregate function twice. In the first calculation, the COUNT aggregate function is calculated on the group identified by the GROUP BY clause of the query, as is the case with the simple COUNT function. In the second calculation, however, the same COUNT aggregate function is calculated on *all* the input records. The final value returned by the PROP-COUNT function is the ratio of the two values.

For example, consider the following query:

```
SELECT SourceName,
       EventID,
       PROPCOUNT(*)
FROM   System
GROUP BY SourceName,
         EventID
```

The value returned by the PROPCOUNT aggregate function in this example is the ratio of the values of the COUNT aggregate functions calculated by the following two queries:

```
SELECT SourceName,
       EventID,
       COUNT(*)
FROM   System
GROUP BY SourceName,
         EventID

SELECT COUNT(*)
FROM   System
```

When the ON keyword is specified, the second COUNT aggregate function is calculated on the group identified by the field-expressions following the ON keyword, rather than on all the input records. In this case, the list of field-expressions used with the ON keyword acts exactly like a separate GROUP BY clause, and identifies a group larger than the GROUP BY group.

For example, consider the following query:

```
SELECT SourceName,
       EventID,
       PROPCOUNT(*) ON SourceName
FROM   System
GROUP BY SourceName,
         EventID
```

The value returned by the PROPCOUNT aggregate function in this example is the ratio of the values of the COUNT aggregate functions calculated by the following two queries:

```
SELECT SourceName,
       EventID,
       COUNT(*)
FROM   System
GROUP BY SourceName,
         EventID


SELECT COUNT(*)
FROM   System
GROUP BY SourceName
```

Since the ON group must be a group larger than the GROUP BY group, its list of field-expressions must be a subset of the GROUP BY field-expressions, starting with the leftmost field-expression and appearing in the same order. In other words, if a query employs the following GROUP BY clause:

```
GROUP BY Field1, Field2, Field3
```

Then there are only two possible ON groups:

```
ON Field1
ON Field1, Field2
```

PROPSUM Aggregate Function

The PROPSUM aggregate function behaves exactly like the PROPCOUNT aggregate function, with the only difference being that PROPSUM returns the ratio of two SUM aggregate functions, rather than the ratio of two COUNT aggregate functions.

The syntax of this function is:

```
PROPSUM( field-expression ) [ ON field-expression [ , field-expression … ] ]
```

The argument of the PROPSUM aggregate function has the same meaning as the argument of the SUM aggregate function, and the ON keyword behaves like the ON keyword in the PROPCOUNT aggregate function.

GROUPING Aggregate Function

The GROUPING aggregate function is used in conjunction with the ROLLUP operator of the GROUP BY clause. Using the ROLLUP operator causes the query to produce additional output rows representing summary aggregate function calculations on the groups being processed, and these rows contain NULL values for the groups being summarized. The GROUPING aggregate function is used to indicate whether or not a NULL value in a row is a legitimate NULL value of the field-expression or if it is a NULL value generated by the ROLLUP operator.

The syntax of this function is:

```
GROUPING( field-expression )
```

The function returns 1 when the value of its argument field-expression is generated as NULL by the ROLLUP operator, and 0 when the value of its argument field-expression is not NULL, or it is NULL and it has not been generated by the ROLLUP operator.

Query Syntax

A Log Parser SQL query is defined as follows:

```
select_clause
[ using_clause ]
[ into_clause ]
from_clause
[ where_clause ]
[ group_by_clause ]
[ having_clause ]
[ order_by_clause ]
```

SELECT Clause

The SELECT clause specifies the field-expressions that will appear in the query *output records*. This syntax of the SELECT clause is:

```
SELECT [ TOP integer ] [ DISTINCT | ALL ] *
SELECT [ TOP integer ] [ DISTINCT | ALL ] selection_list
```

The TOP keyword specifies that the query should return only the first *n* output records.

The DISTINCT keyword specifies that duplicate output records should be discarded, while the ALL keyword (the default) specifies that all the output records will be returned, even duplicate ones.

When used with the * wildcard, the SELECT clause returns all the input record fields. For example, the output records of the following query contain all the fields of the EVT input format:

```
SELECT *
FROM SYSTEM
```

When used with a *selection_list*, the SELECT clause returns only the field-expressions specified in the *selection_list*. A *selection_list* is defined as follows:

```
field-expression [ AS alias ] [ , field-expression [ AS alias ] … ]
```

For example, the output records of the following query contain the specified two field-expressions only:

```
SELECT TO_UPPERCASE(SourceName),
       TimeGenerated
FROM SYSTEM
```

The field-expressions in the *selection_list* can be *aliased* with the AS keyword followed by a user-defined name. When this happens, the field-expression can be referenced anywhere else in the query by making use of its alias.

For example, the field-expression in the WHERE clause of the following query is the alias of a field-expression in the SELECT clause:

```
SELECT TO_LOWERCASE(cs-uri-stem) AS Url
FROM extend1.log
WHERE Url LIKE '%.asp'
```

If a query includes a GROUP BY clause, then the SELECT clause can only specify aggregate functions or field-expressions appearing in the GROUP BY clause.

Together with the FROM clause, the SELECT clause is one of the two mandatory clauses in Log Parser queries.

USING Clause

The USING clause defines a list of aliased field-expressions that can be referenced anywhere else in the query. The USING clause is a non-standard SQL language element, and its use is targeted at improving the readability of queries.

This syntax of the USING clause is:

```
USING field-expression AS alias [ , field-expression AS alias … ]
```

For example, the SELECT and WHERE clauses of the following query reference a field-expression defined in the USING clause:

```
SELECT cs-uri-stem, ClientAddress
USING REVERSEDNS(c-ip) AS ClientAddress
FROM extend1.log
WHERE ClientAddress <> 'CLIENT01'
```

INTO Clause

The INTO clause specifies the output target to which the currently selected output format should send the output records.

The syntax of the INTO clause is:

```
INTO into_entity
```

The *into_entity* element specifies the output target, and its syntax is dependent on the output format selected. For a description of the *into_entity* values supported by each output format, refer to Appendix E.

FROM Clause

The FROM clause specifies the input data source(s) to be processed by the currently selected input format.

The syntax of the FROM clause is:

```
FROM from_entity
```

The *from_entity* element specifies the input data source, and its syntax is dependent on the input format selected. For a description of the *from_entity* values supported by each input format, refer to Appendix D.

Together with the SELECT clause, the FROM clause is one of the two mandatory clauses in Log Parser queries.

WHERE Clause

The WHERE clause specifies one or more filtering conditions on the values of an input record. If the conditions are not satisfied, the input record is discarded.

The syntax of the WHERE clause is:

```
WHERE expression
```

An expression is a combination of "expression terms" joined together using the AND, OR, and NOT logical operators. An "expression term" can have one of eight different forms.

The first form is a simple relational comparison between two field-expressions:

```
field-expression > | < | = | <> | >= | <= field-expression
```

An example of this form would be:

```
WHERE cs-uri-stem = '/default.asp'
```

The second form is a relational comparison between a single field-expression and a list of constant values:

```
field-expression > | < | = | <> | >= | <= [ ALL | ANY ] ( value_rows )
```

The *value_rows* element is a list of *value_row* elements, separated by the semicolon character. In this form, each *value_row* element must be a single constant. The keyword ANY (the default) specifies that the expression term is satisfied when the comparison operator is true for at least *one* of the values in the right term list; the keyword ALL, on the other hand, specifies that the expression term is satisfied when the comparison operator is true for *all* of the values in the right term list.

```
An example of this form would be:
WHERE cs-bytes = ANY ( 100; 200; 500 )
```

The third form is a comparison between a *list* of field-expressions and a list of *lists* of constant values:

```
( field-expression , field-expression … ) > | < | = | <> | >= | <= [ ALL | ANY ] ( value_rows )
```

In this form, each *value_row* element must be a *list* of constants equaling in number the number of field-expressions on the left side, separated by the comma character. This form works similarly to the previous form, with the distinction that the operands of the comparison operator are multi-valued items, rather than single items.

An example of this form would be:

```
WHERE (cs-uri-stem, cs-bytes) = ANY
        ( '/default.asp', 100;
          '/index.htm', 200;
          '/index.htm', 500
        )
```

The fourth form is a case-insensitive string matching comparison:

```
field-expression [ NOT ] LIKE like_mask
```

The *like_mask* element is a string search pattern that can include any number of two special wildcard characters: the underscore character ('_'), meaning "any character", and the percent character ('%'), meaning "any substring".

An example of this form is:

```
WHERE cs-uri-stem LIKE '%.aspx'
```

The fifth form is a test for inclusion of a value in an interval:

```
field-expression [ NOT ] BETWEEN field-expression AND field-expression
```

The BETWEEN operator is satisfied when the value of the left field-expression is included in the interval whose boundaries are specified by the values of the right field-expressions.

An example of this form is:

```
WHERE TimeGenerated BETWEEN
      TIMESTAMP('2004-05-28 12:00:00', 'yyyy-MM-dd hh:mm:ss')
      AND
      TIMESTAMP('2004-06-06 23:59:59', 'yyyy-MM-dd hh:mm:ss')
```

The sixth form is a test for NULL values:

```
field-expression IS [ NOT ] NULL
```

The IS NULL operator is satisfied when the value of the left field-expression is NULL. An example of this form is:

```
WHERE cs-uri-query IS NULL
```

The seventh form is a test for inclusion of a value in a list of constants:

```
field-expression [ NOT ] IN ( value_rows )
```

The IN operator is satisfied when the value of the left field-expression appears in the list of constants on the right side of the operator.

An example of this form is:

```
WHERE c-ip IN ('192.168.1.100'; '192.168.1.101')
```

The eighth form is a test for inclusion of a multi-valued value in a list of multi-valued constants:

```
( field-expression , field-expression … ) [ NOT ] IN ( value_rows )
```

This form is similar to the previous form, with the only difference being that the values being compared are multi-valued items, rather than single values.

An example of this form is:

```
WHERE (cs-uri-stem, c-ip) IN
     ('/default.htm', '192.168.1.100';
      '/default.asp', '192.168.1.101'
     )
```

Since the conditions in a WHERE clause are applied to the values of an input record, these conditions cannot reference aggregate functions; the HAVING clause can be used to impose filtering conditions on the values of aggregate functions.

GROUP BY Clause

The GROUP BY clause specifies a list of field-expressions whose values are to be used as the grouping criteria when aggregating data. Input records that yield identical values for the GROUP BY field-expressions are considered to belong to the same group.

The syntax of the GROUP BY clause is:

```
GROUP BY field-expression [ , field-expression … ] [ WITH ROLLUP ]
```

When a query includes a GROUP BY clause, its SELECT clause can only specify aggregate functions or field-expressions that appear in the GROUP BY clause.

An example of a query using the GROUP BY clause is:

```
SELECT   cs-uri-stem,
         COUNT(*) AS Hits
```

```
FROM     <1>
GROUP BY cs-uri-stem
```

The ROLLUP operator generates additional output records that are constructed by applying group aggregations to all the hierarchical levels specified by the GROUP BY clause. For more information on the ROLLUP operator, consult the Log Parser documentation.

HAVING Clause

The HAVING clause specifies one or more filtering conditions on the values of the records generated by the group aggregation process specified with the GROUP BY clause and with the use of aggregate functions. The HAVING clause works in the same way as the WHERE clause, with the difference being that the conditions in the HAVING clause can reference aggregate functions, while the conditions in the WHERE clause cannot.

The syntax of the HAVING clause is:

```
HAVING expression
```

Expressions in the HAVING clause follow the same rules as the expressions in the WHERE clause. An example of a query using the HAVING clause is:

```
SELECT   cs-uri-stem,
         COUNT(*) AS Hits
FROM     <1>
GROUP BY cs-uri-stem
HAVING   Hits > 10
```

ORDER BY Clause

The ORDER BY clause specifies sorting criteria on output record values.

The syntax of the ORDER BY clause is:

```
ORDER BY field-expression [ , field-expression … ] [ ASC | DESC ]
```

When an ORDER BY clause is used, the query output records are sorted according to the values of the specified field-expressions, in either ascending order (the default), or in descending order, depending on the use of the ASC or DESC keywords.

Different from the standard SQL language, the Log Parser SQL language requires that the field-expressions in the ORDER BY clause appear in the SELECT clause as well.

Appendix C

Function Reference

In This Toolbox

Functions are powerful elements of the Log Parser SQL language; virtually all queries written with the Log Parser SQL language make use of at least one function. Functions take zero or more field-expressions as arguments, process their values, and return a new value. The Log Parser SQL language supports more than 80 functions, ranging from string manipulation functions (for example, SUBSTR, STRCAT) to arithmetical functions (for example, ADD, EXP).

Functions

The ADD function returns the sum of the two argument values.

```
ADD( addend1 <any type>, addend2 <any type> )
```

When the arguments are of the STRING type, the value returned is the concatenation of the strings.

```
BIT_AND( arg1 <INTEGER>, arg2 <INTEGER> )
BIT_NOT( arg <INTEGER> )
BIT_OR( arg1 <INTEGER>, arg2 <INTEGER> )
BIT_SHL( arg1 <INTEGER>, arg2 <INTEGER> )
BIT_SHR( arg1 <INTEGER>, arg2 <INTEGER> )
BIT_XOR( arg1 <INTEGER>, arg2 <INTEGER> )
```

The BIT… functions calculate the specified bitwise operators on the argument values.

```
CASE <field_expression>
  WHEN <field_expression> THEN <field_expression>

    [ ... ]
    [ ELSE <field_expression> ]
  END
```

The CASE function compares the value of the specified field-expression with the values of the field-expressions in the WHEN statements, returning the value of the field-expression specified in a THEN statement when a match is found. If no match is found, the value of the ELSE statement field-expression is returned, or NULL if no ELSE statement is provided.

```
COALESCE( arg1 <any type>, arg2 <any type> [, ....] )
```

The COALESCE function returns the first non-NULL value found among the specified arguments. The following example returns **First Value**:

```
COALESCE( NULL, NULL, 'First value', 'Second value')
```

```
COMPUTER_NAME()
```

The COMPUTER_NAME function returns the name of the local computer.

```
DIV( dividend <INTEGER | REAL>, divisor <INTEGER | REAL> )
```

The DIV function returns the quotient of the two argument values.

```
    EXP( argument <INTEGER | REAL> )
EXP10( argument <INTEGER | REAL> )
```

The EXP and EXP10 functions return the natural exponential and the base-10 exponential of their arguments.

```
    EXTRACT_EXTENSION( filepath <STRING> )

    EXTRACT_FILENAME( filepath <STRING> )
EXTRACT_PATH( filepath <STRING> )
```

These functions return the extension, filename, or path portions of a STRING value representing the full path of a file.

```
EXTRACT_PREFIX( argument <STRING>, index <INTEGER>, separator <STRING> )
```

The EXTRACT_PREFIX function returns the prefix of the specified argument string up to the nth appearance of the specified separator. Negative values of the *index* argument are relative to the end of the string.

```
EXTRACT_SUFFIX( argument <STRING>, index <INTEGER>, separator <STRING> )
```

The EXTRACT_SUFFIX function returns the suffix of the specified argument following the nth appearance – in a right-to-left order - of the specified separator. Negative values of the *index* argument are relative to the beginning of the string.

```
EXTRACT_TOKEN( argument <STRING>, index <INTEGER> [ , separator <STRING> ] )
```

The EXTRACT_TOKEN function returns the portion of the specified argument string enclosed within the nth appearance of the specified separator and the next. Negative values of the *index* argument are relative to the end of the string.

```
EXTRACT_VALUE( argument <STRING>, key <STRING> [ , separator <STRING> ] )
```

The EXTRACT_VALUE function parses *key=value* pairs in the argument string, returning the value of the pair whose key matches the specified argument. The *separator* argument specifies the separator used between the pairs, and its default value is *&*.

```
FLOOR( argument <REAL> )
```

The FLOOR function returns the largest integer less than or equal to the specified value. The following example returns **5**:

```
FLOOR( 5.9 )
```

```
HASHMD5_FILE( filePath <STRING> )
```

The HASHMD5_FILE function returns a string containing the MD5 hash of the content of the specified file.

```
HASHSEQ( value <STRING> )
```

The HASHSEQ function returns a sequential integer for each distinct value of the specified argument.

`HEX_TO_ASC( hexString <STRING> )`

The HEX_TO_ASC function converts a hexadecimal representation of the characters in a string to the string itself, considering only characters belonging to the 0x20–0x7f ASCII character range. Characters outside of this range are returned as period characters.

`HEX_TO_HEX16( hexString <STRING> [ , bigEndian <INTEGER> ] )`

`HEX_TO_HEX32( hexString <STRING> [ , bigEndian <INTEGER> ] )`

`HEX_TO_HEX8( hexString <STRING> )`

These functions convert a hexadecimal representation of an integer to another hexadecimal representation where the individual bytes are grouped together according to the number of bits specified. When the *bigEndian* argument is different than 0, the conversion assumes that the hexadecimal representation of the integer is in the big-endian form.

`HEX_TO_INT( hexString <STRING> )`

The HEX_TO_INT function converts a hexadecimal representation of an integer to the integer itself.

`HEX_TO_PRINT( hexString <STRING> )`

The HEX_TO_PRINT function converts a hexadecimal representation of the characters in a string to the string itself, considering only characters that are printable. Non-printable characters are returned as period characters.

`IN_ROW_NUMBER()`

The IN_ROW_NUMBER returns the sequential index of the input record currently being processed.

`INDEX_OF( string <STRING>, searchStr <STRING> )`

The INDEX_OF function returns the 0–based index of the first appearance of the specified search string in the first argument.

`INT_TO_IPV4( ipV4Address <INTEGER> )`

The INT_TO_IPV4 function converts a 32-bit integer containing the network value of an IPV4 address to the string representation of the address.

`IPV4_TO_INT( ipV4Address <STRING> )`

The IPV4_TO_INT function parses the string representation of an IPV4 address and returns a 32-bit integer containing the network value of the address.

`LAST_INDEX_OF( string <STRING>, searchStr <STRING> )`

The LAST_INDEX_OF function returns the 0–based index of the last appearance of the specified search string in the first argument.

```
  LOG( argument <INTEGER | REAL> )
LOG10( argument <INTEGER | REAL> )
```

The LOG and LOG10 functions return the natural logarithm and the base-10 logarithm of their arguments.

```
LTRIM( string <STRING> )
```

The LTRIM function returns a left-trimmed version of the argument string.

```
MOD( dividend <INTEGER | REAL>, divisor <INTEGER | REAL> )
```

The MOD function returns the remainder of the quotient of its argument.

```
MUL( multiplicand <INTEGER | REAL>, multiplier <INTEGER | REAL> )
```

The MUL function returns the multiplication of its arguments.

```
OUT_ROW_NUMBER()
```

The OUT_ROW_NUMBER function returns the sequential index of the output record being generated. This function can only appear in the SELECT and ORDER BY clauses.

```
QNTFLOOR_TO_DIGIT( value <INTEGER>, digits <INTEGER> )

QNTROUND_TO_DIGIT( value <INTEGER>, digits <INTEGER> )
```

The QNTFLOOR_TO_DIGIT and QNTROUND_TO_DIGIT functions return the first argument value truncated or rounded to the nearest power of ten having the specified number of significant digits. These functions are commonly used in GROUP BY clauses to group input records based on *categories* of numerical values.

The following example returns **12400**:

```
QNTFLOOR_TO_DIGIT( 12475, 3 )
```

The following example returns **10000**:

```
QNTFLOOR_TO_DIGIT( 12475, 1 )
```

The following example returns **12500**:

```
QNTROUND_TO_DIGIT( 12475, 3 )
```

```
QUANTIZE( argument <INTEGER | REAL | TIMESTAMP>,

          quantization <INTEGER | REAL> )
```

The QUANTIZE function returns the multiple of the specified quantization argument nearest to the value of the first argument. When used with an argument of the TIMESTAMP type, the function interprets the quantization argument as a number of seconds.

The following example returns **12460**:

```
QUANTIZE( 12475, 20 )
```

The following example returns **11:35:30**:

```
QUANTIZE( TO_TIMESTAMP( '11:35:47', 'hh:mm:ss' ), 30 )
```

```
REPLACE_CHR( string <STRING>, searchCharacters <STRING>,
        replaceString <STRING> )
```
The REPLACE_CHR function returns its first argument after replacing each instance of any of the characters in the specified search string with an instance of the specified replace string.

```
REPLACE_IF_NOT_NULL( argument <any type>, replaceValue <any type> )
```
The REPLACE_IF_NOT_NULL function returns the second argument when the first argument is not NULL. If the first argument is NULL, the function returns NULL.

```
REPLACE_STR( string <STRING>, searchString <STRING>, replaceString <STRING> )
```
The REPLACE_STR function returns its first argument after replacing each instance of the specified search string with an instance of the specified replace string.

```
RESOLVE_SID( sid <STRING> [ , computerName <STRING> ] )
```
The RESOLVE_SID function resolves the SID specified in the first argument and returns the full account name represented by the SID. The optional *computerName* argument specifies a remote computer where the account is defined.

```
REVERSEDNS( ipAddress <STRING> )
```
The REVERSEDNS function resolves the specified IP address returning the corresponding host name.

```
ROT13( string <STRING> )
```
The ROT13 function returns the ROT13 encoding or decoding of the specified value.

```
ROUND( argument <REAL> )
```
The ROUND function returns the integer nearest to the specified value.

```
RTRIM( string <STRING> )
```
The RTRIM function returns a right-trimmed version of the argument string.

```
SEQUENCE( [ startValue <INTEGER> ] )
```
The SEQUENCE function returns a new sequential integer for each input record. The optional *startValue* argument specifies the initial value of the sequence.

```
SQR( argument <INTEGER | REAL> )
```
The SQR function returns the square of its argument.

```
SQRROOT( argument <INTEGER | REAL> )
```
The SQRROOT function returns the square root of its argument.

`STRCAT( string1 <STRING>, string2 <STRING> )`

The STRCAT function returns the concatenation of the specified strings.

`STRCNT( string <STRING>, token <STRING> )`

The STRCNT function returns the number of times that the specified token appears in the first argument.

`STRLEN( string <STRING> )`

The STRLEN function returns the length of the specified string.

`STRREPEAT( string <STRING>, count <INTEGER> )`

The STRREPEAT function returns a string built by concatenating the first argument with itself for the number of times specified by the second argument.

`STRREV( string <STRING> )`

The STRREV function returns the argument string reversed.

`SUB( minuend <any type>, subtrahend <any type> )`

The SUB function returns the difference of the two arguments. When the arguments are of the STRING type, the value returned is the substring of the first argument that remains after removing the second argument from the beginning of the string.

`SUBSTR( string <STRING>, start <INTEGER> [ , length <INTEGER> ])`

The SUBSTR function returns the substring of the first argument that starts at the character with the specified index. The optional *length* argument specifies the length of the substring to return.

`SYSTEM_DATE()`
`SYSTEM_TIME()`

`SYSTEM_TIMESTAMP()`

These functions return the current date, the current time, and the current full date and time, respectively. The TIMESTAMP value returned is in Universal Time Coordinates (UTC).

`SYSTEM_UTCOFFSET()`

The SYSTEM_UTCOFFSET function returns a TIMESTAMP value representing the absolute bias of the local time zone.

`TO_DATE( timestamp <TIMESTAMP> )`

The TO_DATE function returns a TIMESTAMP value that contains the date portion only of the specified argument.

`TO_HEX( argument <INTEGER | STRING> )`

The TO_HEX function returns a string containing the hexadecimal representation of the specified integer, or of the characters in the specified string.

`TO_INT( argument <any type> )`

The TO_INT function returns its argument converted to an INTEGER value. If the type of its argument is a TIMESTAMP value, the value returned is the number of seconds elapsed since January 1, year 0.

`TO_LOCALTIME( timestamp <TIMESTAMP> )`

The TO_LOCALTIME function returns the result of converting the argument timestamp to local time coordinates.

`TO_LOWERCASE( string <STRING> )`

The TO_LOWERCASE function returns the argument string after converting its alphabetical characters to their corresponding lower-case characters.

`TO_REAL( argument <any type> )`

The TO_REAL function returns its argument converted to a REAL value. If the type of its argument is a TIMESTAMP value, the value returned is the fractional number of seconds elapsed since January 1, year 0.

`TO_STRING( argument <INTEGER | REAL> )`
`TO_STRING( timestamp <TIMESTAMP>, format <STRING> )`

When used with INTEGER or REAL arguments, the TO_STRING function returns a string representing the specified INTEGER or REAL value.
When used with a TIMESTAMP argument, the TO_STRING function returns a string containing the specified TIMESTAMP value formatted according to the specifiers described with the *format* argument.

`TO_TIME( timestamp <TIMESTAMP> )`

The TO_TIME function returns a TIMESTAMP value that contains the time portion only of the specified argument.

`TO_TIMESTAMP( dateTime1 <TIMESTAMP>, dateTime2 <TIMESTAMP> )`
`TO_TIMESTAMP( string <STRING>, format <STRING> )`
`TO_TIMESTAMP( seconds <INTEGER | REAL> )`

When used with TIMESTAMP arguments, the TO_TIMESTAMP function returns a TIMESTAMP value built after merging the data portion and the time portion of the specified arguments.

When used with STRING arguments, the TO_TIMESTAMP function parses the string representation of a date and/or time specified as the first argument according to the format specifiers described with the *format* argument, returning the resulting TIMESTAMP value.
When used with INTEGER or REAL arguments, the TO_TIMESTAMP function returns the TIMESTAMP value of the instant of time corresponding to the specified number of seconds since January 1, year 0.

`TO_UPPERCASE( string <STRING> )`

The TO_UPPERCASE function returns the argument string after converting its alphabetical characters to their corresponding upper-case characters.

`TO_UTCTIME( timestamp <TIMESTAMP> )`

The TO_UTCTIME function returns the result of converting the argument timestamp to Universal Time Coordinates (UTC) time.

`TRIM( string <STRING> )`

The TRIM function returns a left-trimmed and right-trimmed version of the argument string.

`URLESCAPE( url <STRING> [ , codepage <INTEGER> ] )`

The URLESCAPE function returns a hex-encoded version of the argument string. The optional *codepage* argument specifies the target encoding codepage.

`URLUNESCAPE( url <STRING> [ , codepage <INTEGER> ] )`

The URLUNESCAPE function returns a decoded version of the hex-encoded argument string. The optional *codepage* argument specifies the source encoding codepage.

`WIN32_ERROR_DESCRIPTION( win32ErrorCode <INTEGER> )`

The WIN32_ERROR_DESCRIPTION function returns the Windows error message corresponding to the specified error code.

Appendix D

Input Format Reference

- ADS Input Format
- BIN Input Format
- COM Input Format
- CSV Input Format
- ETW Input Format
- EVT Input Format
- FS Input Format
- HTTPERR Input Format
- IIS Input Format
- IISODBC Input Format
- IISW3C Input Format
- NCSA Input Format
- NETMON Input Format
- REG Input Format
- TEXTLINE Input Format
- TEXTWORD Input Format
- TSV Input Format
- URLSCAN Input Format
- W3C Input Format
- XML Input Format

In This Toolbox

Log Parser 2.2 provides 20 input formats that can be used to parse a wide variety of text file formats (all the IIS log file formats, generic NCSA log files, CSV, TSV, and XML text files), to parse specialized binary files (NetMon files, ETW trace files), and to retrieve system information (Event Log, files and directories, registry keys, and Active Directory objects).

ADS Input Format

The Active Directory Services (ADS) input format returns properties of Active Directory objects. This input format works in two different modes. In *property mode*, the ADS input format returns an input record for each property of each Active Directory object enumerated under the Active Directory path specified in the query FROM clause. In *object mode*, users specify the name of an Active Directory object class, and the ADS input format returns an input record for each Active Directory object that is an instance of the specified class found under the Active Directory path specified in the query FROM clause.

From-Entity

The ADS input format accepts FROM clause values with the following syntax:

`[[provider:]//[username:password@]domain]/path [; ...]`

- **Provider** This is the name of the Active Directory provider, for example, LDAP (Lightweight Directory Access Protocol) or IIS. When not specified, IIS is assumed by default.

- **Username and password** This is optional authentication information for the connection to the AD provider. When not specified, the ADS input format uses the current user's credentials.

- **Domain** This is the name of the domain where the provider resides. When not specified, localhost is assumed by default.

- **Path** This is the Active Directory path containing the Active Directory objects that will be enumerated by the ADS input format.

Fields

When working in property mode, the ADS input format generates input records with the following fields:

- ObjectPath
- ObjectName
- ObjectClass
- PropertyName
- PropertyValue

- PropertyType

When working in object mode, the ADS input format generates input records with the following fields:

- ObjectPath
- A field for each property of the specified Active Directory object class

Parameters

- **objClass** Specifies the name of an Active Directory object class to be used in object mode. When this parameter is left unspecified, the ADS input format works in property mode.

- **username** Specifies the username to be used for the connection to the AD provider. If left unspecified, the ADS input format uses the current user's credentials.

- **password** Specifies the password for the user account specified for the **username** parameter.

- **recurse** Specifies the maximum directory depth reached while enumerating Active Directory objects.

- **multiValuedSep** Specifies the string to be used as a separator between the values of multi-valued object properties.

- **ignoreDSErrors** When set to **ON**, the ADS input format ignores errors occurring during the enumeration of Active Directory objects. When set to **OFF**, the ADS input format returns errors as *parse errors*.

- **parseBinary** When set to **ON**, the ADS input format returns object properties that contain binary data. When set to **OFF**, binary properties are not returned.

- **binaryFormat** Specifies the format of binary data as one of the ASC, HEX, or PRINT values.

BIN Input Format

The BIN input format parses the centralized binary log files generated by IIS version 6.0 and later.

From-Entity

The BIN input format accepts FROM clause values with the following syntax:

filename | *siteID* [, *filename* | *siteID* ...]

- **Filename** This is the path to an IIS binary log file; the path can contain wildcards and can be in UNC (universal naming convention) notation if specifying log files on a remote share.

- **SiteID** This is the Metabase path of an IIS virtual site, enclosed in angled brackets; the Metabase path can be a full path that includes a remote server name (for example, **<//Mycomputer/W3SVC/12>**), or it can simply be the site's numeric identifier or the site's **ServerComment** property value (for example, **<12>**, **<www.mysite.com>**), eventually including wildcards.

Fields

The BIN input format generates input records containing the following fields:

- LogFilename
- LogRow
- ComputerName
- SiteID
- DateTime
- ClientIpAddress
- ServerIpAddress
- ServerPort
- Method
- ProtocolVersion

- ProtocolStatus
- SubStatus
- TimeTaken
- BytesSent
- BytesReceived
- Win32Status
- UriStem
- UriQuery
- UserName

COM Input Format

The COM input format encapsulates custom input format plug-ins, making it possible for users to interact with these plug-ins through the Log Parser command-line executable.

From-Entity

The COM input format accepts any FROM clause value supported by the custom input format plug-in being used.

Parameters

- **iProgID** Specifies the progID of the COM object implementing the custom input format being used.

- **iCOMParams** Specifies values for the optional properties exposed by the custom input format plug-in. The value specified for this parameter has the following format:

  property_name=value[,property_name=value…]

- **iCOMServer** Specifies the computer name on which the COM object implementing the custom input format plug-in should be initiated.

CSV Input Format

The CSV input format parses comma-separated values text files. This input format works with a two-stage approach. During an initial *inspection stage*, the input format inspects a configurable number of lines in the CSV files to determine the number of fields, the field types, and the field names of the columns contained in the files. After the number of fields, their types, and their names has been determined, the real *parsing stage* begins, in which the files are parsed again from beginning to end, and input records are generated to be processed by the query.

From-Entity

The CSV input format accepts FROM clause values with the following syntax:

```
filename [, filename …] |
http://url              |
STDIN
```

- **Filename** This is the path to a CSV file; the path can contain wildcards and can be in UNC notation if specifying files on a remote share.

- **URL** This is the URL (uniform resource locator) of a resource formatted as CSV text.

- **STDIN** This special keyword specifies that the CSV input format should read the input data from the console input. This value is mostly used when piping commands and using the output of a command as the input of a Log Parser query.

Fields

The CSV input format generates input records containing the following fields:

- Filename
- RowNumber
- A field for each column in the input CSV file(s)

Parameters

- **headerRow** When set to **ON**, the CSV input format assumes that the file(s) being parsed contain a header line declaring the names of the columns in the file(s), and it extracts the column names from this line. When set to **OFF**, the CSV input format assumes that each file being parsed begins with the first line of data.

- **iHeaderFile** Specifies the path to a CSV text file containing a header line declaring the names of the columns in the file(s) being parsed. The column names found in the specified header file override the eventual column names declared by the header line in the file(s) being parsed.

- **fixedFields** When set to **ON**, the CSV input format assumes that all the lines in the CSV file(s) being parsed contain the same number of fields, and thus it determines the number of fields by inspecting the very first line in the file(s) being parsed. When set to **OFF**, lines can have a variable number of fields, and the CSV input format determines the number of fields by inspecting the number of initial lines specified by the value of the **dtLines** parameter.

- **nFields** This parameter can be used to specify directly the number of fields (columns) contained in the CSV file(s) being parsed. When this parameter is set to **–1** (the default value), the CSV input format determines the number of fields automatically during the initial inspection stage.

- **dtLines** Specifies the number of initial lines to be inspected during the initial inspection stage to determine the number of fields, the field types, and the field names of the columns contained in the file(s).

- **iDQuotes** When set to **AUTO**, the CSV input format properly processes field values enclosed in double-quote characters, ignoring spaces and comma characters within the values, and stripping the double-quote characters before returning the values; when set to **OFF**, the CSV input format returns field values as they appear in the file(s) being processed, ignoring the presence of eventual double-quote characters.

- **nSkipLines** This parameter specifies the number of lines that the CSV input format should skip in each file before it starts parsing its data.

- **comment** Specifies the prefix of comment lines that should not be parsed as data.

- **iCodepage** Specifies the numeric identifier of the codepage of the file(s) being parsed.

- **iTsFormat** Specifies the format of the timestamp values contained in the file(s) being parsed.

- **iCheckpoint** Specifies the path of the checkpoint file to use when parsing the input file(s) incrementally.

ETW Input Format

The ETW input format parses Enterprise Tracing for Windows trace log files and live tracing sessions. ETW traces contain debugging and performance information generated by one or more *providers*. This input format works in four different modes, selectable through the **fMode** parameter. In *compact* mode, the ETW input format returns an input record for each event found in the trace being parsed; the input record contains a few fields common to all the ETW events, and a single **UserData** field containing the values of all the event-specific properties concatenated with each other. In *fnames* mode, the ETW input format behaves exactly as in the compact mode, but each event-specific property value is prefixed by the name of the property. In *full* mode, the ETW input format returns the value of each event-specific property as a field of its own. Finally, in *meta* mode, the ETW input format returns meta-information about the events being parsed; in this mode, input records correspond to individual properties of events.

When the full or meta modes are selected, the ETW input format works with a two-stage approach. During an initial inspection stage, the input format inspects a configurable number of events in the trace files to determine the providers whose events are contained in the traces. After the providers have been identified, the real parsing stage begins, in which the traces are parsed again from beginning to end, and input records are generated to be processed by the query.

From-Entity

The ETW input format accepts FROM clause values with the following syntax:

```
filename [, filename ...] |
session
```

- **Filename** This is the path to an ETW trace log file (.etl file). The path can contain wildcards and can be in UNC notation if specifying log files on a remote share.
- **Session** This is the name of a live ETW trace session.

Fields

In compact and fnames modes, the ETW input format generates input records containing the following fields:

- EventNumber
- EventName
- EventTypeName
- Timestamp
- UserData

In full mode, the ETW input format generates input records containing the following fields:

- TraceName
- EventNumber
- Timestamp
- InstanceID
- ParentInstanceID
- ParentGUID
- ProviderDescription
- ProviderGUID
- EventName
- EventDescription
- EventVersion
- EventGUID

- EventType
- EventTypeName
- EventTypeDescription
- EventTypeLevel
- ThreadID
- ProcessID
- KernelTime
- UserTime
- A field for each property of each event of each provided detected in the input trace(s)

In meta mode, the ETW input format generates input records containing the following fields:

- ProviderDescription
- ProviderClassName
- ProviderGUID
- EventName
- EventDescription
- EventVersion
- EventClassName
- EventGUID
- EventType

- EventTypeName
- EventTypeDescription
- EventTypeClassName
- EventTypeLevel
- FieldName
- FieldDescription
- FieldIndex
- FieldType

Parameters

- **fMode** Specifies one of the four possible ETW input format operation modes described above; possible values are compact, fnames, full, and meta.

- **providers** Specifies the providers whose events are contained in the trace(s) being parsed. This parameter can be specified as a comma-separated list of provider names or GUIDs, or as the path of a text file containing a provider GUID on each line. If this parameter is not specified, the ETW input format detects the providers automatically by inspecting the first dtEventsLog or dtEventsLive events in the trace(s) being parsed. This parameter is used in the full or meta modes only.

- **dtEventsLog** Specifies the number of events to pre-process during the inspection stage in order to determine which providers have logged events in the trace log file(s) being parsed. This parameter is used in the full or meta modes only when the **providers** parameter is not specified.

- **dtEventsLive** Specifies the number of events to pre-process during the inspection stage in order to determine which providers have logged events in the live trace session being parsed. This parameter is used in the full or meta modes only when the **providers** parameter is not specified.

- **flushPeriod** Frequency of live session buffer flushes, in milliseconds.

- **ignoreEventTrace** When set to **ON**, the ETW input format ignores the **EventTrace** event that appears at the beginning of ETW trace files. When set to **OFF**, these **EventTrace** events are returned to the user instead.

- **compactModeSep** Separator to be used between the event property values returned in the **UserData** field when operating in compact or fnames modes.

- **expandEnums** When **ON**, the ETW input format expands enumeration values; when **OFF**, enumeration values are returned as unprocessed integer values.

- **ignoreLostEvents** When this parameter is set to **ON**, the number of lost events reported by the ETW infrastructure is ignored. When set to **OFF**, the ETW input format returns a final warning containing the total number of lost events reported by the ETW infrastructure while parsing the input trace(s).

- **schemaServer** Specifies the name of a remote computer whose Windows Management Instrumentation (WMI) repository contains the schema description of the events in the trace(s) being parsed. When this parameter is not specified, the ETW input format uses the WMI repository on the computer where the trace(s) are being parsed from.

EVT Input Format

The EVT input format parses the Windows Event Log and Event Log (.evt) backup files, returning an input record for each event being parsed.

From-Entity

The EVT input format accepts FROM clause values with the following syntax:

`[\\computername\] eventlogname | filename [,…]`

- **Computername** Optional, this is the name of the remote computer containing the event log to be parsed.

- **Eventlogname** Name of the event log to be parsed, such as standard Event Log names (System, Security, Application) or custom Event Log names.

- **Filename** Path to an .evt Event Log backup file; the path can contain wildcards and can be in UNC notation if specifying Event Log backup files on a remote share.

Fields

The EVT input format generates input records containing the following fields:

- EventLog
- EventNumber
- TimeGenerated
- TimeWritten
- EventID
- EventType
- EventTypeName
- EventCategory
- EventCategoryName
- SourceName
- Strings
- ComputerName
- SID
- Message
- Data

Parameters

- **fullText** When set to **ON** (the default), the EVT input format retrieves the text of the event log message; when set to **OFF**, the EVT input format does not retrieve the message text.

- **resolveSIDs** When set to **ON**, the EVT input format resolves the event log SID into a full account name. When set to **OFF** (the default), the EVT input format returns the SID in alphanumerical form.

- **formatMsg** When set to **ON**, the EVT input format removes multiple white space characters and carriage-return/line-feed characters from the event log message to preserve readability. When set to **OFF**, the event log message is returned as is.

- **msgErrorMode** Setting this parameter to **NULL** causes the **Message** or **EventCategoryName** fields to be returned as NULL when their text value cannot be retrieved. Setting this parameter to **ERROR** causes the EVT input format to return a *parse error* in these situations, and setting this parameter to **MSG** causes the EVT input format to return an error message as the value of the **Message** or **EventCategoryName** fields.

- **fullEventCode** When set to **ON**, the EVT input format returns the full 32-bit value of the EventID field. When set to **OFF** (the default), the EVT input format returns only the lower 16 bits of the **EventID** field, as displayed by the Windows Event Viewer.

- **direction** When set to **FW** (the default), events are returned from the oldest to the newest. When set to **BW**, events are returned from the newest to the oldest.

- **stringsSep** This parameter specifies the string used as a separator between the values of the **Strings** field. The default value is the pipe (|) character.

- **iCheckpoint** Specifies the path of the checkpoint file to use when parsing the input file(s) incrementally.

- **binaryFormat** Specifies the format of the binary data returned in the **Data** field as one of the **ASC**, **HEX**, or **PRINT** values.

FS Input Format

The FS input format returns properties of files and directories.

From-Entity

The FS input format accepts FROM clause values with the following syntax:

`path [, path ...]`

- **Path** Path to a file or to a directory, eventually containing wildcards.

Fields

The FS input format generates input records with the following fields:

- Path
- Name
- Size
- Attributes
- CreationTime
- LastAccessTime
- LastWriteTime

- FileVersion
- ProductVersion
- InternalName
- ProductName
- CompanyName
- LegalCopyright
- LegalTrademarks
- PrivateBuild
- SpecialBuild
- Comments
- FileDescription
- OriginalFilename

Parameters

- **recurse** Specifies the number of subdirectories to recurse into. The special **-1** value means *unlimited recursion*.

- **preserveLastAccTime** Specifying **ON** for this value causes the FS input format to restore the last access time attribute of each file visited during the enumeration. When this parameter is **OFF**, files that are visited by the FS input format will have their last access time attribute modified.

- **useLocalTime** Specifying **ON** for this value causes the FS input format to return timestamp values relative to the local time zone. When this parameter is **OFF**, timestamp values are returned in Universal Time Coordinates (UTC) time.

HTTPERR Input Format

The HTTPERR input format parses the HTTP Error log files generated by the Http.sys Windows HTTP driver. These log files contain entries for HTTP (Hypertext Transfer Protocol) requests that generated abnormal errors on the server computer, such as 400 errors, and connections that hit a timeout.

From-Entity

The HTTP input format accepts FROM clause values with the following syntax:

```
filename [, filename ...] |
```

HTTPERR

- **Filename** Path to an HTTP Error log file.
- **HTTPERR** This keyword specifies that the user wants to parse all the HTTP Error log files available on the local computer.

Fields

The HTTPERR input format generates input records with the following fields:

- LogFilename
- LogRow
- date
- time
- s-computername
- c-ip
- c-port
- s-ip
- s-port
- cs-version
- cs-method
- cs-uri

- cs(User-Agent)
- cs(Cookie)
- cs(Referer)
- cs-host
- sc-status
- sc-bytes
- cs-bytes
- time-taken
- s-siteid
- s-reason
- s-queuename

Parameters

- **iCodepage** Specifies the numeric identifier of the codepage of the file(s) being parsed.
- **minDateMod** Specifies the minimum value of the last date modified attribute of a log file for the file to be parsed.
- **dirTime** When set to **ON**, the HTTPERR input format fills in missing **date** and **time** field values with the value of the **#Fields** directive.
- **iCheckpoint** Specifies the path of the checkpoint file to use when parsing the input file(s) incrementally.

IIS Input Format

The IIS input format parses IIS log files in the Microsoft IIS Log File Format.

From-Entity

The IIS input format accepts FROM clause values with the following syntax:

filename | siteID [, filename | siteID ...]

- **Filename** This is the path to a log file in the Microsoft IIS Log File Format; the path can contain wildcards and can be in UNC notation if specifying log files on a remote share.

- **SiteID** This is the Metabase path of an IIS virtual site, enclosed in angled brackets; the Metabase path can be a full path that includes a remote server name (for example, **<//Mycomputer/W3SVC/12>**), or it can simply be the site's numeric identifier or the site's **ServerComment** property value (for example, **<12>**, **<www.mysite.com>**), eventually including wildcards.

Fields

The IIS input format generates input records containing the following fields:

- LogFilename
- LogRow
- UserIP
- UserName
- Date
- Time
- ServiceInstance
- HostName
- ServerIP

- TimeTaken
- BytesSent
- BytesReceived
- StatusCode
- Win32StatusCode
- RequestType
- Target
- Parameters

Parameters

- **iCodepage** Specifies the numeric identifier of the codepage of the file(s) being parsed. The special **–1** value means UNICODE, and the special **–2** value causes the IIS input format to automatically detect the codepage from the log file name and from the **LogInUTF8** property of the virtual site.

- **recurse** Specifies the number of subdirectories to recurse into. The special **–1** value means *unlimited recursion*.

- **minDateMod** Specifies the minimum value of the last date modified attribute of a log file for the file to be parsed.

- **locale** The 3-letter Locale ID whose date and time format has been used to generate values for the **Date** and **Time** fields.

- **iCheckpoint** Specifies the path of the checkpoint file to use when parsing the input file(s) incrementally.

IISODBC Input Format

The IISODBC input format returns records from the database tables to which Microsoft IIS logs Web requests when configured to log using the ODBC Log Format.

From-Entity

The IISODBC input format accepts FROM clause values with the following syntax:

```
siteID [,siteID …] |
table:tablename;username:username;password:password;dsn:dsn
```

- **SiteID** This is the Metabase path of an IIS virtual site, enclosed in angled brackets; the Metabase path can be a full path that includes a remote server name (for example, **<//Mycomputer/W3SVC/12>**), or it can simply be the site's numeric identifier or the site's **ServerComment** property value (for example, **<12>**, **<www.mysite.com>**), eventually including wildcards.

- **Tablename** Name of the table where the IIS Web server logs web requests.

- **Username** User account to be used when connecting to the database.

- **Password** Password for the database connection.

- **DSN** Data Source Name containing information about the database connection.

Fields

The IISODBC input format generates input records containing the following fields:

- ClientHost
- Username
- LogTime
- Service
- Machine
- ServerIP
- ProcessingTime

- BytesRecvd
- BytesSent
- ServiceStatus
- Win32Status
- Operation
- Target
- Parameters

IISW3C Input Format

The IISW3C input format parses IIS log files in the W3C Extended Log File Format.

From-Entity

The IISW3C input format accepts FROM clause values with the following syntax:

```
filename | siteID [, filename | siteID ...]
```

- **Filename** This is the path to an IIS log file in the W3C Extended Log File Format; the path can contain wildcards and can be in UNC notation if specifying log files on a remote share.

- **SiteID** This is the Metabase path of an IIS virtual site, enclosed in angled brackets; the Metabase path can be a full path that includes a remote server name (for example, **<//Mycomputer/W3SVC/12>**), or it can simply be the site's numeric identifier or the site's **ServerComment** property value (for example, **<12>**, **<www.mysite.com>**), eventually including wildcards.

Fields

The IISW3C input format generates input records containing the following fields:

- LogFilename
- LogRow
- date
- time
- c-ip
- cs-username
- s-sitename
- s-computername
- s-ip
- s-port
- cs-method
- cs-uri-stem
- cs-uri-query
- sc-status
- sc-substatus
- sc-win32-status
- sc-bytes
- cs-bytes
- time-taken
- cs-version
- cs-host
- cs(User-Agent)
- cs(Cookie)
- cs(Referer)
- s-event
- s-process-type
- s-user-time
- s-kernel-time
- s-page-faults
- s-total-procs
- s-active-procs
- s-stopped-procs

Parameters

- **iCodepage** Specifies the numeric identifier of the codepage of the file(s) being parsed. The special **-1** value means UNICODE, and the special **-2** value causes the IIS input format to automatically detect the codepage from the log file name and from the **LogInUTF8** property of the virtual site.

- **recurse** Specifies the number of subdirectories to recurse into. The special **-1** value means *unlimited recursion*.

- **minDateMod** Specifies the minimum value of the last date modified attribute of a log file for the file to be parsed.

- **dQuotes** When **ON**, the IISW3C input format expects string fields in the file(s) being parsed to be surrounded by double-quote characters.

- **dirTime** When set to **ON**, the IISW3C input format fills in missing **date** and **time** field values with the value of the #**Fields** directive.

- **consolidateLogs** When log files from multiple virtual sites are parsed in a single query, setting this parameter to **ON** causes the IISW3C input format to return log entries ordered by date and time across all the input files.

- **iCheckpoint** Specifies the path of the checkpoint file to use when parsing the input file(s) incrementally.

NCSA Input Format

The NCSA input format parses log files in the NCSA Common, Combined, and Extended Log File Formats.

From-Entity

The NCSA input format accepts FROM clause values with the following syntax:

filename | siteID [, filename | siteID ...]

- **Filename** This is the path to a log file in any of the supported NCSA Log File Formats; the path can contain wildcards and can be in UNC notation if specifying log files on a remote share.

- **SiteID** This is the Metabase path of an IIS virtual site, enclosed in angled brackets; the Metabase path can be a full path that includes a remote server name (for example, **<//Mycomputer/W3SVC/12>**), or it can simply be the site's numeric identifier or the site's **ServerComment** property value (for example, **<12>**, **<www.mysite.com>**), eventually including wildcards.

Fields

The NCSA input format generates input records containing the following fields:

- LogFilename
- LogRow
- RemoteHostName
- RemoteLogName
- UserName
- DateTime
- Request
- StatusCode
- BytesSent
- Referer
- User-Agent
- Cookie

Parameters

- **iCodepage** Specifies the numeric identifier of the codepage of the file(s) being parsed. The special **–1** value means UNICODE, and the special **–2** value causes the IIS input format to automatically detect the codepage from the log file name and from the **LogInUTF8** property of the virtual site.

- **recurse** Specifies the number of subdirectories to recurse into. The special **–1** value means *unlimited recursion*.

- **minDateMod** Specifies the minimum value of the last date modified attribute of a log file for the file to be parsed.

- **iCheckpoint** Specifies the path of the checkpoint file to use when parsing the input file(s) incrementally.

NETMON Input Format

The NETMON input format returns properties of TCP packets and connections from NetMon capture files (.cap files). This input format works in two different modes. In *TCPIP* mode, the NETMON input format returns an input record for each TCP/IP *packet* found in the capture file(s) being parsed. In *TCPConn* mode, the NETMON input format returns an input record for each TCP/IP *connection* found in the capture file(s) being parsed. In the latter mode, the NETMON input format reconstructs the whole TCP connection from the packets, returning aggregate fields such as the total payloads exchanged during the connection, and the total duration of the connection.

From-Entity

The NETMON input format accepts FROM clause values with the following syntax:

`filename [, filename ...]`

- **Filename** Path to a NetMon capture file (.cap file).

Fields

When working in TCPIP mode, the NETMON input format generates input records with the following fields:

- CaptureFilename
- Frame
- DateTime
- FrameBytes
- SrcMAC
- SrcIP
- SrcPort
- DstMAC
- DstIP
- DstPort

- IPVersion
- TTL
- TCPFlags
- Seq
- Ack
- WindowSize
- PayloadBytes
- Payload
- Connection

When working in TCPConn mode, the NETMON input format generates input records with the following fields:

- CaptureFilename
- StartFrame
- EndFrame
- Frames
- DateTime
- TimeTaken
- SrcMAC
- SrcIP

- SrcPort
- SrcPayloadBytes
- SrcPayload
- DstMAC
- DstIP
- DstPort
- DstPayloadBytes
- DstPayload

Parameters

- **fMode** This parameter controls the operation mode of the NETMON input format; the possible values for this parameter are **TCPIP** and **TCPConn**.

- **binaryFormat** Specifies the format of binary data as one of the **ASC**, **HEX**, or **PRINT** values.

REG Input Format

The REG input format returns properties of registry keys and values.

From-Entity

The REG input format accepts FROM clause values with the following syntax:

```
[\\computername]\[rootname[\subkeypath]]  [,...]
```

- **Computername** Optional computer name; used when enumerating keys from a remote registry.

- **Rootname** Name of the registry root; can be on the following values: **HKCR**, **HKCU**, **HKLM**, **HKCC**, or **HKU**.

- **Subkeypath** Path to a registry key below the specified root.

Fields

The REG input format generates input records with the following fields:

- ComputerName
- Path
- KeyName
- ValueName
- ValueType
- Value
- LastWriteTime

Parameters

- **recurse** Specifies the number of subdirectories to recurse into. The special **–1** value means *unlimited recursion*.

- **multiSZSep** This parameter specifies the string used as a separator between the elements of MULTI_SZ key values. The default value is the pipe (|) character.

- **binaryFormat** Specifies the format of binary data as one of the **ASC**, **HEX**, or **PRINT** values.

TEXTLINE Input Format

The TEXTLINE input format parses generic text files returning whole lines as a single input record field.

From-Entity

The TEXTLINE input format accepts FROM clause values with the following syntax:

```
filename [, filename …] |
http://url             |
STDIN
```

- **Filename** This is the path to a text file; the path can contain wildcards and can be in UNC notation if specifying log files on a remote share.

- **URL** This is the URL of a resource formatted as a text file.

- **STDIN** This special keyword specifies that the TEXTLINE input format should read the input data from the console input. This value is mostly used when piping commands and using the output of a command as the input of a Log Parser query.

Fields

The TEXTLINE input format generates input records containing the following fields:

- LogFilename
- Index
- Text

Parameters

- **iCodepage** Specifies the numeric identifier of the codepage of the file(s) being parsed.

- **recurse** Specifies the number of subdirectories to recurse into. The special **-1** value means *unlimited recursion*.

- **splitLongLines** Setting this parameter to **ON** causes the TEXTLINE input format to return lines longer than the maximum allowed as multiple input records. Setting this parameter to

OFF causes the TEXTLINE input format to truncate long lines, returning only their initial section.

■ **iCheckpoint** Specifies the path of the checkpoint file to use when parsing the input file(s) incrementally.

TEXTWORD Input Format

The TEXTWORD input format parses generic text files returning each word as a single input record field.

From-Entity

The TEXTWORD input format accepts FROM clause values with the following syntax:

```
filename [, filename …] |
http://url              |
STDIN
```

■ **Filename** This is the path to a text file; the path can contain wildcards and can be in UNC notation if specifying log files on a remote share.

■ **URL** This is the URL of a resource formatted as a text file.

■ **STDIN** This special keyword specifies that the TEXTWORD input format should read the input data from the console input. This value is mostly used when piping commands and using the output of a command as the input of a Log Parser query.

Fields

The TEXTWORD input format generates input records containing the following fields:

■ LogFilename

■ Index

■ Text

Parameters

■ **iCodepage** Specifies the numeric identifier of the codepage of the file(s) being parsed.

■ **recurse** Specifies the number of subdirectories to recurse into. The special **–1** value means *unlimited recursion*.

■ **iCheckpoint** Specifies the path of the checkpoint file to use when parsing the input file(s) incrementally.

TSV Input Format

The TSV input format parses tab-separated and space-separated values text files. This input format works with a two-stage approach. During an initial inspection stage, the input format inspects a configurable number of lines in the TSV files to determine the number of fields, the field types, and the field names of the columns contained in the files. After the number of fields, their types, and their names has been determined, the real parsing stage begins, in which the files are parsed again from beginning to end, and input records are generated to be processed by the query.

From-Entity

The TSV input format accepts FROM clause values with the following syntax:

```
filename [, filename …] |
http://url               |
STDIN
```

- **Filename** This is the path to a TSV file; the path can contain wildcards and can be in UNC notation if specifying files on a remote share.
- **URL** This is the URL of a resource formatted as TSV text.
- **STDIN** This special keyword specifies that the TSV input format should read the input data from the console input. This value is mostly used when piping commands and using the output of a command as the input of a Log Parser query.

Fields

The TSV input format generates input records containing the following fields:

- Filename
- RowNumber
- A field for each column in the input TSV file(s)

Parameters

- **iSeparator** Specifies the separator character used in the text file being parsed. The parameter can be set to **tab**, **space**, or to a custom character.
- **nSep** Specifies the number of separator characters that must appear to signify a field separator. This parameter is usually set to a value greater than one when parsing text files that use multiple space characters as separators, and whose field values can contain a single space character, as is the case with the output of the netstat utility.
- **fixedSep** When set to **ON**, the TSV input format assumes that the number of separator characters between fields is fixed, and equal to the value specified for the **nSep** parameter. Setting

this parameter to **OFF** causes the TSV input format to assume that the number of separator characters between fields is variable, in which case the **nSep** parameter is assumed to indicate the *minimum* number of separator characters between fields.

- **headerRow** When set to **ON**, the TSV input format assumes that the file(s) being parsed contain a header line declaring the names of the columns in the file(s), and it extracts the column names from this line. When set to **OFF**, the TSV input format assumes that each file being parsed begins with the first line of data.

- **iHeaderFile** Specifies the path to a TSV text file containing a header line declaring the names of the columns in the file(s) being parsed. The column names found in the specified header file override the eventual column names declared by the header line in the file(s) being parsed.

- **nFields** This parameter can be used to specify directly the number of fields (columns) contained in the TSV file(s) being parsed. When this parameter is set to **-1** (the default value), the TSV input format determines the number of fields automatically during the initial inspection stage.

- **dtLines** Specifies the number of initial lines to be inspected during the initial inspection stage to determine the number of fields, the field types, and the field names of the columns contained in the file(s).

- **nSkipLines** This parameter specifies the number of lines that the TSV input format should skip in each file before it starts parsing its data.

- **lineFilter** Specifies a comma-separated list of prefixes of lines to be considered or ignored when parsing the input file(s). If the value specified for this parameter starts with "+", the TSV input format only parses lines that begin with one of the specified prefixes; if the value starts with "-", the TSV input format ignores all the lines that begin with one of the specified prefixes.

- **iCodepage** Specifies the numeric identifier of the codepage of the file(s) being parsed.

- **iTsFormat** Specifies the format of the timestamp values contained in the file(s) being parsed.

- **iCheckpoint** Specifies the path of the checkpoint file to use when parsing the input file(s) incrementally.

URLSCAN Input Format

The URLSCAN input format parses the log files created by the URLScan IIS filter.

From-Entity

The URLSCAN input format accepts FROM clause values with the following syntax:

```
filename [, filename ...] |
URLSCAN
```

- **Filename** Path to a URLScan log file.
- **URLSCAN** This keyword specifies that the user wants to parse all the URLScan log files available on the local computer.

Fields

The URLSCAN input format generates input records with the following fields:

- LogFilename
- LogRow
- Date
- ClientIP
- Comment
- SiteInstance
- Url

Parameters

- **iCheckpoint** Specifies the path of the checkpoint file to use when parsing the input file(s) incrementally.

W3C Input Format

The W3C input format parses log files in the W3C Extended Log File Format. Examples of log files in this format include Exchange Tracking log files, Personal Firewall log files, and Windows Media Server log files.

This input format inspects the **#Fields** directive contained in the header of the W3C log files to determine the number of fields and the field names contained in the log. During this initial inspection stage, the input format also inspects a configurable number of lines in the W3C files to determine the field types. After the number of fields, their types, and their names has been determined, the real parsing stage begins, in which the files are parsed again from beginning to end, and input records are generated to be processed by the query.

From-Entity

The W3C input format accepts FROM clause values with the following syntax:

```
filename [, filename …] |
http://url              |
STDIN
```

- **Filename** This is the path to a W3C file; the path can contain wildcards and can be in UNC notation if specifying files on a remote share.

- **URL** This is the URL of a resource formatted as a W3C log file.

- **STDIN** This special keyword specifies that the W3C input format should read the input data from the console input. This value is mostly used when piping commands and using the output of a command as the input of a Log Parser query.

Fields

The W3C input format generates input records containing the following fields:

- Filename
- RowNumber
- A field for each column in the input W3C file(s)

Parameters

- **dtLines** Specifies the number of initial lines to be inspected during the initial inspection stage to determine the types of the columns contained in the file(s).

- **dQuotes** When **ON**, the W3C input format expects string fields in the file(s) being parsed to be surrounded by double-quote characters.

- **iCodepage** Specifies the numeric identifier of the codepage of the file(s) being parsed.

- **separator** Specifies the separator character used in the text file being parsed. The parameter can be set to **tab**, **space**, to a custom character, or to **auto**, which causes the W3C input format to determine the separator character automatically.

XML Input Format

The XML input format parses XML documents, returning the values of elements and attributes. This input format works in three different modes. In *Branch* mode, the XML input format returns the values of the elements and attributes found along the paths that start at the document root node and end at the document leaf nodes. In *Tree* mode, the XML input format returns the values of the elements and attributes contained in entire subtrees that satisfy particular conditions. In *Node* mode, the XML input format only considers instances of a user-specified node, returning its value and its attributes. For more information on the difference operation modes, consult the Log Parser documentation.

The XML input format works with a two-stage approach. During an initial inspection stage, the input format inspects a configurable number of nodes in the XML documents to determine the number of nodes and attributes, their types, and their names; the different nodes and attributes names found during this stage become the fields contained in the XML input format records. After the number of fields, their types, and their names has been determined, the real parsing stage begins, in which the documents are parsed again from beginning to end, and input records are generated to be processed by the query.

From-Entity

The XML input format accepts FROM clause values with the following syntax:

```
filename[#XPath]  |  url[#XPath]  [, …]
```

- **Filename** Path to an XML document.
- **XPath** Optional XPath specifying which nodes in the document are to be considered root nodes.
- **URL** URL of an XML resource.

Fields

The XML input format generates input records with field names corresponding to the names of the elements and attributes found in the document(s) being parsed.

Parameters

- **rootXPath** XPath selecting the nodes in the document that should be considered root nodes. The value of this parameter is overridden by the optional XPath specified in the FROM clause.
- **fMode** This parameter controls the operation mode of the XML input format; the possible values for this parameter are **Branch**, **Tree**, **Node**, and **Auto**, which specifies that the XML input format should select the best operation mode suitable for the schema of the document being parsed.
- **iTsFormat** Specifies the format of the timestamp values contained in the document(s) being parsed.
- **dtNodes** Specifies the number of initial leaf nodes to be inspected during the inspection stage to determine the number, types, and names of the input record fields.
- **fNames** When this parameter is set to **Compact**, fields are named after the name of the element or attribute they represent. When this parameter is set to **XPath**, fields are named after the full XPath to the element or attribute they represent.

Output Format Reference

- CHART Output Format

- CSV Output Format

- DATAGRID Output Format

- IIS Output Format

- NAT Output Format

- SQL Output Format

- SYSLOG Output Format

- TPL Output Format

- TSV Output Format

- W3C Output Format

- XML Output Format

In This Toolbox

Log Parser 2.2 provides 11 output formats that can be used to format query output records in a wide variety of text file formats (CSV, TSV, XML, W3C, IIS, and custom formats), to display results to the screen (NAT and DATAGRID output formats), to create image files containing charts, to upload results to a SQL database, and to send results to a SysLog server.

CHART Output Format

The CHART output format creates GIF and JPG image files containing chart representations of the output records of a query. In order to use the CHART output format, the computer running the Log Parser query must have the Microsoft Office Web Components installed, which are distributed with Microsoft Office 2000 and later versions.

Into-Entity

The CHART output format accepts INTO clause values with the following syntax:

`filename`

- **Filename** This is the path to the output GIF or JPG filename.

Parameters

- **chartType** Specifies the type of the desired output chart. The available values depend on the version of the Office Web Components installed; for a comprehensive list of chart type available on your computer, type the following command:

  ```
  LogParser -h -o:CHART
  ```

- **categories** Setting this parameter to **ON** causes the CHART output format to utilize the values of the first output record field as the labels of the categories on the x-axis. Setting this parameter to **OFF** causes the CHART output format to not display category labels, and to process the first output record field as a series of the chart. Setting this parameter to **AUTO** causes the CHART output format to automatically assume an **ON** value when the first output record field contains values of the STRING data type.

- **maxCategoryLabels** This parameter helps reduce clutter in the output chart by specifying the maximum number of category labels displayed on the x-axis. Specifying **-1** causes the CHART output format to display as many category labels as the number of output records; specifying **0** causes the CHART output format to automatically adjust the number of displayed category labels based on the geometrical dimensions of the chart.

- **legend** Setting this parameter to **ON** causes the CHART output format to display a legend for each numerical series plotted on the chart. Setting this parameter to **AUTO** causes the

CHART output format to display a legend only when there are more than one numerical series to be plotted. When this parameter is set to **OFF**, the chart legend is never displayed.

- **values** Specifying **ON** or **OFF** for this parameter causes the CHART output format to display or not display value labels on the chart. Specifying **AUTO** causes the CHART output format to display value labels depending on the chart type selected.

- **groupSize** Specifies the dimensions of the target image, in pixels. This parameter has the following syntax:

    `widthXheight`

- **fileType** Can be **GIF**, **JPG**, or **AUTO**, in which case the CHART output format selects the format based on the extension of the filename provided for the INTO clause.

- **config** This parameter can be used to specify a comma-separated list of JScript or VBScript scripts that are executed immediately before rendering the chart, allowing users to customize the chart as desired.

- **chartTitle** Specifies a title for the chart.

- **oTsFormat** Format in which output record fields of the TIMESTAMP type are formatted.

- **view** Setting this parameter to **ON** causes the CHART output format to display the chart image after it has been saved to disk.

CSV Output Format

The CSV output format creates text file formatted according to the CSV (Comma-Separated-Values) convention.

Into-Entity

The CSV output format accepts INTO clause values with the following syntax:

```
filename |
STDOUT
```

- **Filename** This is the path to the output CSV text file. Since the CSV output format supports the *multiplex* feature, users can specify asterisk (*) wildcards in the output filename, causing the CSV output format to write its output to different output files whose names are created after substituting the wildcards with the first values of the output records.

- **STDOUT** Specifying this keyword causes the CSV output format to write its output to the console.

Parameters

- **headers** Specifying **ON** causes the CSV output format to begin the output with a header line containing the names of the fields. Specifying **OFF** disables the header altogether, and specifying **AUTO** causes the CSV output format to write a header only when not appending output to an existing file.

- **oDQuotes** Specifying **ON** for this parameter causes the CSV output format to enclose each field value within double-quote characters. Specifying **OFF** disables double-quoting altogether, and specifying **AUTO** causes the CSV output format to only double-quote those fields that contain comma characters.

- **tabs** Specifying **ON** for this parameter causes the CSV output format to write a tab character immediately after each separator comma.

- **oTsFormat** Specifies how TIMESTAMP field values should be formatted in the output.

- **oCodepage** This parameter specifies the codepage of the output file. Specifying **-1** causes the CSV output format to write UNICODE text files.

- **fileMode** Setting this parameter to **0** causes the CSV output format to append its output to a file when the file already exists. Specifying **1** causes the CSV output format to overwrite existing files, and specifying **2** causes the CSV output format to not modify an existing file.

DATAGRID Output Format

The DATAGRID output format displays output records in a window, allowing users to browse through the records, and to copy selected records to the clipboard.

Into-Entity

The DATAGRID output format accepts INTO clause values with the following syntax:

```
DATAGRID
```

- **DATAGRID** This keyword identifies the DATAGRID output format.

Parameters

- **rtp** Specifies the number of output records that should be displayed before waiting for the user to press the **Next N rows** button. Specifying **-1** causes the DATAGRID output format to display all the output records without interruption.

- **autoScroll** Specifying **ON** causes the DATAGRID output format to automatically scroll the window when new output records are displayed. Specifying **OFF** causes the

DATAGRID output format to display new output records without scrolling the window.

IIS Output Format

The IIS output format creates text file formatted according to the Microsoft IIS Log File Format.

Into-Entity

The IIS output format accepts INTO clause values with the following syntax:

```
filename |
STDOUT
```

- **Filename** This is the path to the output text file. Since the IIS output format supports the multiplex feature, users can specify asterisk (*) wildcards in the output filename, causing the IIS output format to write its output to different output files whose names are created after substituting the wildcards with the first values of the output records.

- **STDOUT** Specifying this keyword causes the IIS output format to write its output to the console.

Parameters

- **rtp** When the IIS output format is writing to STDOUT, this parameter specifies the number of output records that should be displayed before waiting for the user to press a key. Specifying **-1** causes the IIS output format to display all the output records without interruption.

- **oCodepage** This parameter specifies the codepage of the output file. Specifying **-1** causes the IIS output format to write UNICODE text files.

- **fileMode** Setting this parameter to **0** causes the IIS output format to append its output to a file when the file already exists. Specifying **1** causes the IIS output format to overwrite existing files, and specifying **2** causes the IIS output format to not modify an existing file.

NAT Output Format

The NAT output format displays output records to the console window in a tabulated readable format.

Into-Entity

The NAT output format accepts INTO clause values with the following syntax:

```
filename |
STDOUT
```

- **Filename** This is the path to an output text file. Since the NAT output format supports the multiplex feature, users can specify asterisk (★) wildcards in the output filename, causing the NAT output format to write its output to different output files whose names are created after substituting the wildcards with the first values of the output records.

- **STDOUT** Specifying this keyword causes the NAT output format to write its output to the console. When no INTO clause is specified, the NAT output format uses "STDOUT" by default.

Parameters

- **rtp** When the NAT output format is writing to STDOUT, this parameter specifies the number of output records that should be displayed before waiting for the user to press a key. Specifying **–1** causes the NAT output format to display all the output records without interruption.

- **headers** Specifying **ON** causes the NAT output format to begin each group of output lines with a header line containing the names of the fields. Specifying **OFF** disables the header altogether.

- **spaceCol** Specifying **ON** causes the NAT output format to space columns uniformly within each group of output lines. Specifying **OFF** causes the NAT output format to separate columns using a single space character.

- **rAlign** Specifying **ON** causes the NAT output format to right-justify values within their columns. Specifying **OFF** causes the NAT output format to left-justify the output values.

- **colSep** This parameter specifies the string to be used as a separator between the columns.

- **direct** When this parameter is set to **ON**, the NAT output format disables its internal buffering mechanism used to group rows together and to calculate the uniform spacing between columns.

- **oCodepage** This parameter specifies the codepage of the output file. Specifying **–1** causes the NAT output format to write UNICODE text files.

- **fileMode** Setting this parameter to **0** causes the NAT output format to append its output to a file when the file already exists. Specifying **1** causes the NAT output format to overwrite existing files, and specifying **2** causes the NAT output format to not modify an existing file.

SQL Output Format

The SQL output format uploads output records to a table in an ODBC-compliant database.

Into-Entity

The SQL output format accepts INTO clause values with the following syntax:

```
tablename
```

- **Tablename** This is the name of the target table.

Parameters

- **server** Specifies the name of the database server.
- **database** Specifies the database name.
- **driver** Specifies the ODBC driver to use.
- **dsn** Specifies a Data Source Name that contains information on the database connection.
- **username** Specifies the name of a SQL account to use for the connection. When this parameter is not specified, the SQL output format uses Integrated Windows Authentication utilizing the current user's credentials.
- **password** Specifies the password for the SQL account specified with the **username** parameter.
- **oConnString** This parameter can be used as an alternative to the previous parameters to specify a connection string containing the ODBC parameters for the database connection.
- **createTable** Setting this parameter to **ON** causes the SQL output format to create the target table in case it does not already exists in the database. When the SQL output format creates a table, the SQL column types are derived from the data types of the query output records. For more information on the mappings between the Log Parser data types and the SQL column types, see the Log Parser documentation.
- **clearTable** Setting this parameter to **ON** causes the SQL output format to delete all the existing entries from the target table before uploading the query output records.
- **fixColNames** Setting this parameter to **ON** causes the SQL output format to process the output record field names and remove illegal characters before creating column names for the target table.

- **maxStrFieldLen** This parameter specifies the maximum number of characters for the **string** SQL column types that are created when the target table does not already exist.

- **transactionRowCount** Specifies the number of output records to enclose in SQL transactions. Specifying **-1** causes the SQL output format to enclose *all* the output records in a single transaction, while specifying **0** causes the SQL output format to enable *auto commit* mode, in which each output record uploaded to the target table is individually committed.

- **ignoreMinWarns** Setting this parameter to **ON** causes the SQL output format to ignore minor warnings that might occur at run time. Specifying **OFF** causes the SQL output format to report these minor warnings when the command execution is complete.

- **ignoreIdCols** When uploading to an existing table, the SQL output requires that the number of fields in the output records match exactly the number of columns in the target table, and it uploads output record fields to each column in the target table. Setting this parameter to **ON** causes the SQL output format to ignore target table columns of the **identity** type, and it uploads output record fields only to those columns that are not of the **identity** type.

SYSLOG Output Format

The SYSLOG output format can be used to send output records to a SYSLOG server, to send SYSLOG messages to a user, or to create text files containing entries formatted according to the SYSLOG specifications.

Into-Entity

The SYSLOG output format accepts INTO clause values with the following syntax:

```
@server[:port] | filename | username [, ...]
```

- **Server** This is the name of the SYSLOG server.
- **Port** This is the optional port on which the SYSLOG server listens for messages.
- **Filename** This is the path to an output text file to which SYSLOG messages will be written to.
- **Username** This is the account name to which SYSLOG messages will be sent, using the Windows *net send* mechanism.

Parameters

- **conf** Specifies the path to a SYSLOG configuration file containing the actions to perform for different SYSLOG messages. For more information, consult the Log Parser documentation.

- **severity** Severity level of the message. Can be specified as a number, as a severity level name, or as the **$** character followed by the name of an output record field containing the severity value.

- **facility** Facility of the message. Can be specified as a number, as a facility name, or as the **$** character followed by the name of an output record field containing the facility value.

- **oTsFormat** Format of the SYSLOG message **timestamp** field.

- **hostname** Value of the SYSLOG message **hostname** field. Can also be specified as the **$** character followed by the name of an output record field containing the value of the **hostname** field.

- **processName** Value of the SYSLOG message **processname** or **TAG** field. Can also be specified as the **$** character followed by the name of an output record field containing the value of the **processname** field.

- **separator** Separator to be used between the SYSLOG message fields.

- **maxPacketSize** Maximum message size, in bytes.

- **protocol** Protocol to use when sending messages to a SYSLOG server; possible values are **TCP** and **UDP**.

- **sourcePort** Source port for messages sent to SYSLOG server. Specifying "★" causes the SYSLOG output format to use the first available port.

- **ignoreDspchErrs** Setting this parameter to **ON** causes the SYSLOG output format to buffer errors that occur while dispatching messages to their destination, reporting all of them as warnings when the execution is completed. Setting this parameter to **OFF** causes the SYSLOG output format to report errors when they occur, aborting the execution of the current query.

- **discardOversized** Setting this parameter to **ON** causes the SYSLOG output format to discard messages exceeding the maximum size specified with the **maxPacketSize** parameter. Setting this parameter to **OFF** causes the SYSLOG output format to truncate messages and dispatch them.

- **oCodepage** This parameter specifies the codepage of the messages. Specifying **-1** causes the SYSLOG output format to write UNICODE messages.

TPL Output Format

The TPL output format creates text file formatted according to user-defined templates. Template files specify the text that should be output once at the beginning (the *header*), repeatedly for each output record (the *body*), and once at the end (the *footer*).

Each of the three sections can contain variables that are substituted with output record values. The variables that can be specified in any section are:

- **%FIELDNAME_N%** Name of the specified output record field.
- **%FIELDS_NUM%** Number of fields in the output records.
- **%SYSTEM_TIMESTAMP%** Date and time at which the output is created.
- **%*environment_variable*%** Value of the specified environment variable.

The variables that can be specified in the body section only are:

- **%FIELD_N%** Value of the specified output record field.
- **%*field_name*%** Value of the specified output record field.

Template files can be specified as three different files (header, body, and footer), or as a single file containing tags delimiting the three sections. In the latter case, the tags are:

- <LPHEADER>…</LPHEADER>: delimits the header section.
- <LPBODY>…</LPBODY>: delimits the body section.
- <LPFOOTER>…</LPFOOTER>: delimits the footer section.

Into-Entity

The TPL output format accepts INTO clause values with the following syntax:

```
filename |
STDOUT
```

- **Filename** This is the path to the output text file. Since the TPL output format supports the multiplex feature, users can specify asterisk (*) wildcards in the output filename, causing the TPL output format to write its output to different output files whose names are created after substituting the wildcards with the first values of the output records.
- **STDOUT** Specifying this keyword causes the TPL output format to write its output to the console.

Parameters

- **tpl** This parameter specifies either the template file for the body section, or the single template file containing the three sections together, delimited by the <LPHEADER>, <LPBODY>, and <LPFOOTER> tags.

- **tplHeader** This parameter specifies the template file containing the header section.

- **tplFooter** This parameter specifies the template file containing the footer section.

- **noEmptyFile** When the query does not produce output records, setting this parameter to **ON** prevents the TPL output format from creating an empty file.

- **oCodepage** This parameter specifies the codepage of the output file. Specifying **–1** causes the TPL output format to write UNICODE text files.

- **fileMode** Setting this parameter to **0** causes the TPL output format to append its output to a file when the file already exists. Specifying **1** causes the TPL output format to overwrite existing files, and specifying **2** causes the TPL output format to not modify an existing file.

TSV Output Format

The TSV output format creates text file formatted according to the TSV (Tab–Separated–Values) convention.

Into-Entity

The TSV output format accepts INTO clause values with the following syntax:

```
filename |
STDOUT
```

- **Filename** This is the path to the output TSV text file. Since the TSV output format supports the multiplex feature, users can specify asterisk (★) wildcards in the output filename, causing the TSV output format to write its output to different output files whose names are created after substituting the wildcards with the first values of the output records.

- **STDOUT** Specifying this keyword causes the TSV output format to write its output to the console.

Parameters

- **headers** Specifying **ON** causes the TSV output format to begin the output with a header line containing the names of the fields. Specifying **OFF** disables the header altogether, and specifying **AUTO** causes the TSV output format to write a header only when not appending output to an existing file.

- **oSeparator** This parameter specifies the separator to use between the field values. Specifying **tab** causes the TSV output format to use a single tab character between the fields, while specifying **space** causes the TSV output format to use a single space character between the fields.

- **oTsFormat** Specifies how TIMESTAMP field values should be formatted in the output.

- **oCodepage** This parameter specifies the codepage of the output file. Specifying **-1** causes the TSV output format to write UNICODE text files.

- **fileMode** Setting this parameter to **0** causes the TSV output format to append its output to a file when the file already exists. Specifying **1** causes the TSV output format to overwrite existing files, and specifying **2** causes the TSV output format to not modify an existing file.

W3C Output Format

The W3C output format creates text file formatted according to the W3C Extended Log File Format.

Into-Entity

The W3C output format accepts INTO clause values with the following syntax:

```
filename |
STDOUT
```

- **Filename** This is the path to the output W3C text file. Since the W3C output format supports the multiplex feature, users can specify asterisk (*****) wildcards in the output filename, causing the W3C output format to write its output to different output files whose names are created after substituting the wildcards with the first values of the output records.

- **STDOUT** Specifying this keyword causes the W3C output format to write its output to the console.

Parameters

- **rtp** When the W3C output format is writing to STDOUT, this parameter specifies the number of output records that should be displayed before waiting for the user to press a key. Specifying **-1** causes the W3C output format to display all the output records without interruption.

- **oDQuotes** Specifying **ON** for this parameter causes the W3C output format to enclose string field values within double-quote characters. Specifying **OFF** causes the W3C output format to never enclose fields within double-quote characters.

- **oDirTime** This parameter specifies the value that the W3C output format should use when writing the **#Date** directive at the beginning of the W3C output. When this parameter is not specified, the W3C output format uses the current date and time.

- **encodeDelim** Setting this parameter to **ON** causes the W3C output format to substitute space characters in field values with plus characters.

- **oCodepage** This parameter specifies the codepage of the output file. Specifying **-1** causes the W3C output format to write UNICODE text files.

- **fileMode** Setting this parameter to **0** causes the W3C output format to append its output to a file when the file already exists. Specifying **1** causes the W3C output format to overwrite existing files, and specifying **2** causes the W3C output format to not modify an existing file.

XML Output Format

The XML output format creates XML text files formatting the output record fields as XML nodes and attributes.

Into-Entity

The XML output format accepts INTO clause values with the following syntax:

```
filename |
STDOUT
```

- **Filename** This is the path to the output XML text file. Since the XML output format supports the multiplex feature, users can specify asterisk (*) wildcards in the output filename, causing the XML output format to write its output to different output files whose names are created after substituting the wildcards with the first values of the output records.

- **STDOUT** Specifying this keyword causes the XML output format to write its output to the console.

Parameters

- **structure** This parameter specifies the structure of the output XML document. Specifying **1** or **2** causes the XML output format to create nodes with the names of the output record fields, and to save the field values as values of these nodes. When **2** is specified, nodes contain a **TYPE** attribute with the data type of the field. Specifying **3** or **4** causes the XML output format to create nodes named **FIELD** having a **NAME** attribute with the name of the field, and to save the field values as values of these nodes; when **4** is specified, nodes contain an additional **TYPE** attribute with the data type of the field.

- **rootName** This parameter specifies the name of the document root node.

- **rowName** This parameter specifies the name of the node containing the field value nodes.

- **fieldName** This parameter specifies the name of the node containing the output record field values when the **structure** parameter is set to **3** or **4**.

- **xslLink** This parameter specifies the path to an XSL file a link to which is placed at the beginning of the XML document.

- **schemaType** Specifying **0** causes the XML output format to not write any schema in the XML document. Specifying **1** causes the XML output format to write an inline DTD schema in the XML document.

- **compact** Specifying **ON** for this parameter causes the XML output format to write compact XML output suppressing indentation space characters and carriage-return/line-feed characters.

- **noEmptyField** Specifying **ON** for this parameter prevents the XML output format from writing empty nodes when the corresponding output record field values are NULL.

- **standAlone** Specifying **ON** causes the XML output format to write an XML header and a root node that contains all the output record nodes. Specifying **OFF** causes the XML output format to write only the output record nodes.

- **oCodepage** This parameter specifies the codepage of the output file. Specifying **–1** causes the XML output format to write UNICODE text files.

- **fileMode** Setting this parameter to **0** causes the XML output format to append its output to a file when the file already exists. Specifying **1** causes the XML output format to overwrite existing files, and specifying **2** causes the XML output format to not modify an existing file.

Index